CHESTER
THROUGH TIME
Paul Hurley *&* Len Morgan

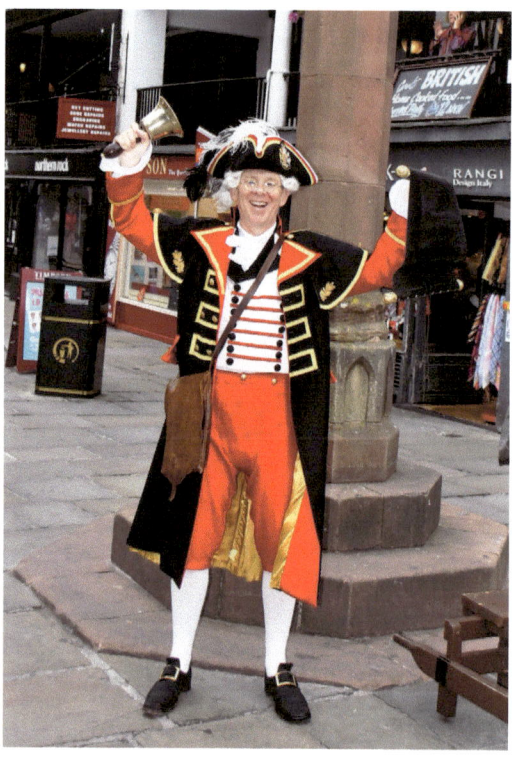

Photograph of the Chester Town Crier at The Cross
The City of Chester is the only place in Britain to have retained the tradition of regular midday proclamations at a fixed place and time – Tuesday to Saturday from May to August, at noon, at the Chester Cross (10.30 a.m. on Race Days). The present Town Crier is David Mitchell and he shares the duties with his Town Crier wife Julie. It was at this spot in 1646, after the Great Siege of Chester, that King Charles I was proclaimed a traitor.

First published 2010
Reprinted 2011

Amberley Publishing
The Hill, Stroud
Gloucestershire, GL5 4EP

www.amberley-books.com

Copyright © Paul Hurley & Len Morgan, 2010

The right of Paul Hurley & Len Morgan to be identified as the Authors of this work has been asserted in accordance with the Copyrights, Designs and Patents Act 1988.

ISBN 978 1 84868 664 9

All rights reserved. No part of this book may be reprinted or reproduced or utilised in any form or by any electronic, mechanical or other means, now known or hereafter invented, including photocopying and recording, or in any information storage or retrieval system, without the permission in writing from the Publishers.

British Library Cataloguing in Publication Data.
A catalogue record for this book is available from the British Library.

Typeset in 9.5pt on 12pt Celeste.
Typesetting by Amberley Publishing.
Printed in the UK.

Appointed GPSR EU Representative: Easy Access System Europe Oü, 16879218
Address: Mustamäe tee 50, 10621, Tallinn, Estonia
Contact Details: gpsr.requests@easproject.com, +358 40 500 3575

Introduction

Chester, that ancient walled city was once one of the most important Roman Fortress towns in Great Britain and is the county town of beautiful Cheshire. It stands astride the mighty River Dee, with its castle facing the Welsh border from whence in days of yore the invaders would come. Little of the original castle remains; it served the city well and held back the Welsh hordes well, most of them anyway! During the Civil War it was the viewing area for one of the last major battles at Rowton Moor and the events around Chester on the 24 September 1645 ended all hope of a Royalist victory. The castle was rebuilt in 1788 by the architect Thomas Harrison who was also responsible for the Grosvenor Bridge, opened in 1832 by Princess Victoria. At the time the largest single arch stone bridge in the world. The 200 foot span cost £50,000 when it was built. Before 1832 the only bridge across the river was the ancient Dee Bridge dating from the fourteenth century and then in 1852 the suspension bridge was built for pedestrians only. But those are routes into Chester, what do you find when you get here? The city is surrounded by a continuous wall, parts of which date to Roman times but the majority is medieval and Victorian. It once formed the city's fortifications but is now a pleasant circular walk around the city centre which is raised for most of its length and is around 2 miles long. There are many vantage points to be enjoyed including the Chester amphitheatre which has recently been suspected of being the true location of King Arthur's Round Table! Stand under the huge clock above the Eastgate and look down on the city centre streets of Eastgate and Foregate. This clock is reported to be second only to Big Ben in the number of photographs taken of it.

Then into the city centre proper where we find the famous Chester Rows, shops and other business premises on two levels, some with cellars that still bear evidence of Roman occupation. The Rows are quite unique in the world and give a good vantage point to lean on the rail and watch the world go by in the city centre street below. Ancient pubs abound in Chester such as the seventeenth century Bear and Billet, once home to the Earls of Shrewsbury and The Falcon, originally built as a house in 1200. But should we be talking of pubs when we are in one of the oldest and most unique cities in Britain? Well yes, because of its uniqueness Chester attracts many visitors throughout the year. Visitors, who want to take a leisurely stroll on the walls, visit the museums, the ancient sites, ride the unique old fashioned city tour bus and see the Roman Centurions in full uniform leading groups of happy schoolchildren around the city, but most of all to delight in the experiences on offer. At one time the famous Roodee racecourse was filled with water and was part of Chester's port in the days when the River Dee was navigable and ships could moor against the wall near to the Watergate but now it is one of the most famous racecourses in the country.

This is a book that can be enjoyed by all and looks specifically at Chester City, most of the city has been altered with care and consideration for what was there before. From the turn of the last century and earlier the city was transformed when in the capable hands of architects such as John Douglas and Thomas Lockwood. Extensive use was made of black and white but after the second war the quality of new buildings left a lot to be desired alterations and renovations made now however are in the main quite acceptable.

Paul and Len have compiled a book that can be enjoyed by all, take a walk using the book and seek out the buildings featured, compare them with what we have today but above all, take time to enjoy it.

Acknowledgements

Paul and Ken would like to thank their respective wives for their patience during the time consuming compilation of this book, also the staff in the Chester Heritage Centre, the former St Michael's Church, for their advice and help. We would also like to thank the photographers of old who left us with these snapshots of the time in which they lived. The old images were chosen from Len's archive as we both passionately believe that they should be viewed and enjoyed. The modern photographs were all taken by the authors.

About the Authors

Paul Hurley is a freelance writer and member of the Society of Authors. He has a novel, magazine and book credits to his name and lives at Winsford in Cheshire, he is married to Rose and has two sons and two daughters.

Books by the same author

Fiction
Liverpool Soldier

Non-Fiction
Middlewich Through Time
Northwich Through Time
Winsford Through Time
Villages of Mid Cheshire Through Time
Frodsham and Helsby Through Time
Nantwich Through Time

Len Morgan is a popular local historian who was born within the city walls so is a true Cestrian! He writes a weekly column in the Chester Leader looking at different aspects of Chester history, he contributes to other publications and also lectures on the subject. In 2005 he co-compiled a book titled *Twentieth Century Handbridge* with Noel St John Williams. Len still lives in Chester and has been married to Joan for over fifty-five years and they have three children and eight grandchildren.

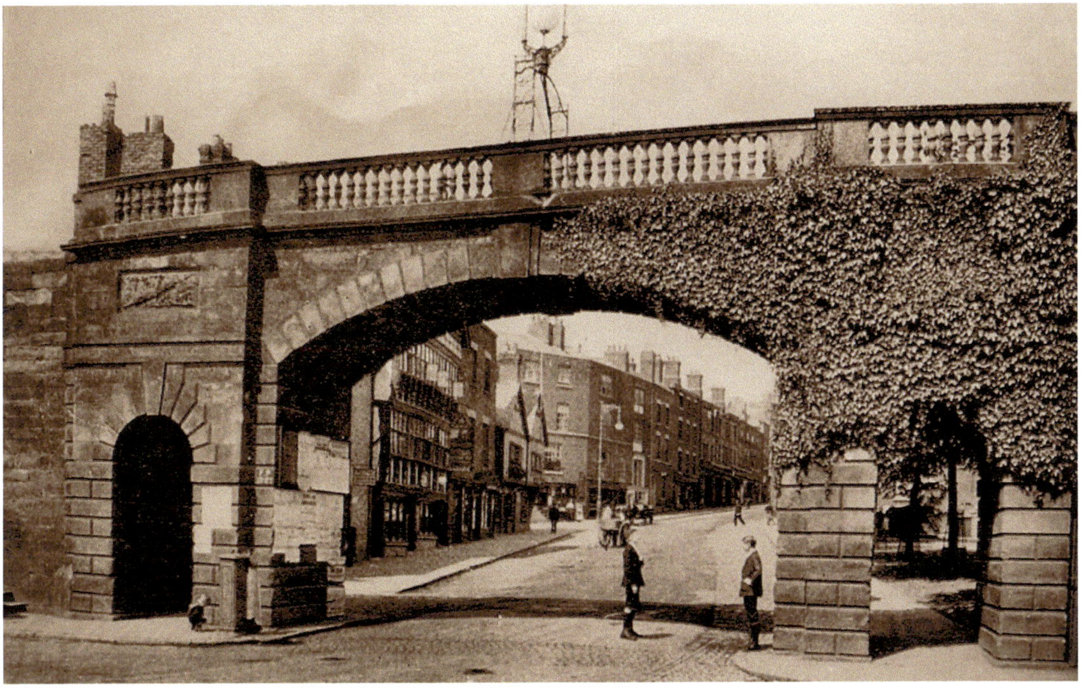

Bridgegate 1900 and 2010

The Bridgegate in Lower Bridge Street was once the main route from the city over the old Dee and through it people would pass on the way to North Wales. It was built in 1782 to replace a medieval gate and the architect of this one was John Turner. The previous bridge had a tower containing machinery to lift water from the Dee for the city. It was destroyed in the siege of Chester in 1644-45. Notice the ornate gas lamp that sits on the top.

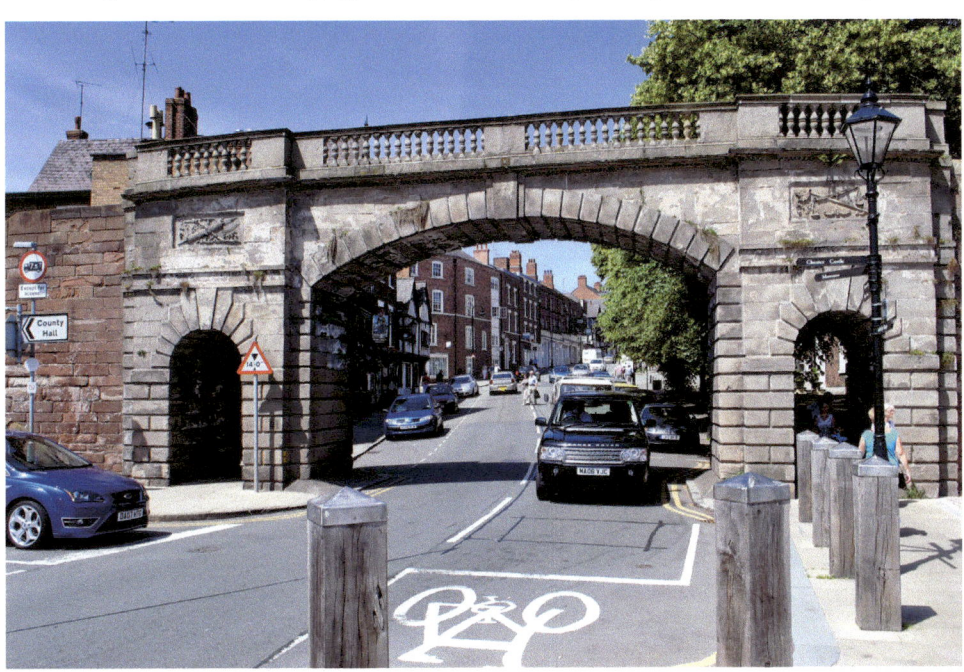

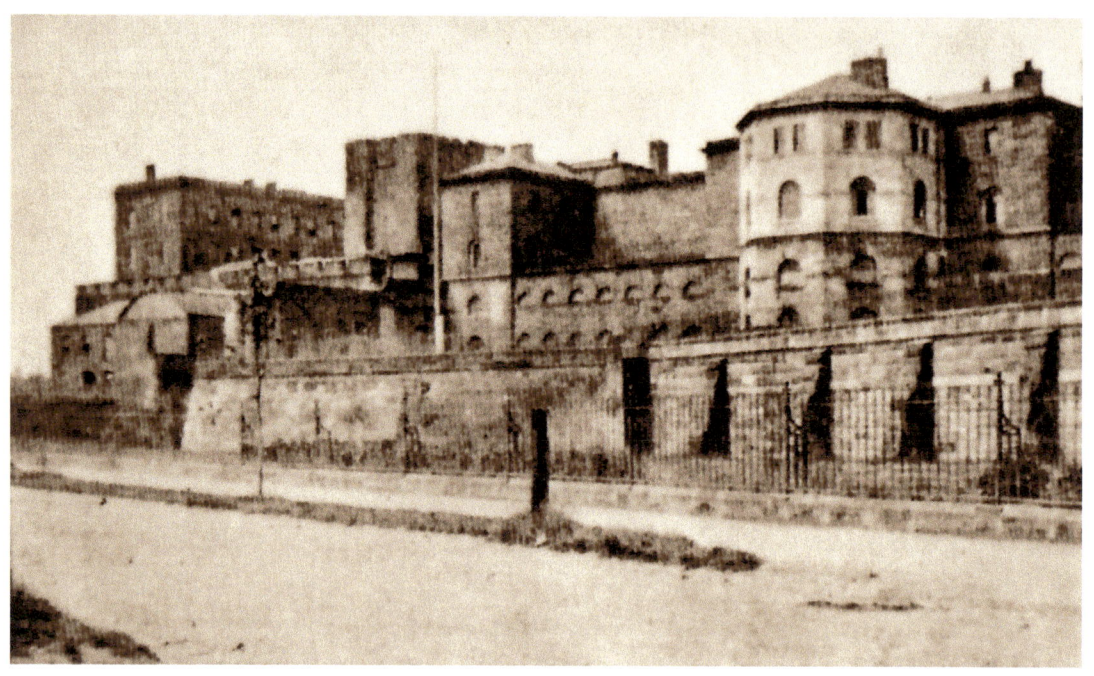

Site of the County Jail 1903 and undated
Castle drive in a 1903 photograph showing the County Jail, the main buildings of the jail had been demolished in 1900 leaving some of the cells and the courts which were used by the County Hall to store documents. The County Hall shown in the modern photograph was later built on the site and opened by the Queen in 1957; it was sold to the university in 2010.

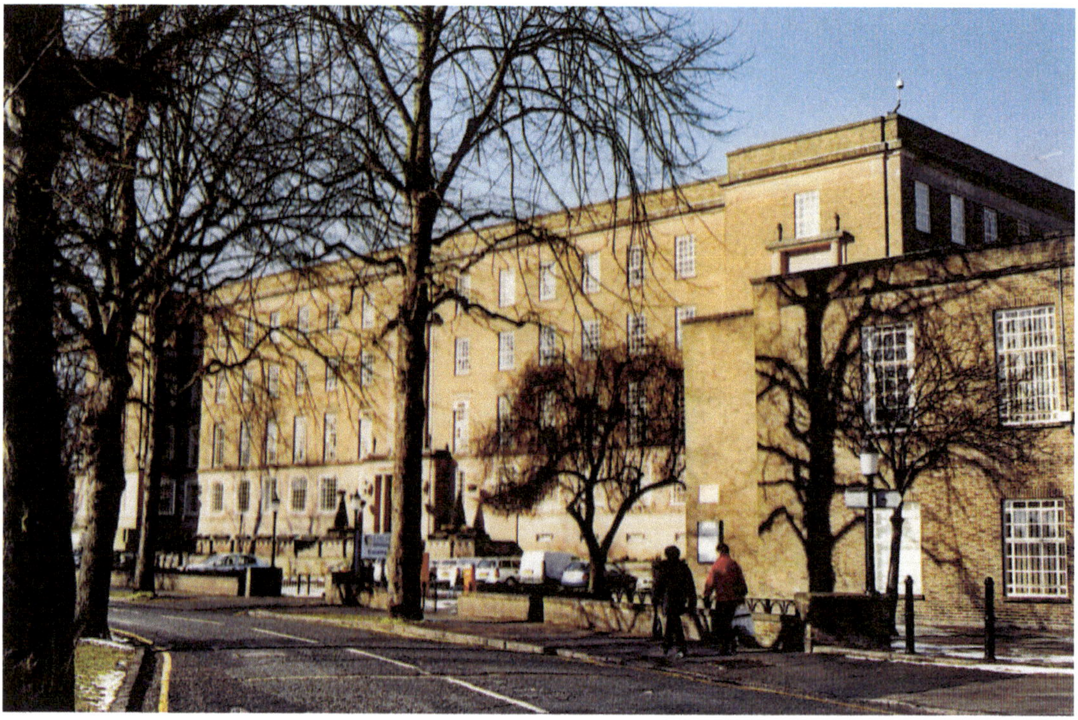

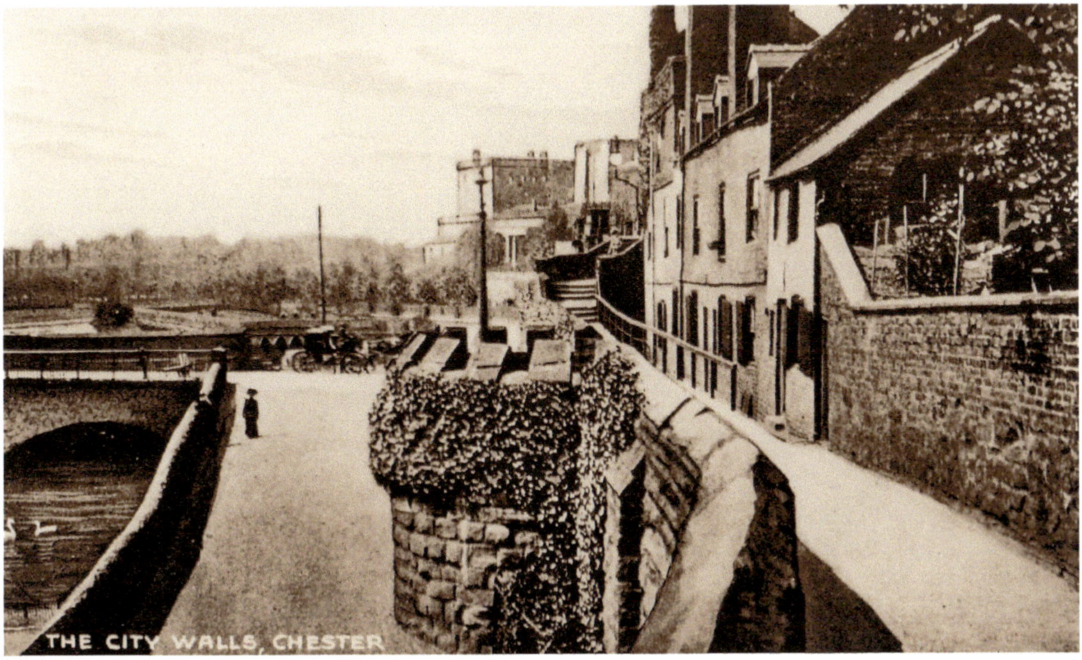

City Walls at Bridgegate 1912 and 2010
This is a section of the city walls that circle the city, the steps that can be seen, cross the Bridgegate which passes over Lower Bridge Street at the start of the old Dee Bridge. This bridge is the oldest in Chester and the first one was built in AD 922. Legend has it that when King Edward I passed over it on his way to fight the Welsh he demanded that it be replaced by a stone bridge or he would sack the city. By 1280 the current bridge was in place making the king happy!

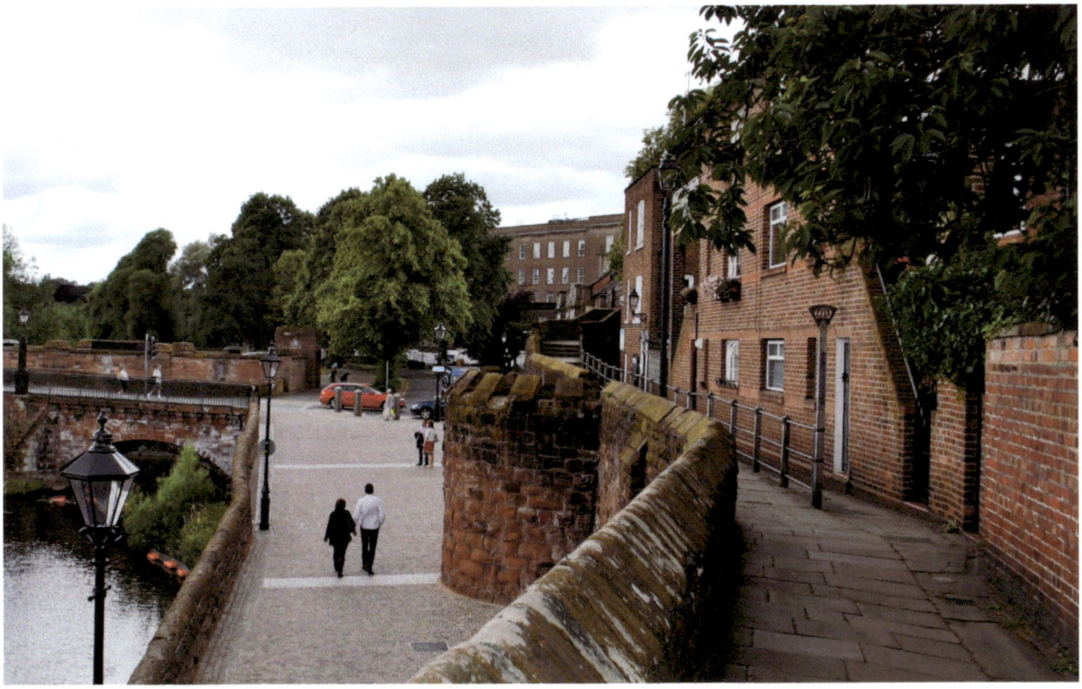

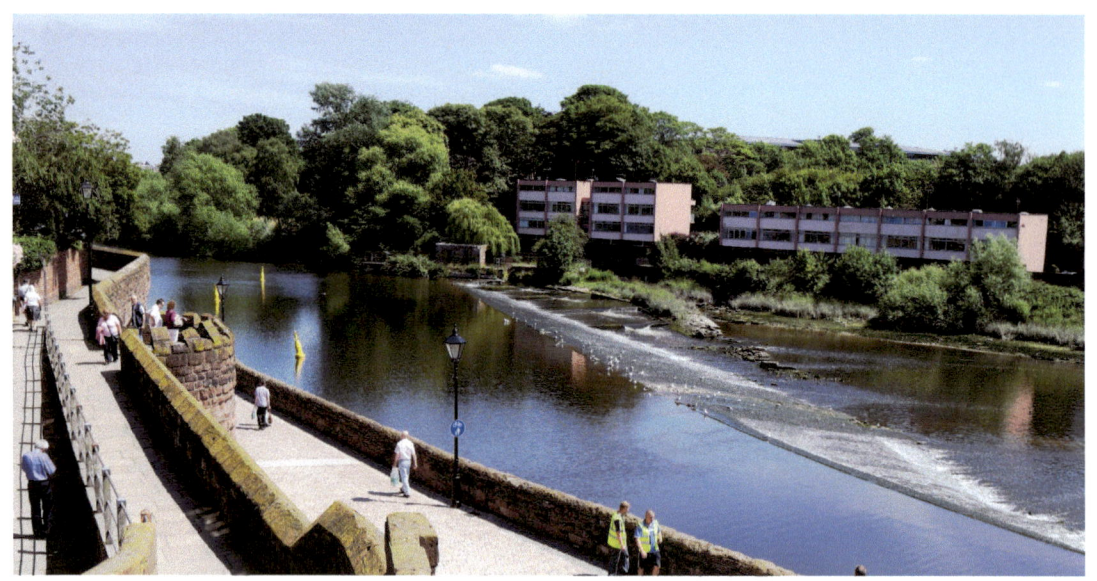

The River Dee with Tobacco Works 1948 and 2010

The old photograph here shows the very attractive Nichols Tobacco and Snuff Mills in 1948, many local people were employed here making all forms of tobacco products. The firm was established in 1780, it was closed and was unoccupied when there was a fire in June 1950 and it was demolished. At a later date in an era not renowned for architectural excellence planning permission was granted for the building of the extremely un-attractive Salmon's Leap blocks of flats as seen in the modern photograph. What would the brilliant architect John Douglas have thought of them?

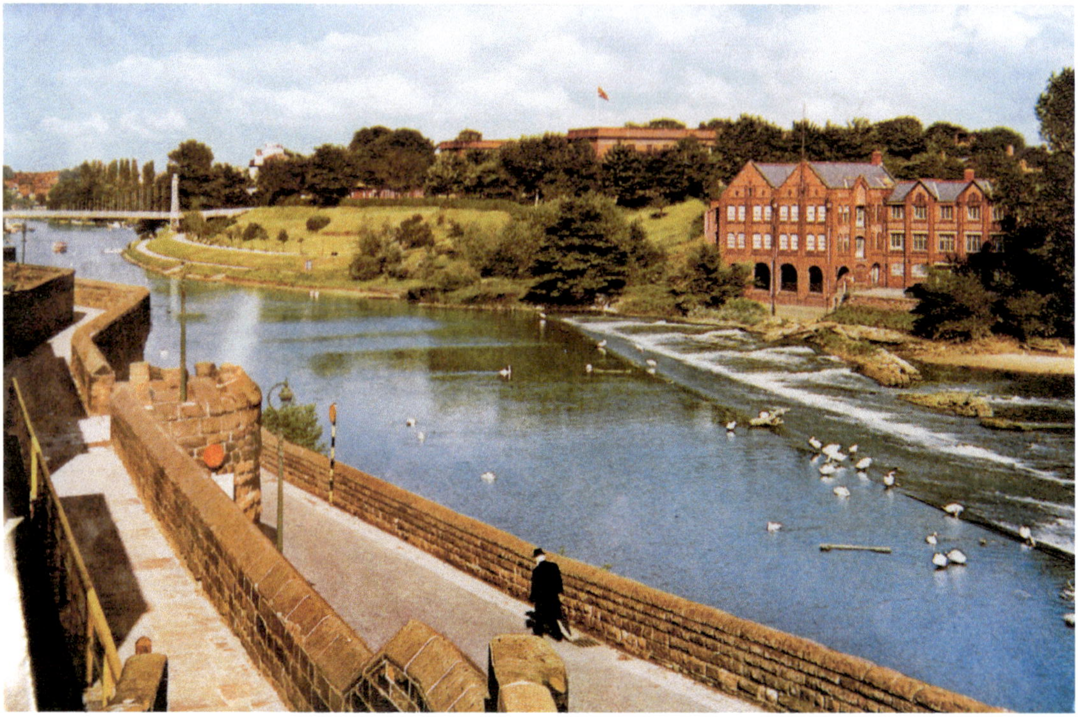

Lower Bridge Street 1920s and 2010

Now we peruse a photograph taken from the walls crossing the Bridgegate and looking down into Lower Bridge Street. The Bear and Billet public house is in the foreground, one of Chester's oldest pubs it dates from 1664 and was once the home of the Earls of Shrewsbury. The wheel of the cart has been turned into the pavement to save the full weight from pushing the horse down the hill as it rests.

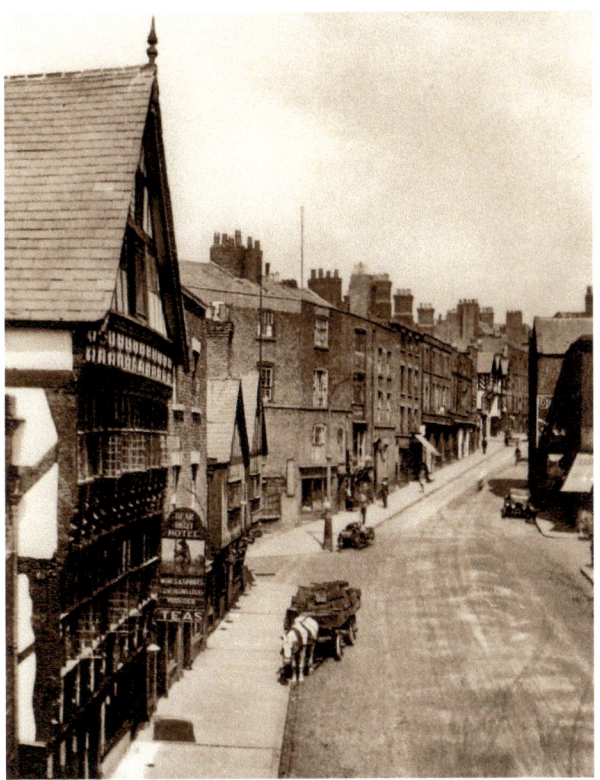

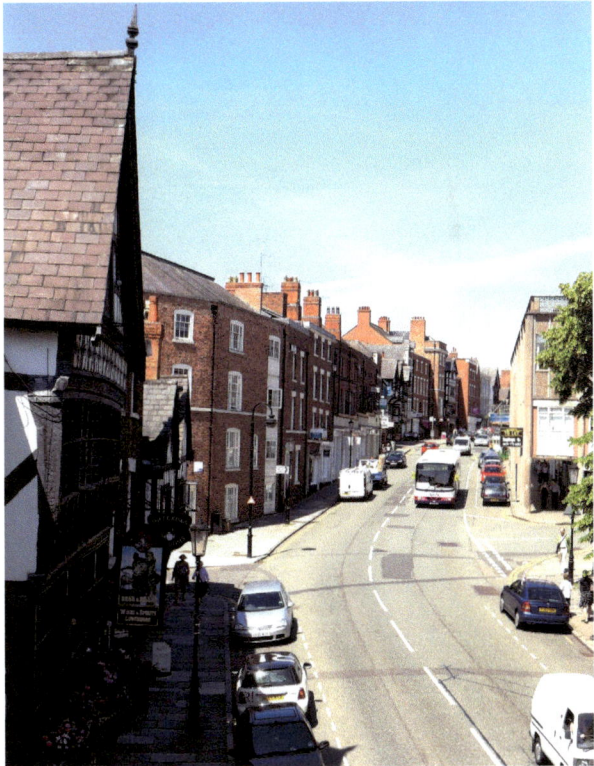

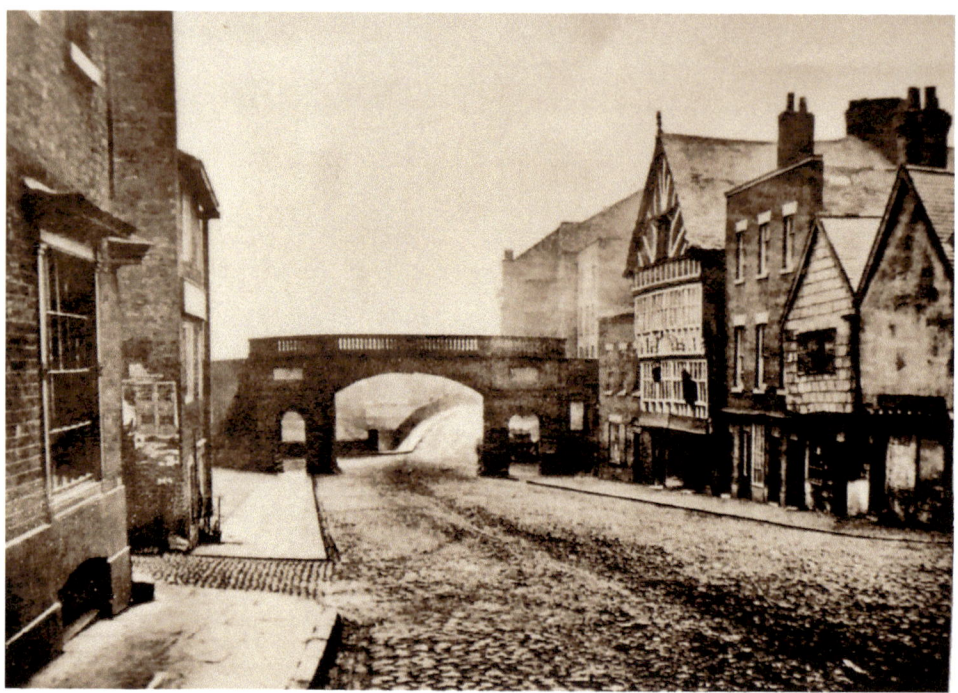

Lower Bridge Street 1860 and 2010

We look down now towards Bridgegate in what is another of the very early photographs. The large building is the Bear and Billet public house which became a public house in the eighteenth century. Originally called The Lower White Bear and later the Bear and Billet with the inn sign being a bear shackled to a billet (post). Nearer the camera is Ye Old Edgar dating from 1570 and one of the best examples of a late Tudor building. It is now two dwellings albeit that the inn name survives on the side. Dee Mills can be seen beyond the gate.

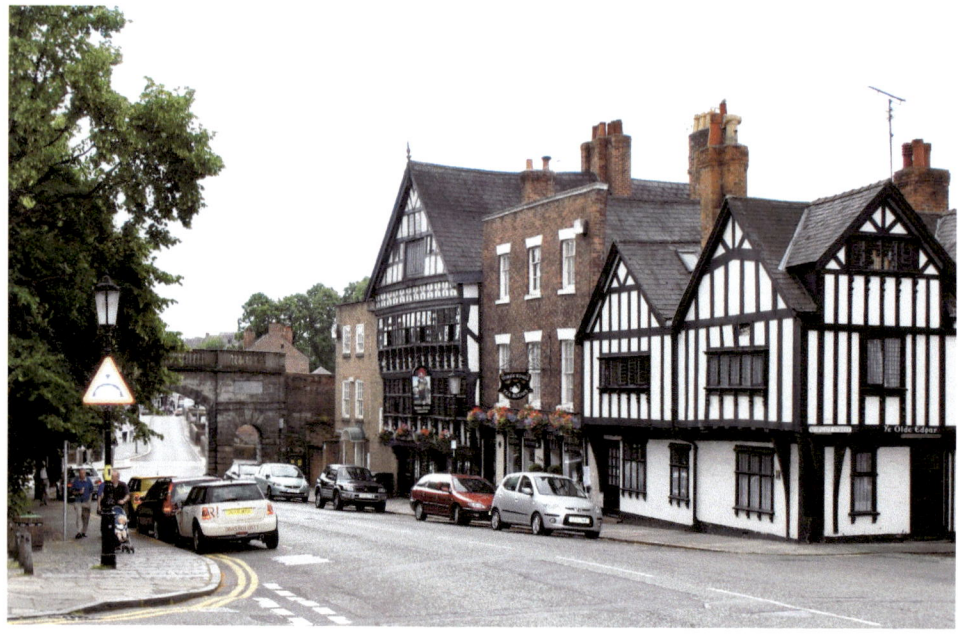

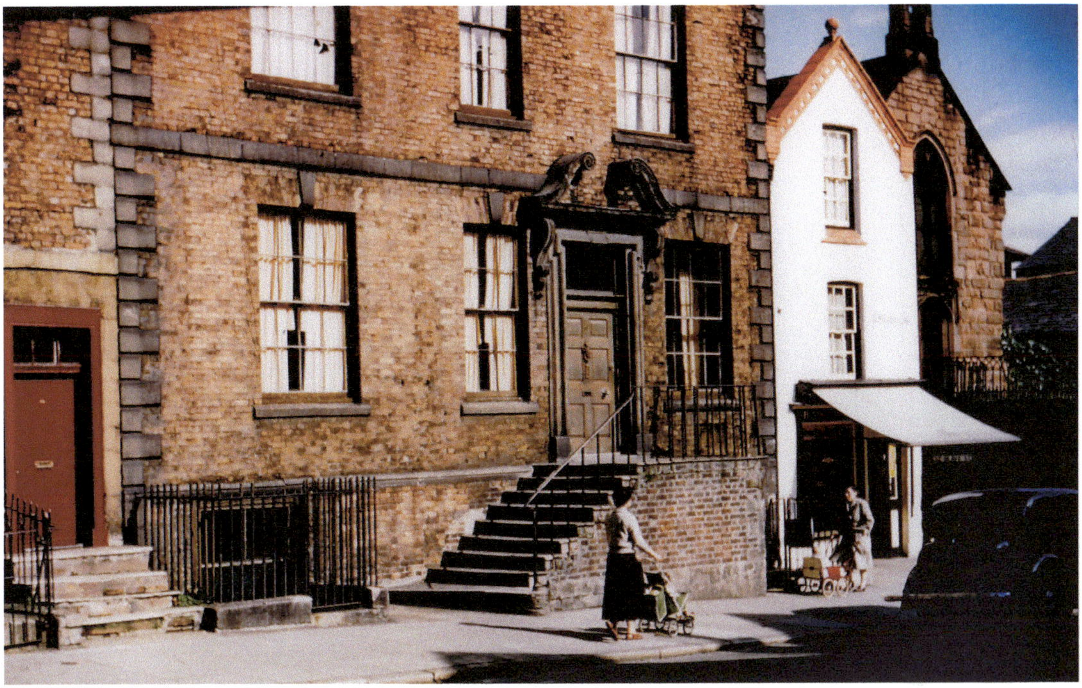

Lower Bridge Street 1956 and 2009
The year is 1956 and everything still looks very much the same due to careful restoration. On the right is St Olav's church, it is believed that there was once a Scandinavian community in this area hence the name. In 1841 the parish was amalgamated with St Michael's.

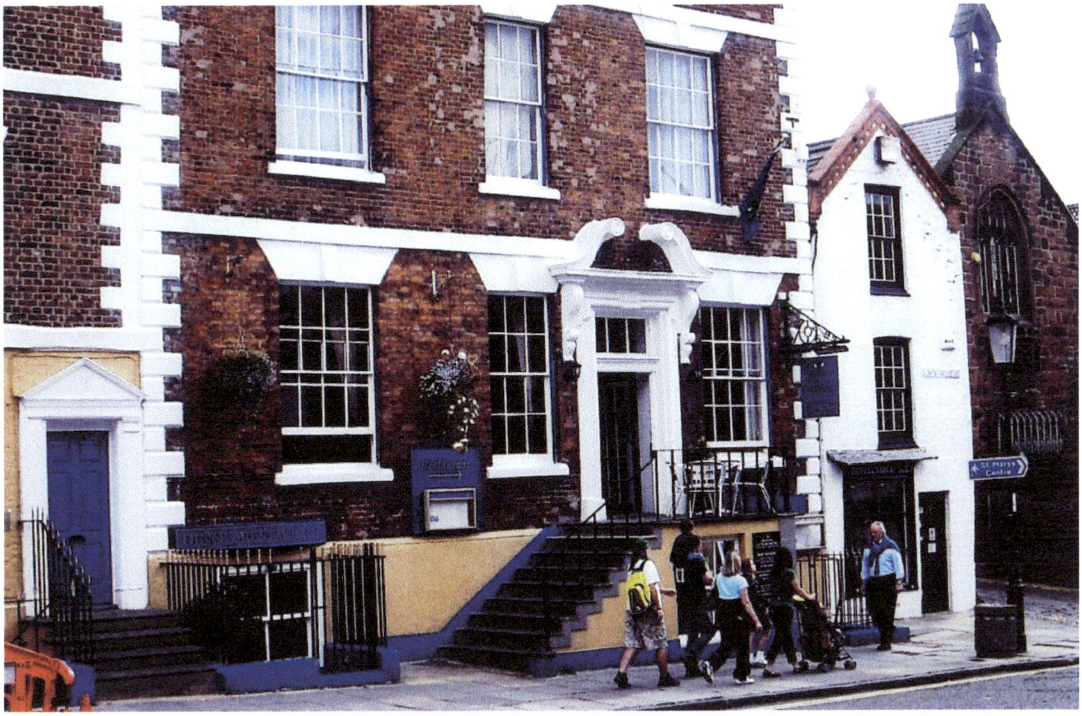

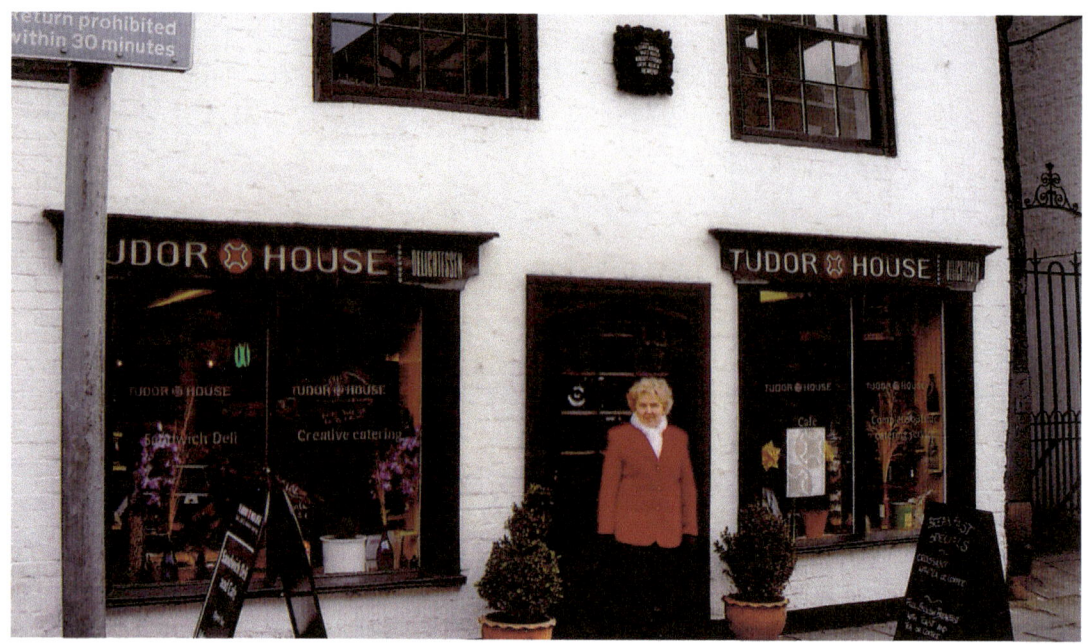

Lower Bridge Street Tudor House 1890 and 2010
This building on the east side of Bridge Street is believed to be the oldest house in Chester. Below the gable an inscription reads 1503 but is more likely to be 1603.

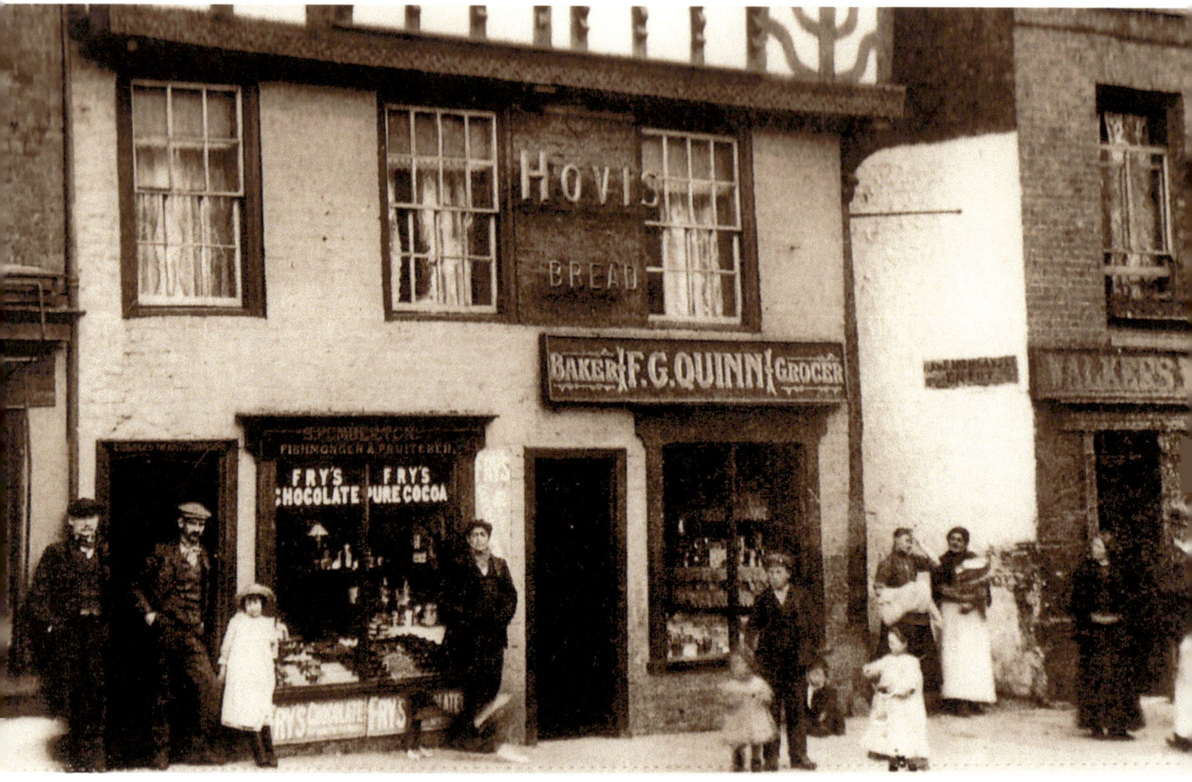

Liverpool House Lower Bridge Street 1960 and 2010

This former lodging house had a sign across the front which read, 'Clean beds and good kitchen.' In the period 1960 photograph a Vauxhall Velox saloon and an Arial Leader motorbike adorn the front hard standing. The building is more evidence of sympathetic alteration and upgrading.

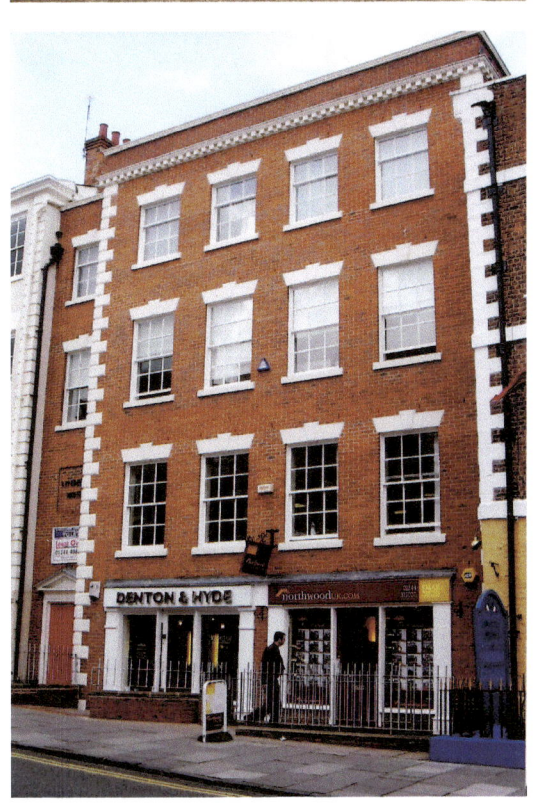

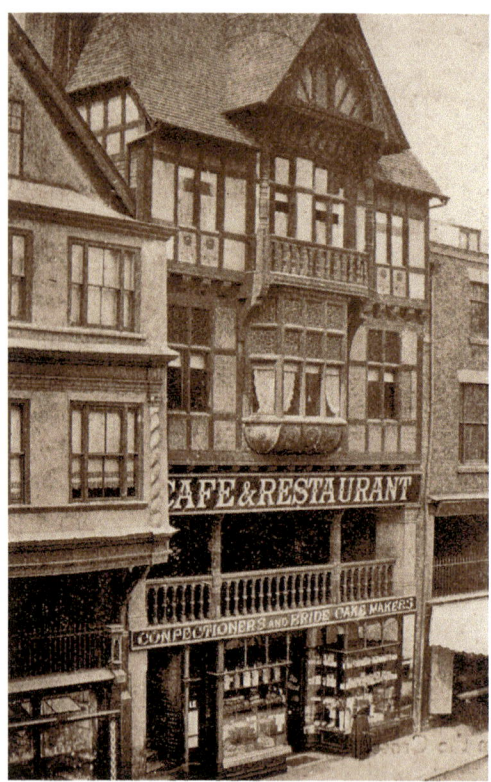

Lower Bridge Street café restaurant 1920 and 2010

This is number 20 Bridge Street and in the 1920 photograph we see a fine Victorian black and white building, part of a group of buildings known as 'The Dutch Houses.' In 1920 it was a café and confectioners, later becoming the Plain Tree Café, then Burger King and now the Yorkshire Building Society. The Plain Tree sign still survives in the modern photograph.

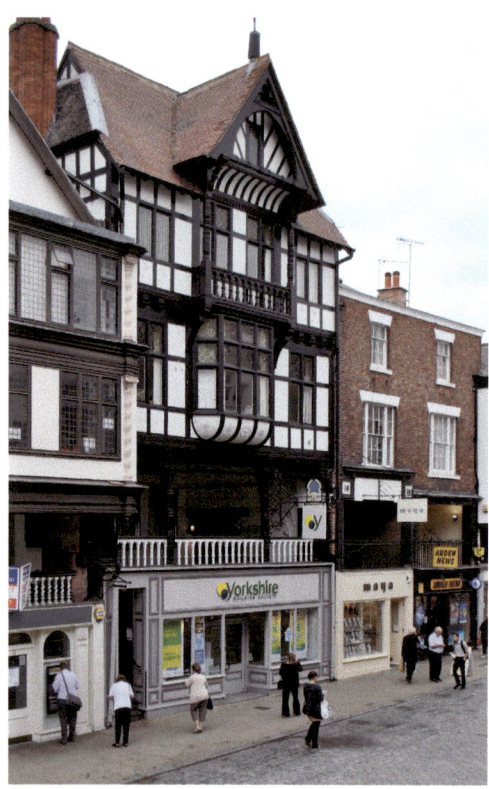

Lower Bridge Street 1900 and 2010

This whole area underwent a major redevelopment during 1984/1985 with many of the new buildings keeping a similar look to the old ones. Note the bowed window above the shop front. The 1900 photograph is a poor one but included because of its period charm.

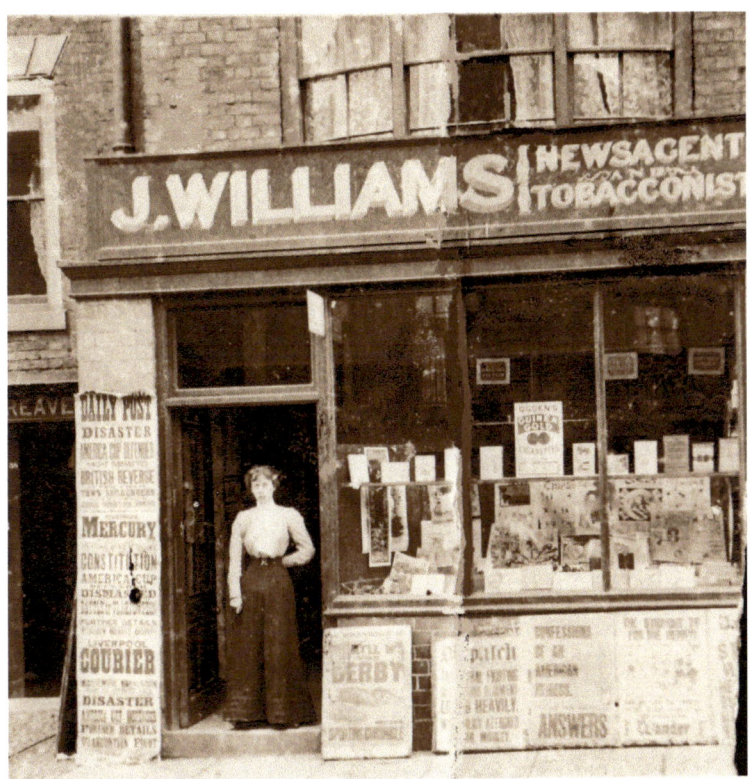

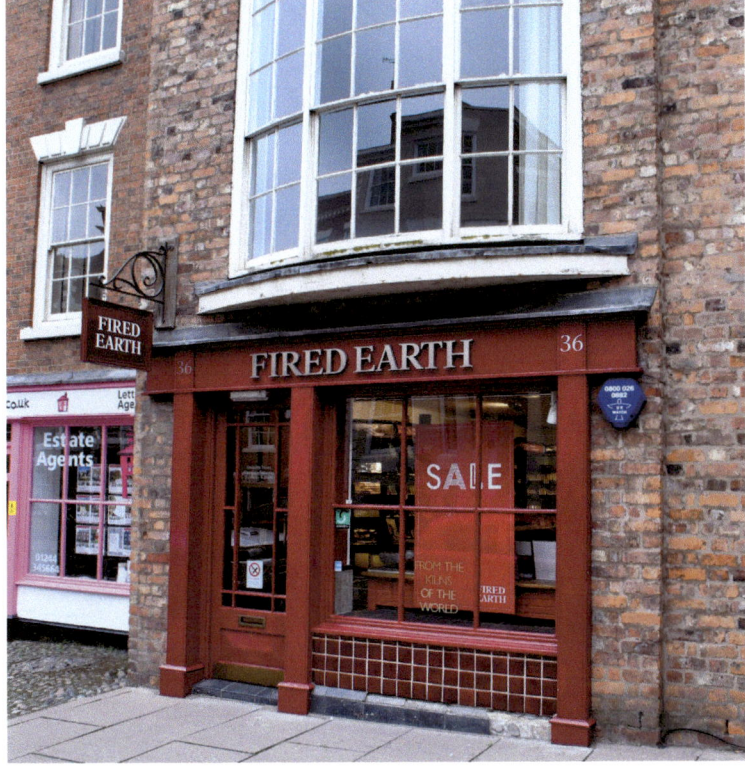

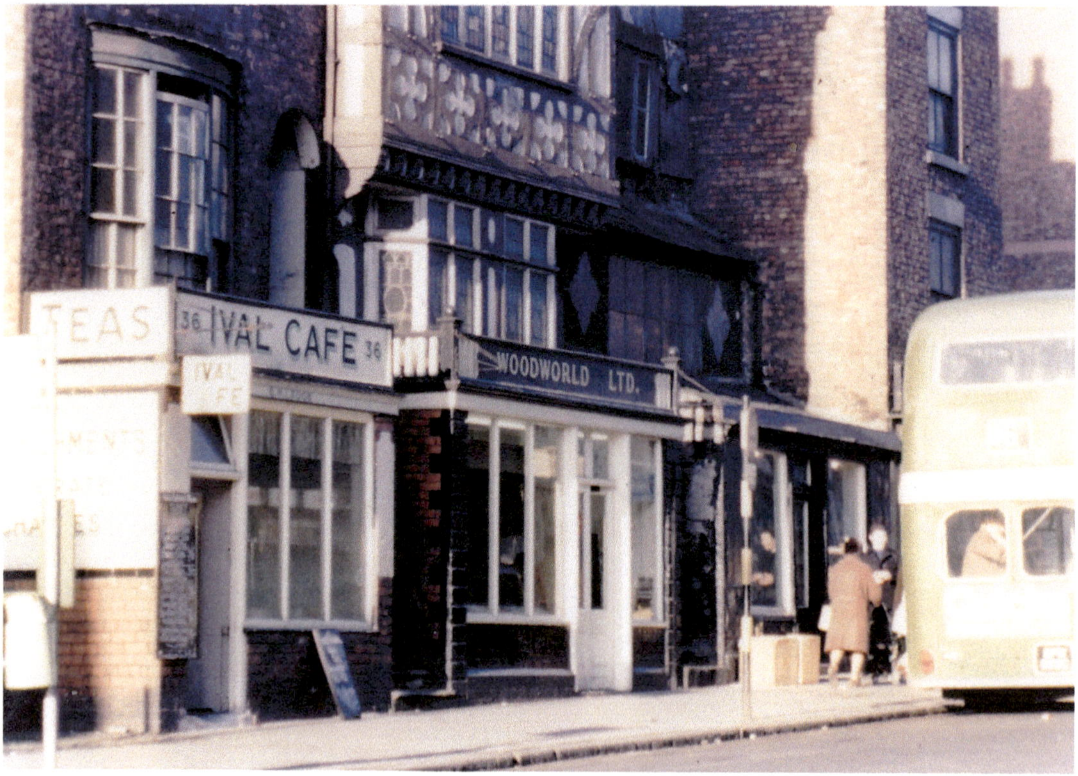

Lower Bridge Street 1967 and 2010
The old photograph was taken prior to redevelopment and the former Woodworld Ltd. shop has gone to make the access to a small office complex called Heritage Court opened in March 1985 by the Duke of Westminster. A Crosville double decker bus has stopped to pick up passengers.

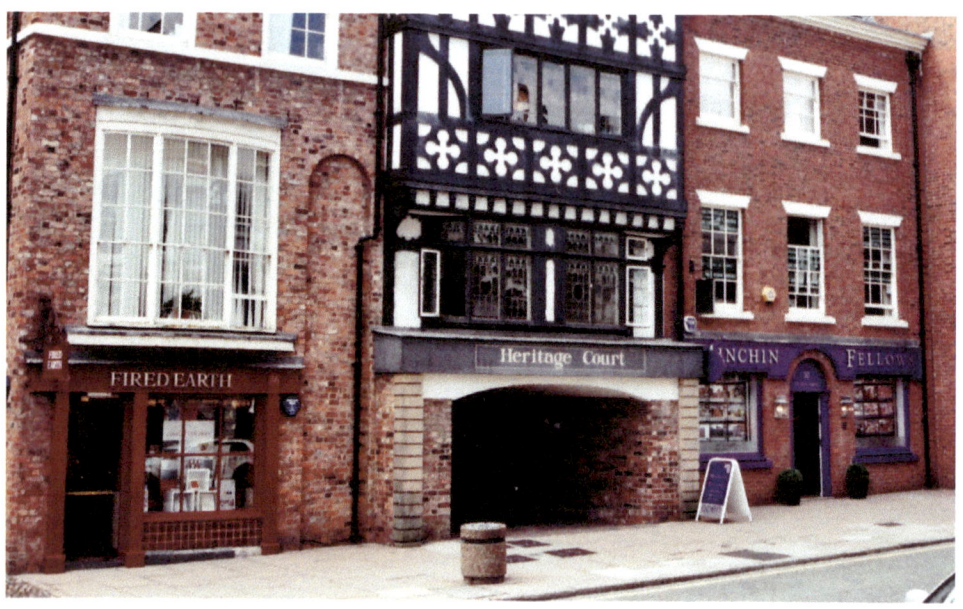

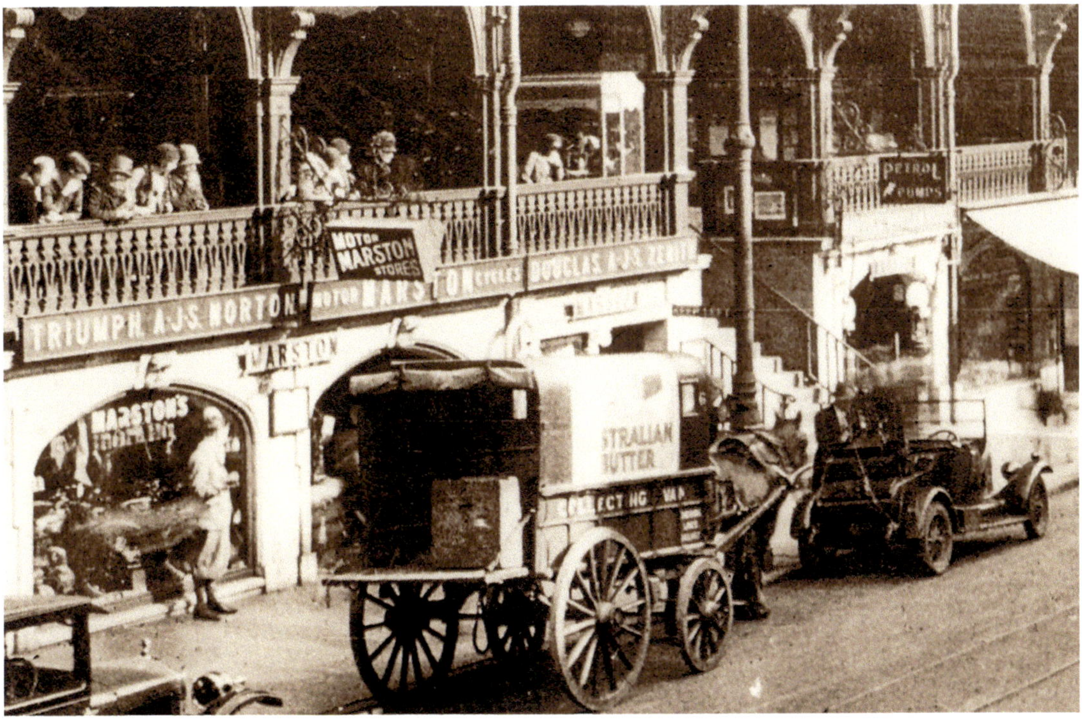

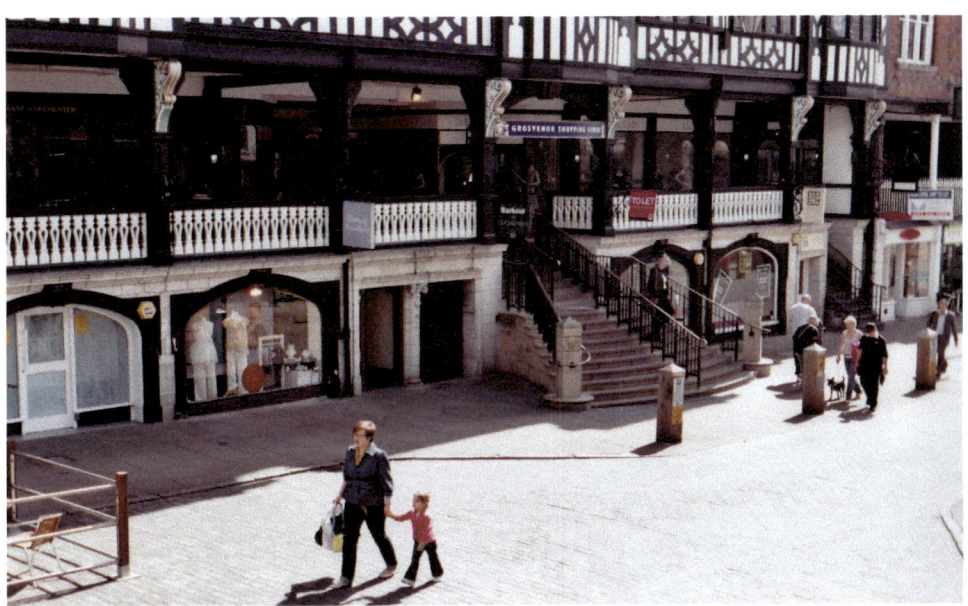

Lower Bridge Street 1920s and 2009
A photograph simply oozing period charm from the 1920s; horse-drawn traffic is still in use but motorcars are starting to predominate. The shop beneath the Row is catering for this upsurge in the mechanically propelled vehicle and deals in motorcycles. The company is Marston's and they offer for sale Douglas, Triumph, AJS and Norton motorcycles. Oh those memorable days when the British motorcycle industry was the best in the world but at least we still have Triumph and Norton.

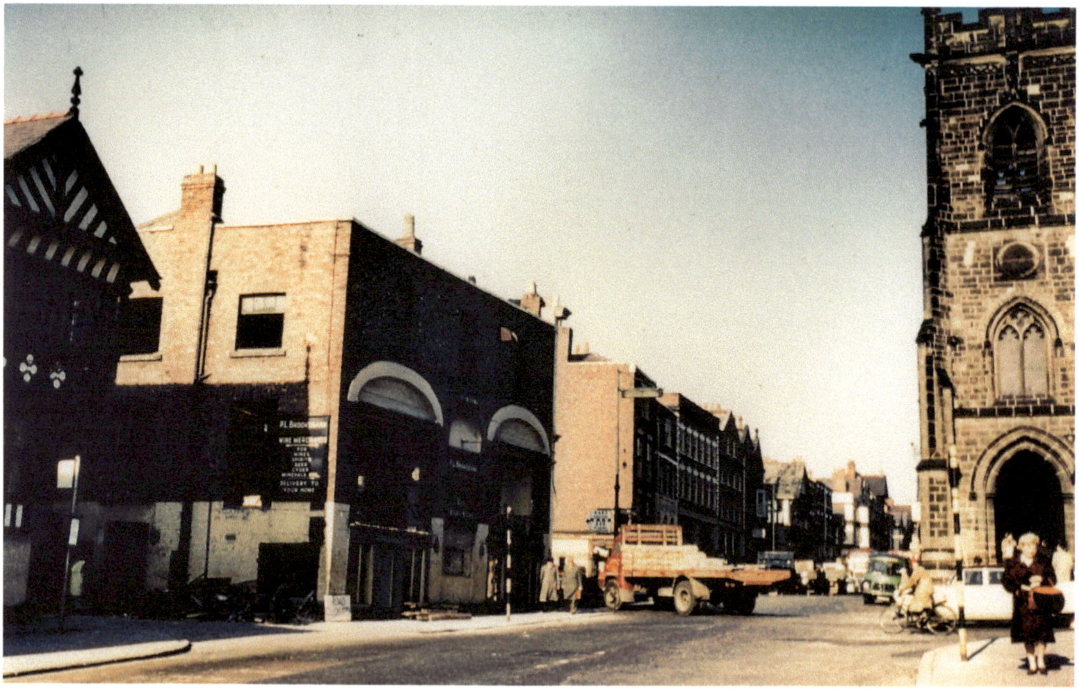

Bridge Street Junction 1964 and 2010

Looking now up Bridge Street with the Falcon pub on the extreme left, the large building beyond the Falcon has gone to make way for the ring road. On the opposite junction and on the right is the Chester Heritage Centre, this was originally St Michael's church which is one of nine medieval churches in Chester. It stands on the southern gateway of the Roman Fortress and was completely overhauled between 1849 and 1861. It became Britain's first Heritage Centre in 1975 but is now reputed to be under threat.

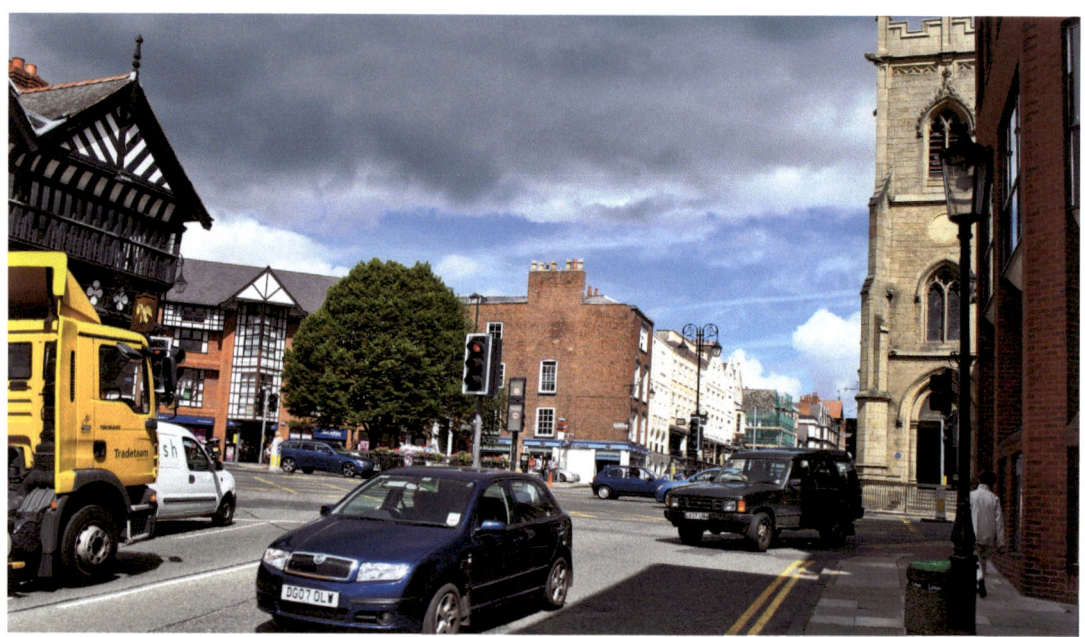

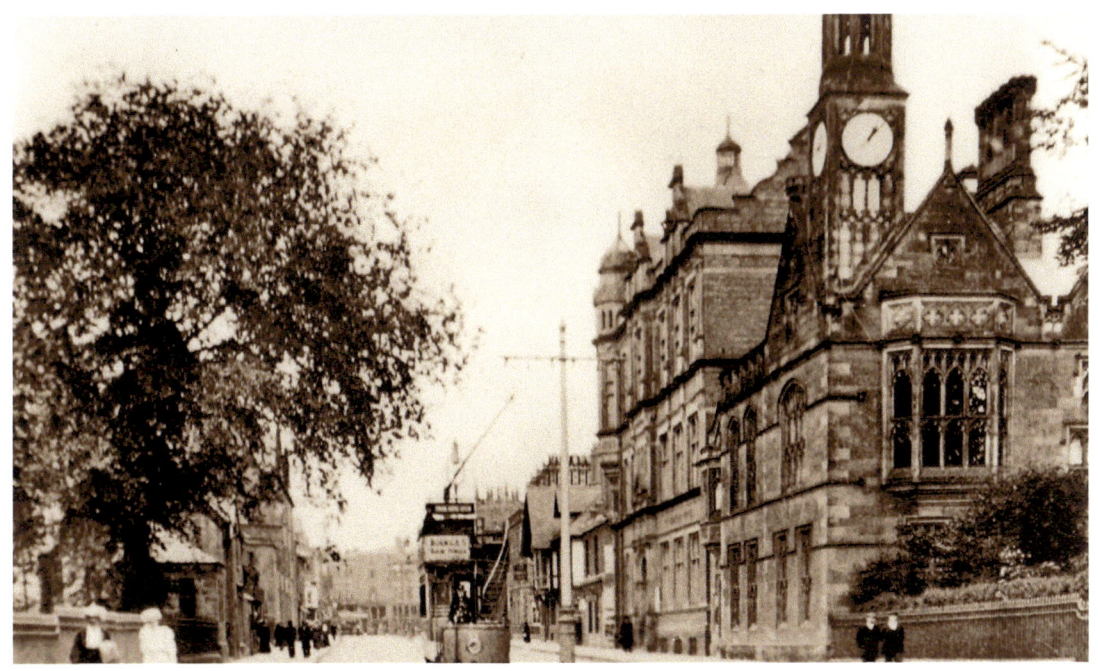

Grosvenor Street 1906 and 2009
The tram is returning from Saltney and is passing the former Trustee Saving Bank which was next to the Grosvenor Museum. The museum was founded in 1885 possibly under the auspices of The Chester Society for Natural Sciences, Literature and Arts which had been instituted by Charles Kingsley, Canon of Chester Cathedral from 1871 to 1873. It now has around 100,000 visitors a year.

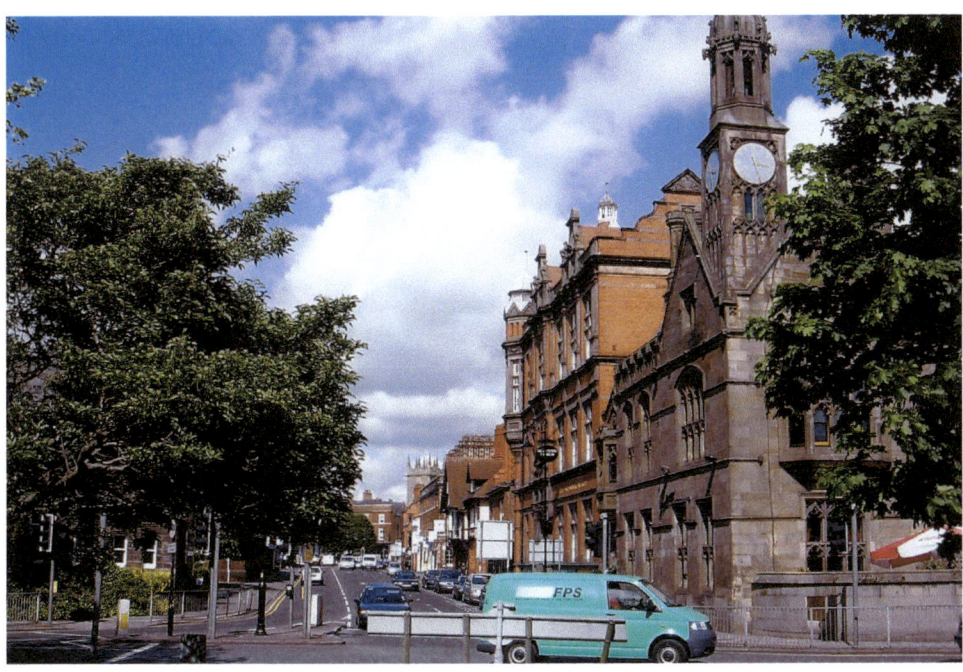

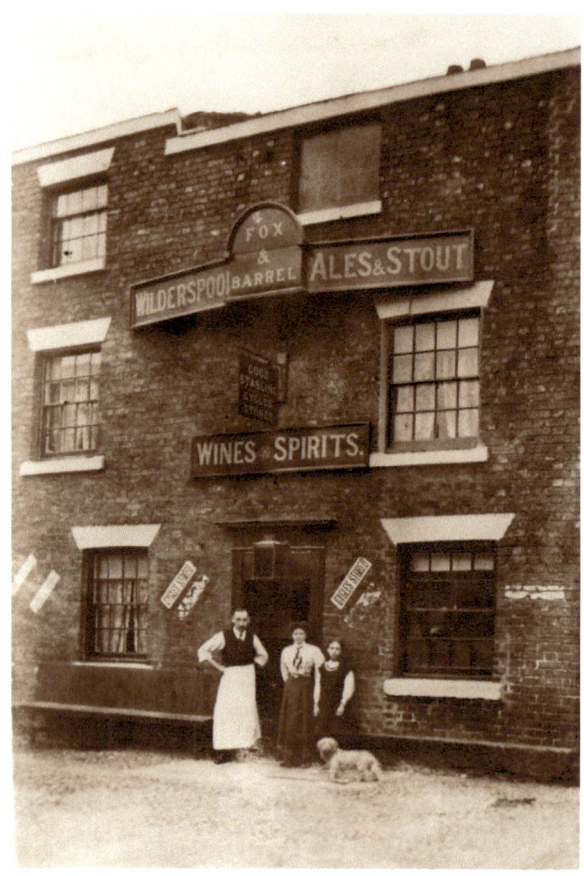

Fox and Barrel, Grosvenor Street 1902 and 2010

This photograph of Grosvenor Street at the junction with Cuppin Street shows in the 1902 photograph the Fox and Barrel public house. At the time Mrs Elizabeth Jones was the licensee, probably the lady in the photograph. The pub walls are adorned with posters offering *'Cycles stored and good stabling.'* The building has been greatly altered over the intervening years and in July 2010 a steakhouse is in occupation.

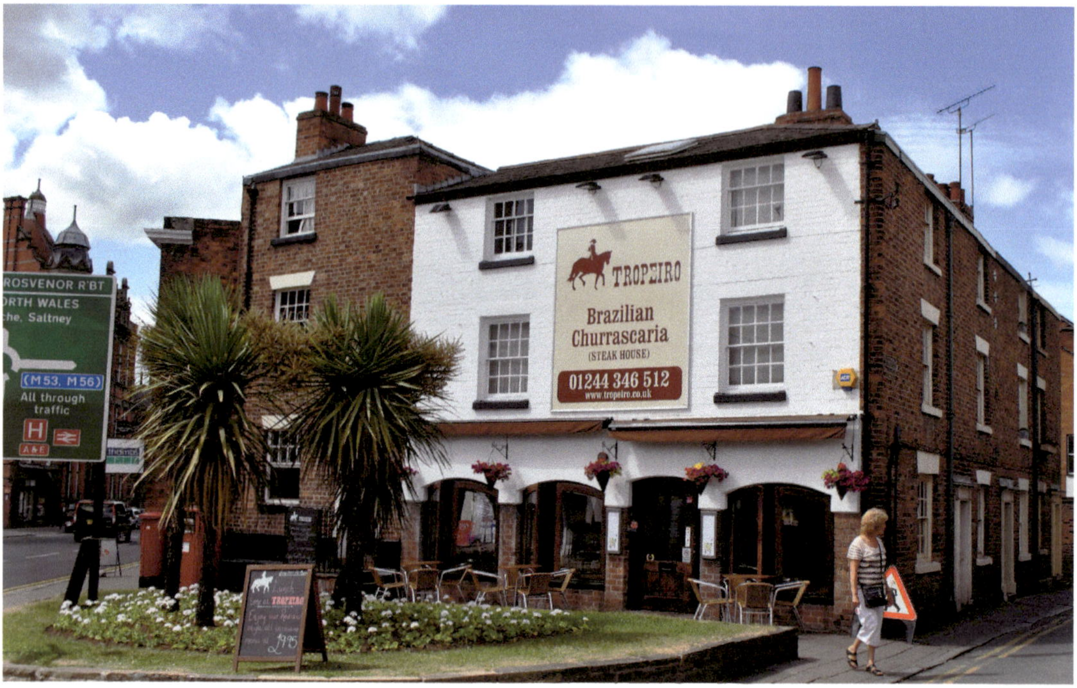

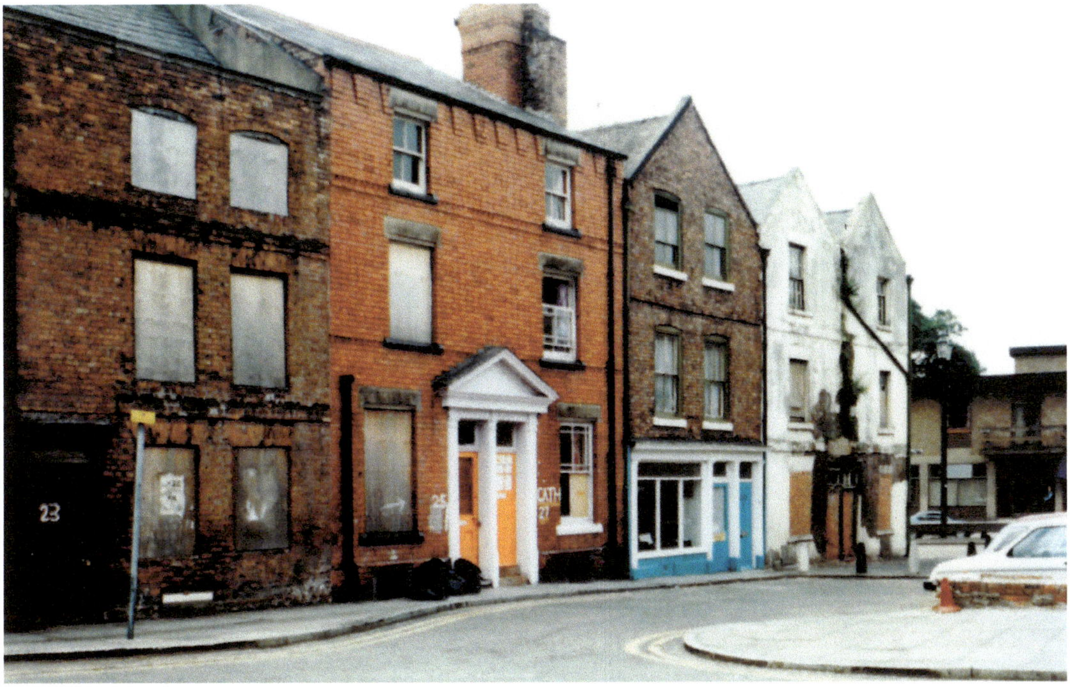

Cuppin Street 1982 and 2008
Cuppin Street is accessed from Grosvenor Street and once went through to Nicholas Street which can be seen at the end of the old photograph. During the building of the ring road it was sealed off and became a car park, part of this was the site of St Martin's Church and graveyard. To pinpoint the locaton, see the balcony on the left facing. This balcony is shown again on page 43.

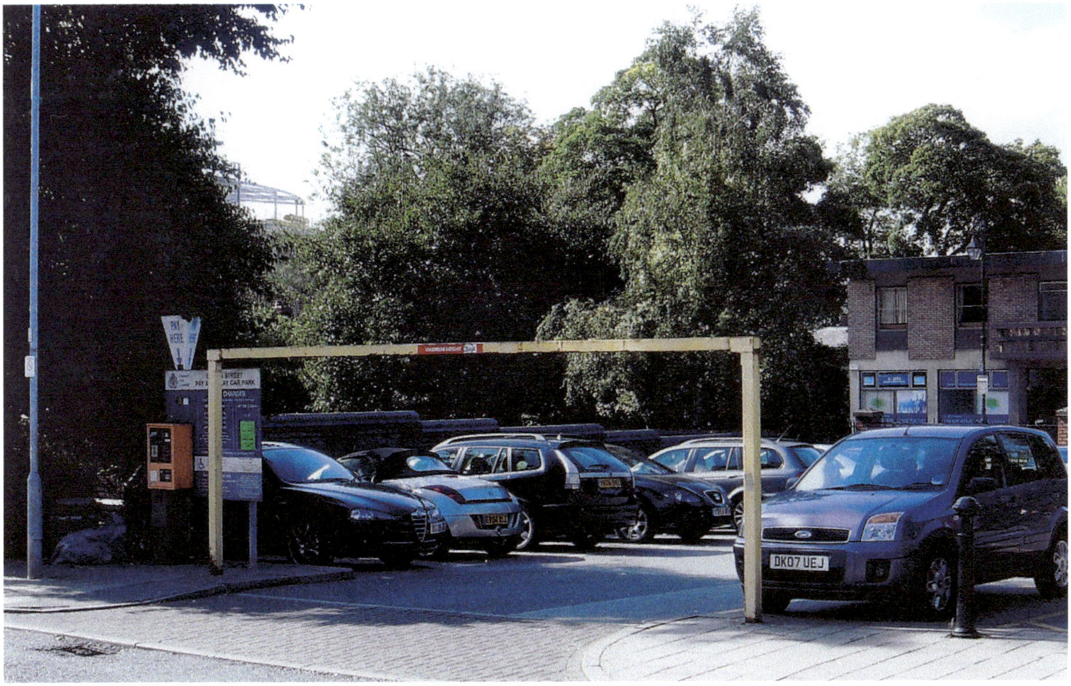

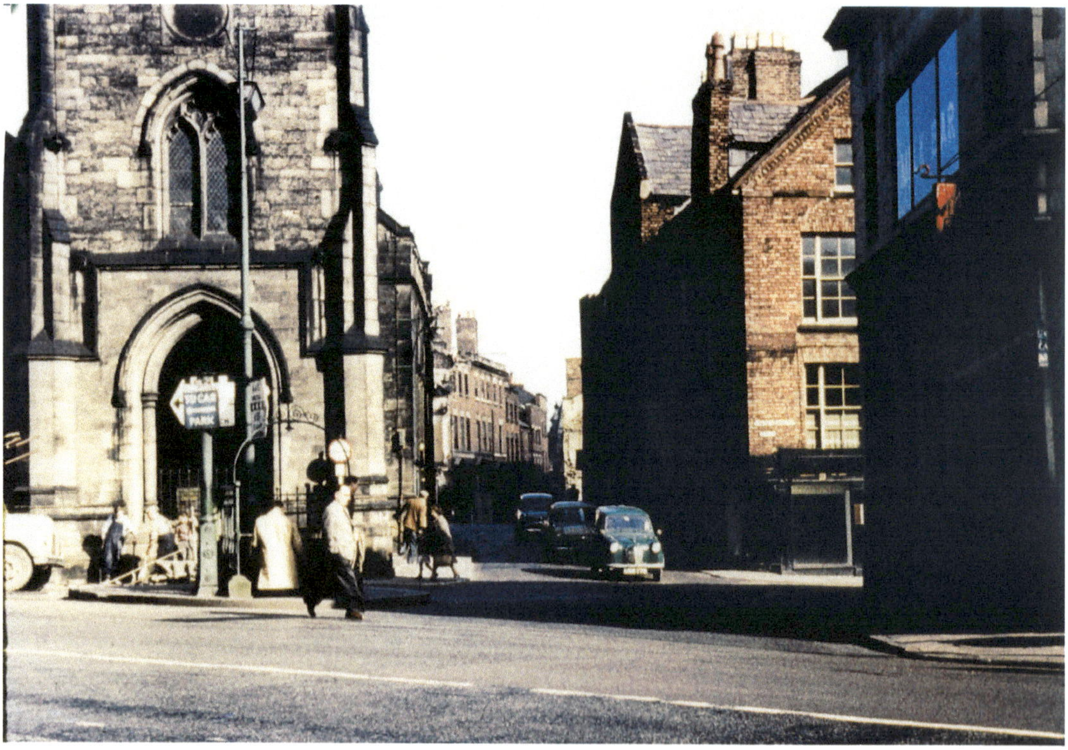

Grosvenor Street into Pepper Street 1960s and 2010

Seen here is the junction of Grosvenor Street, Bridge Street and Pepper Street in the town centre. In the old photograph the underground gents' toilet can be seen. Many buildings on both sides of Pepper Street were demolished to make way for this section of the ring road which was opened in 1966.

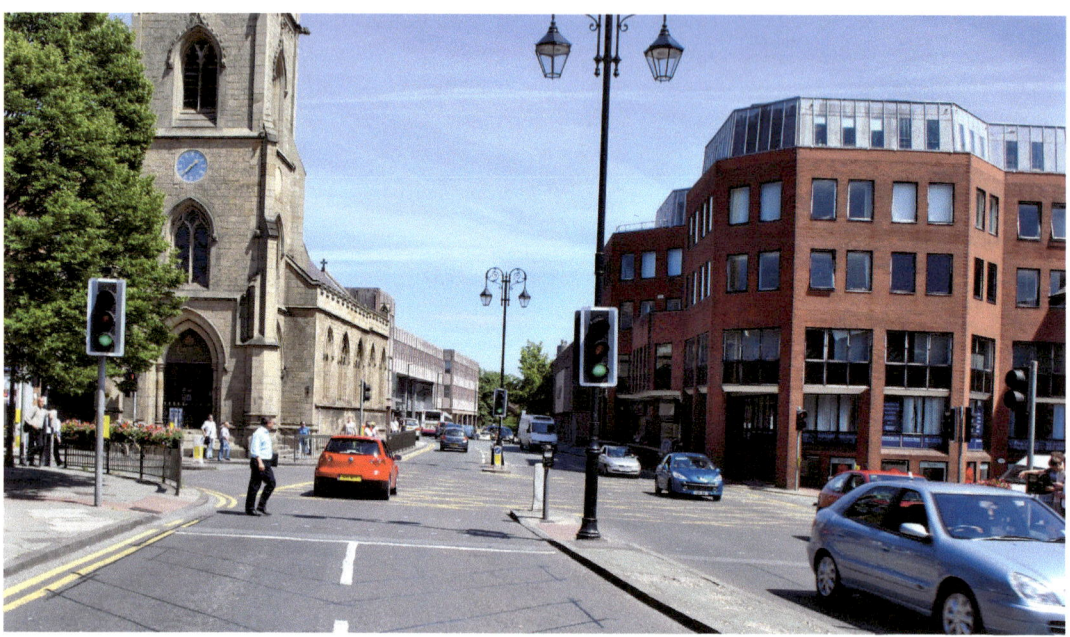

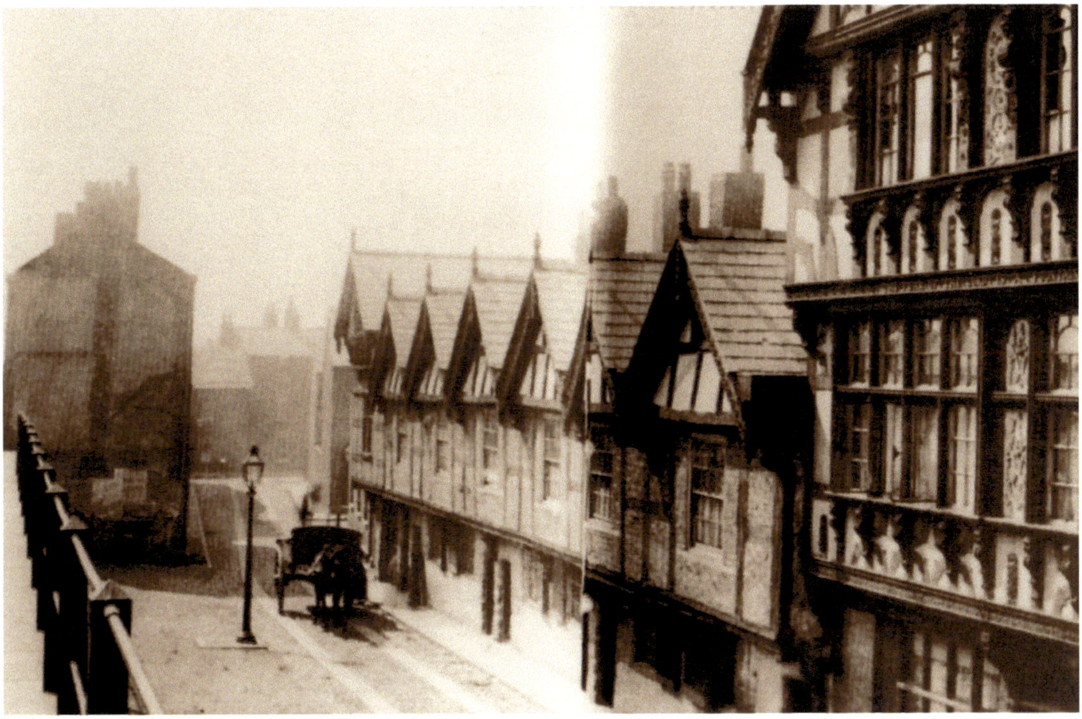

Park Street 1908 and 2009
Park Street is off Pepper Street and runs parallel with the walls from which these photographs were taken. The row of cottages was built in 1650 and was known as The Nine Houses although only six have survived. They were restored and modernised in 1968/69.

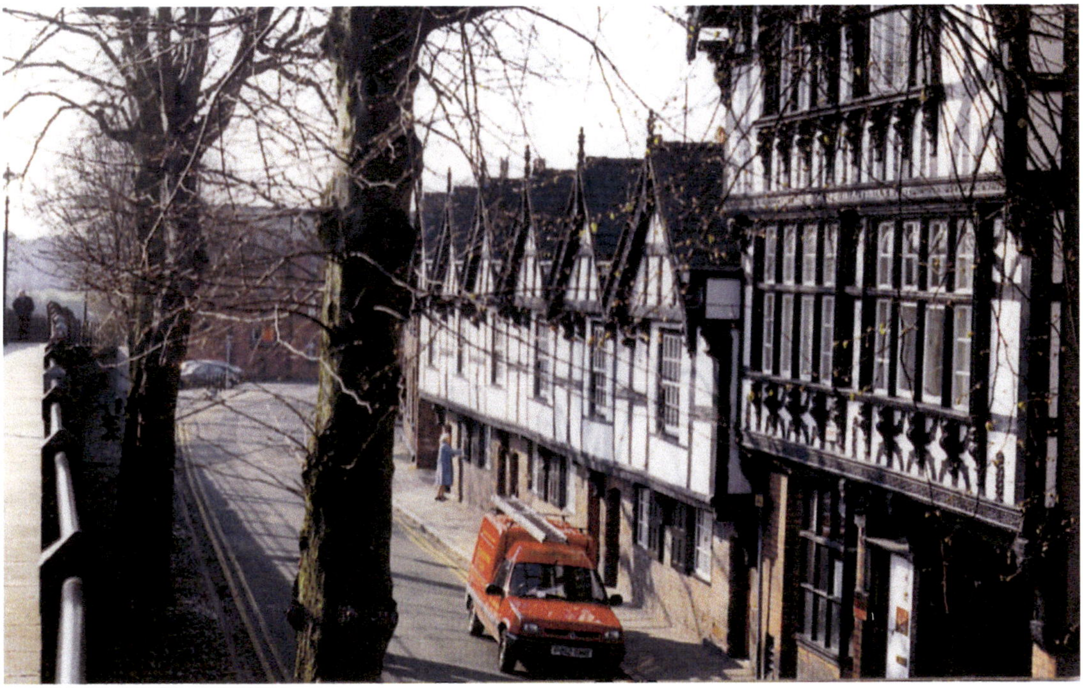

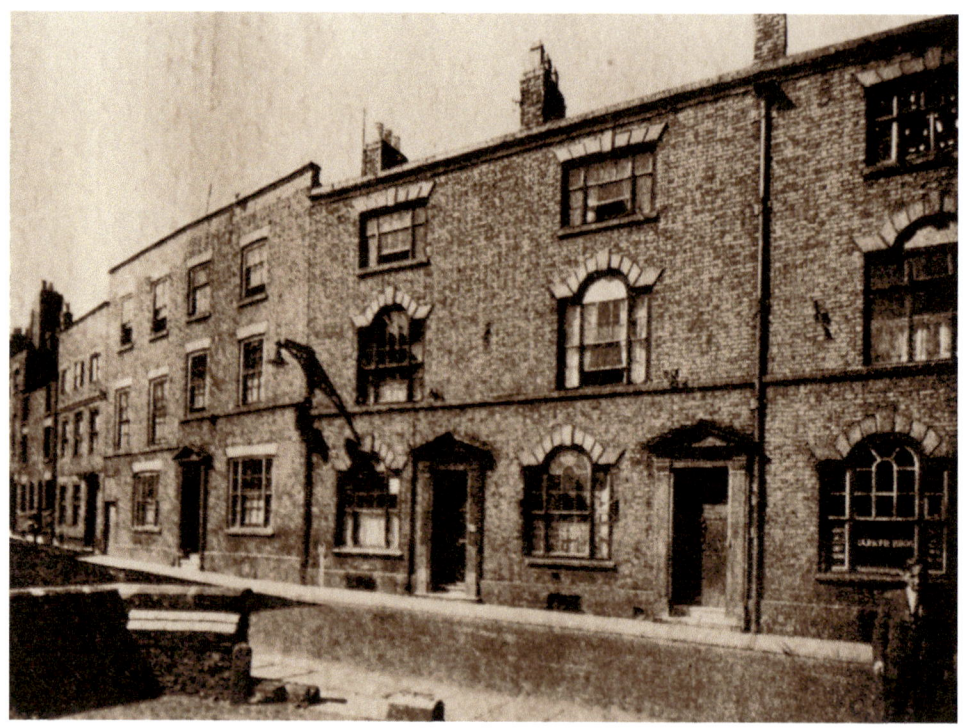

Pepper Street 1950 and undated

Now here we have considerable alterations on a street that is the main one through the city. The buildings in the 1950 photograph were demolished and the new ones erected, at the same time, the road was widened to become a section of the ring road. The old houses were replaced by the Grosvenor Shopping Centre.

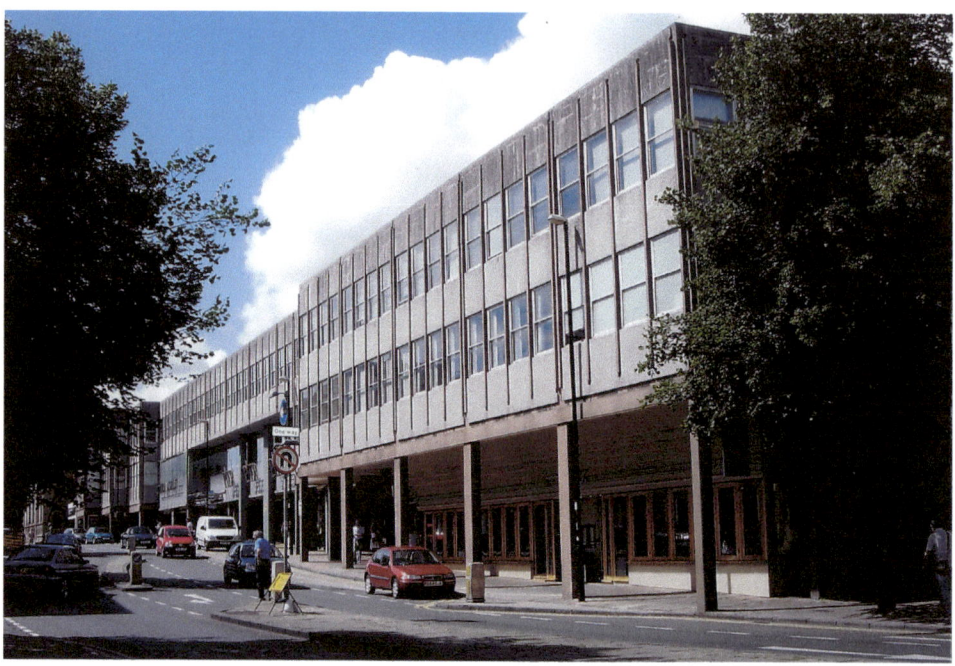

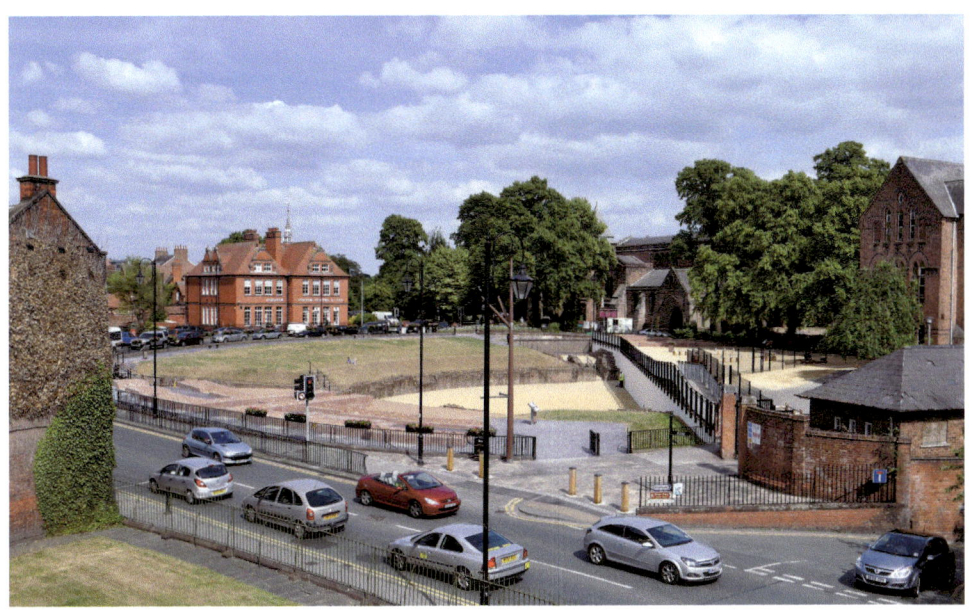

Site of the Roman Amphitheatre 1947 and 2010
This is the partially-excavated remains of the largest stone-built Roman military amphitheatre in Britain. The first amphitheatre on the site was built soon after the establishment of the fortress itself in the late 70s AD. Chester's Roman amphitheatre was discovered in 1929, when a short stretch of the curved outer wall was discovered. Little St John Street was to be straightened out and driven across the site but was cancelled after much campaigning. Now experts are suggesting that it was the site of King Arthur's Round Table (after the Romans had finished with it of course).

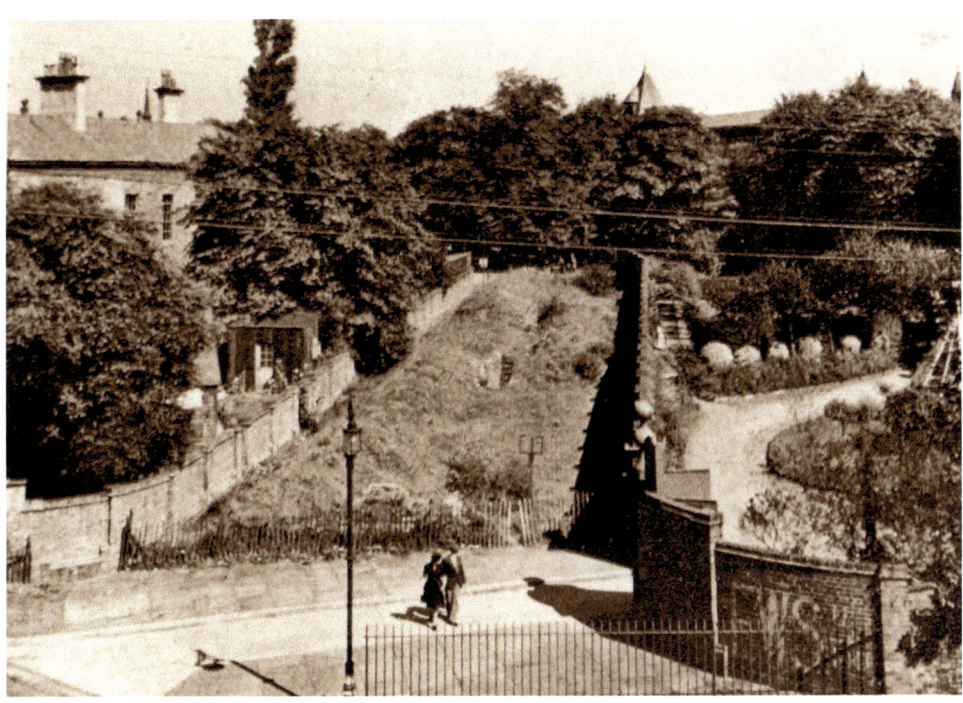

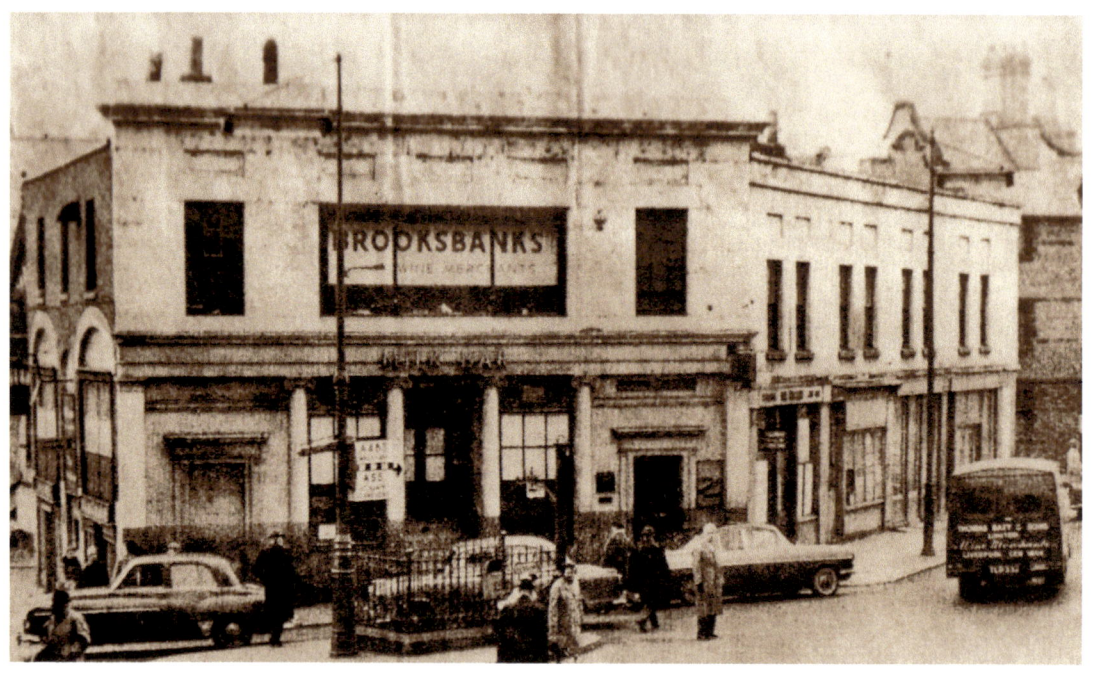

Corner of Lower Bridge Street 1950s and 2010
Not the best photograph but one that shows the building that stood in front of The Falcon Inn until road widening swept it away. You can just see the roof of The Falcon behind it. In front of it on the road is an underground gents' toilet which is still under the road somewhere on the traffic lights, albeit that it has been filled in.

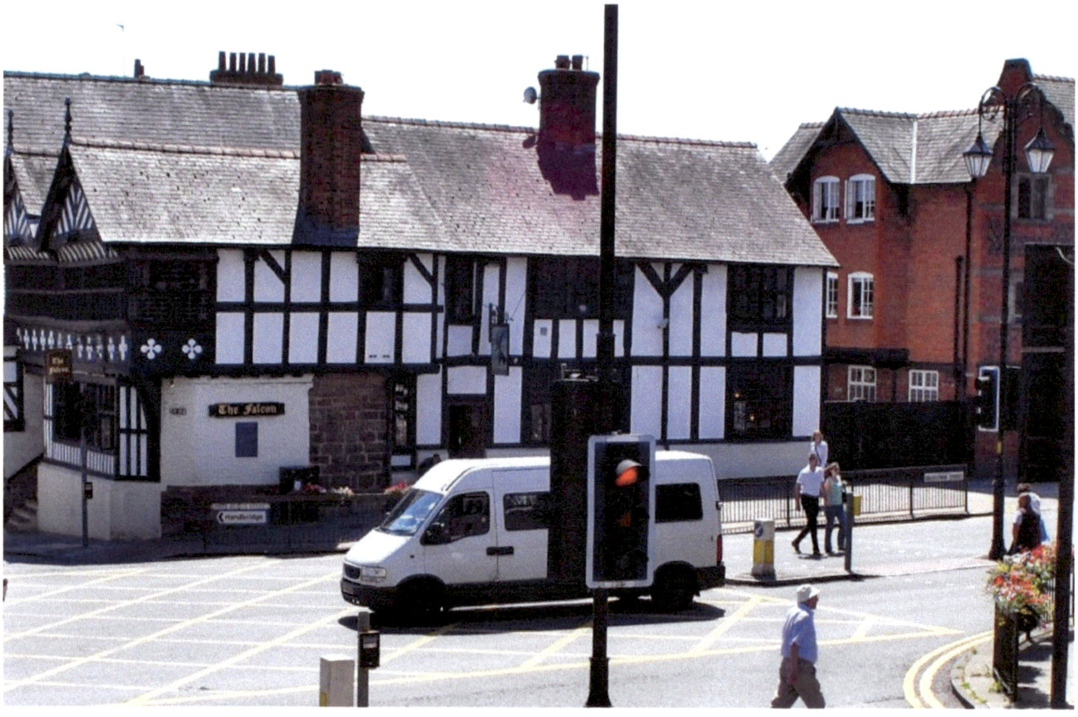

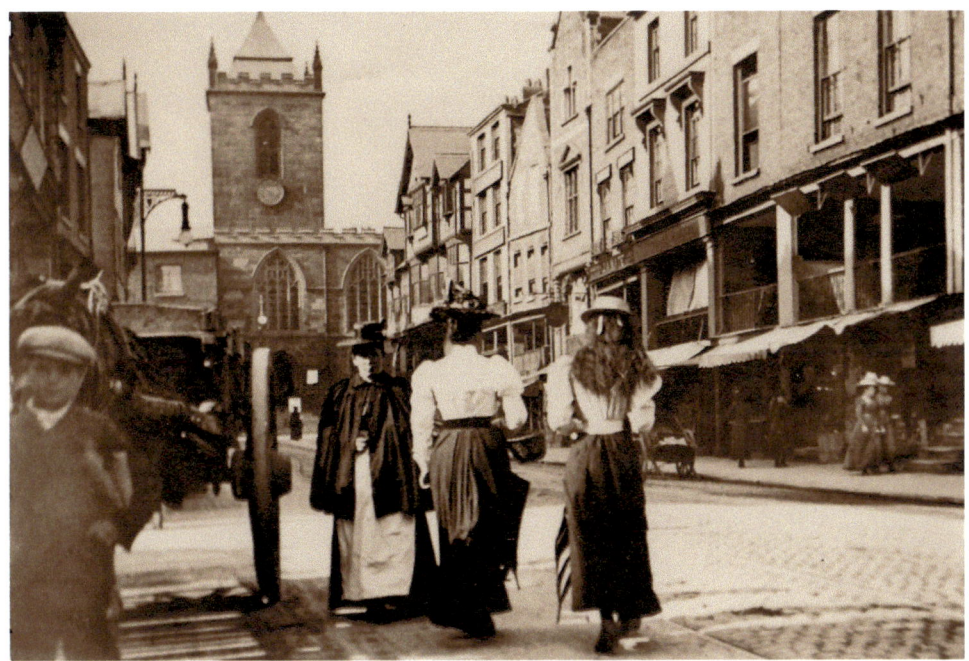

Bridge Street 1890s and 2010

Another view up Bridge Street towards St Peter's Church at The Cross as we see the ladies in their Victorian finery walking past a heavy horse drawn cart. Little has changed as far as the buildings are concerned and the road surface sill consists of stone sets although whether they are original is another matter!

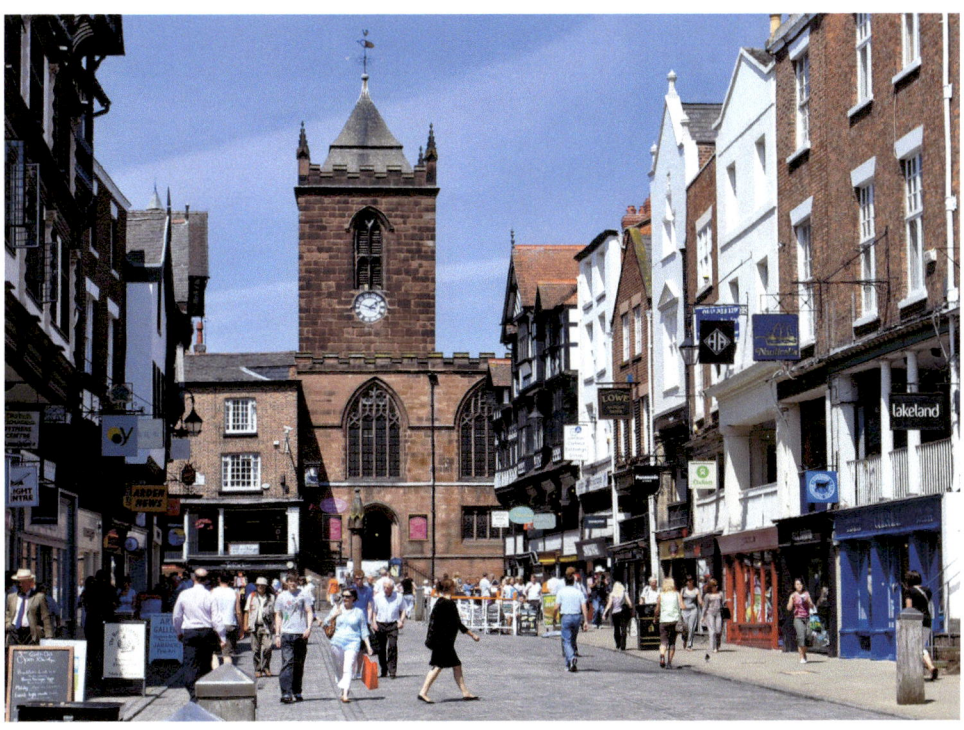

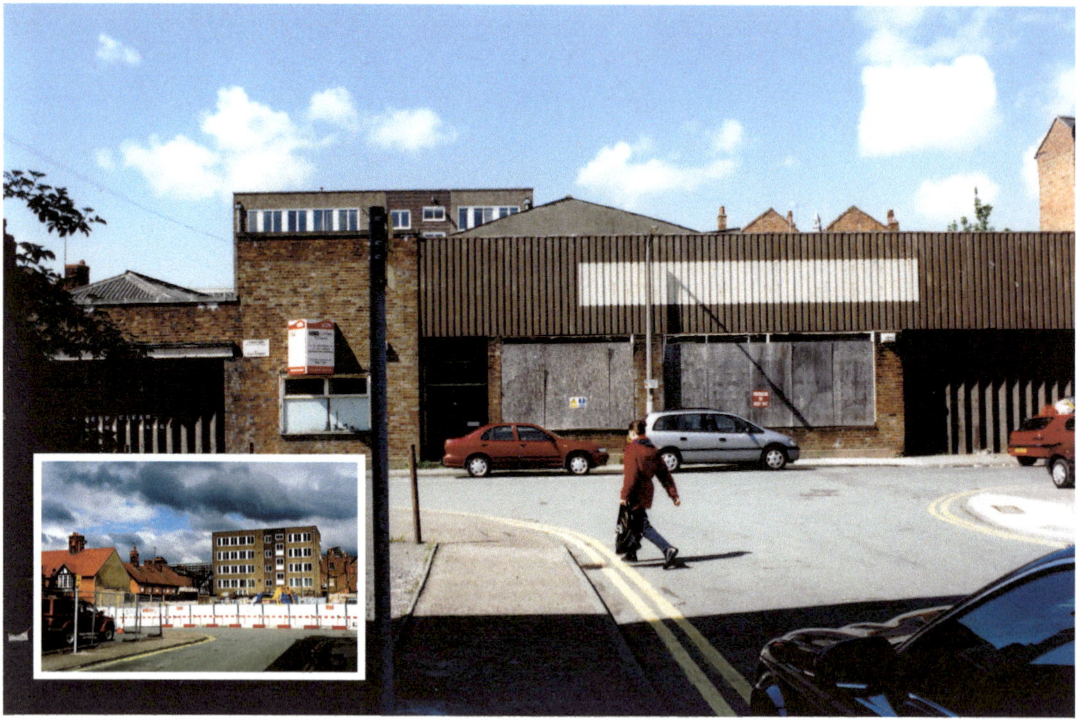

Commonhall Street 2003
Commonhall Street is off Bridge Street and this series of photographs show the demolition of a former warehouse and the erection of a new block of flats with shops beneath. It is an example of the improved quality of design so lacking in the latter part of the last century.

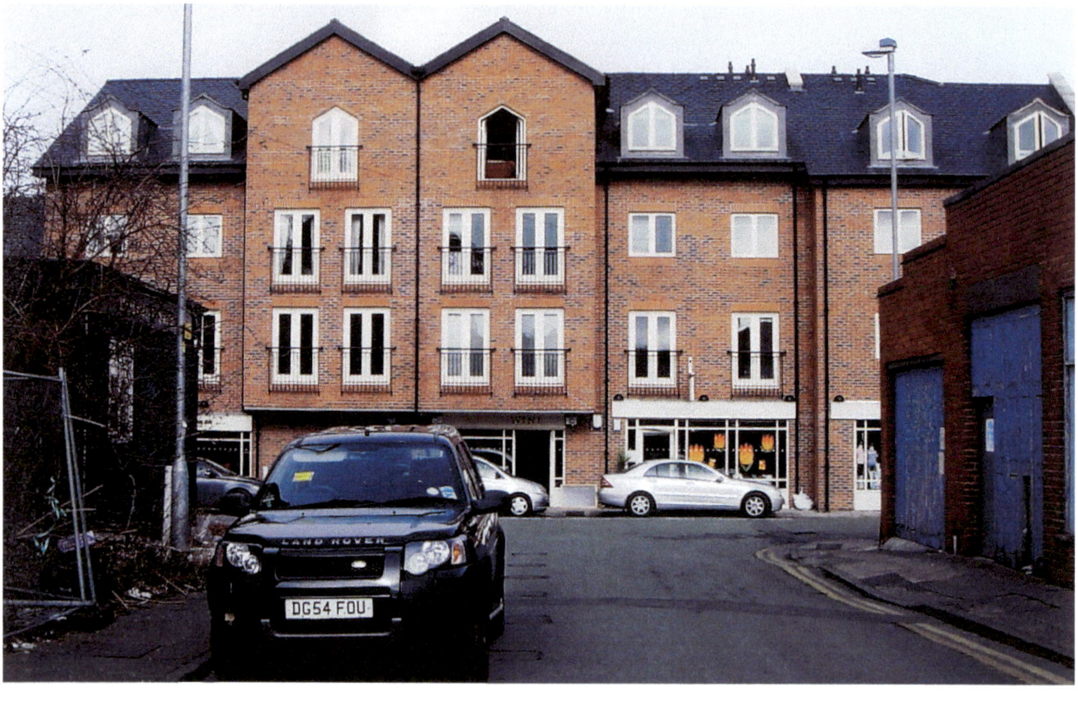

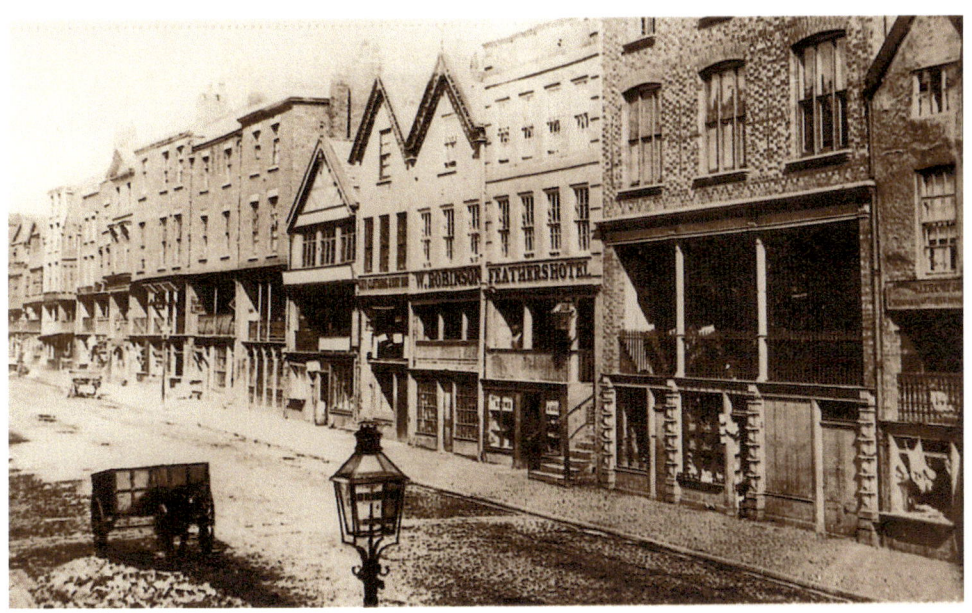

Bridge Street Feathers Hotel 1860 and 2010

One of the oldest photographs in the book shows the old Feathers Hotel on the east side of Bridge Street. It was once a famous coaching inn but was demolished in 1863. It now forms one of the entrances to the Grosvenor Shopping Centre. The buildings around it are still *in situ*.

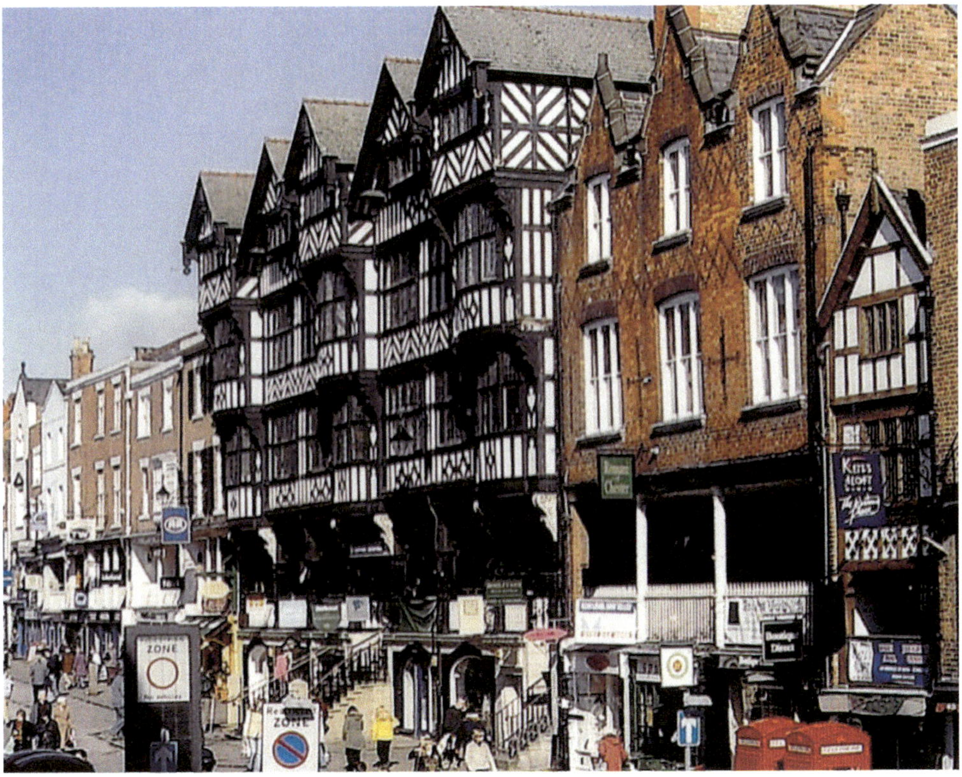

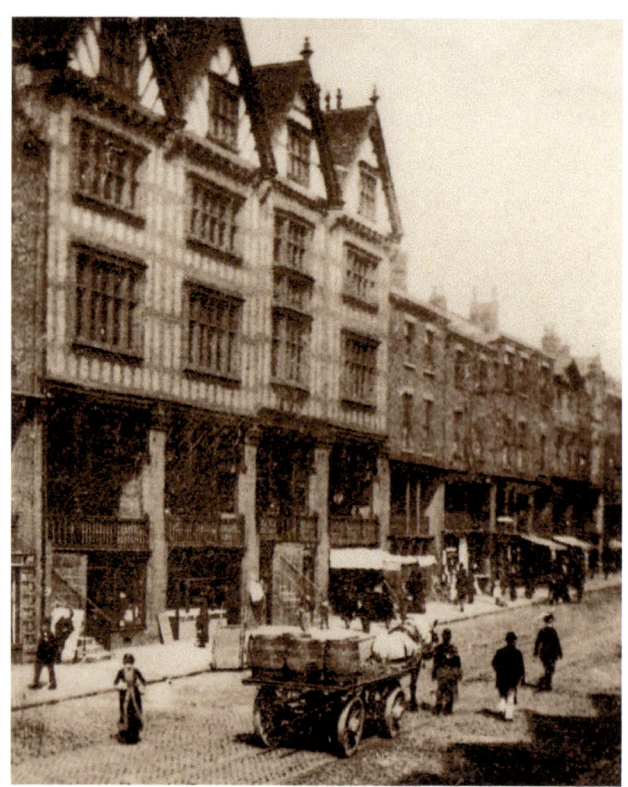

Bridge Street Site of Feathers Hotel 1880s and 2010

We now look at the site of the Feathers Hotel from the opposite side and after the replacement had been built. This replacement is a beautiful black and white building but as can be seen from the old photograph, this hasn't always been the case and some alterations have been carried out to the front elevation.

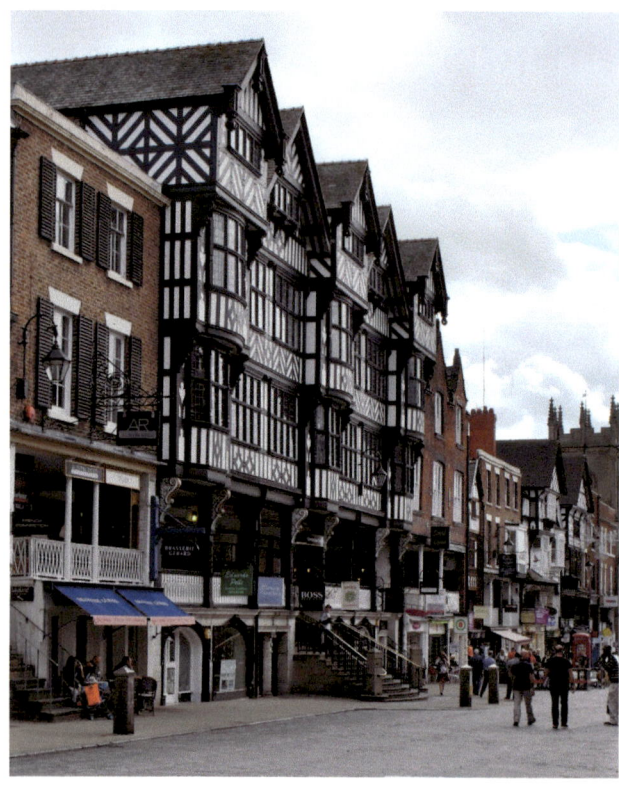

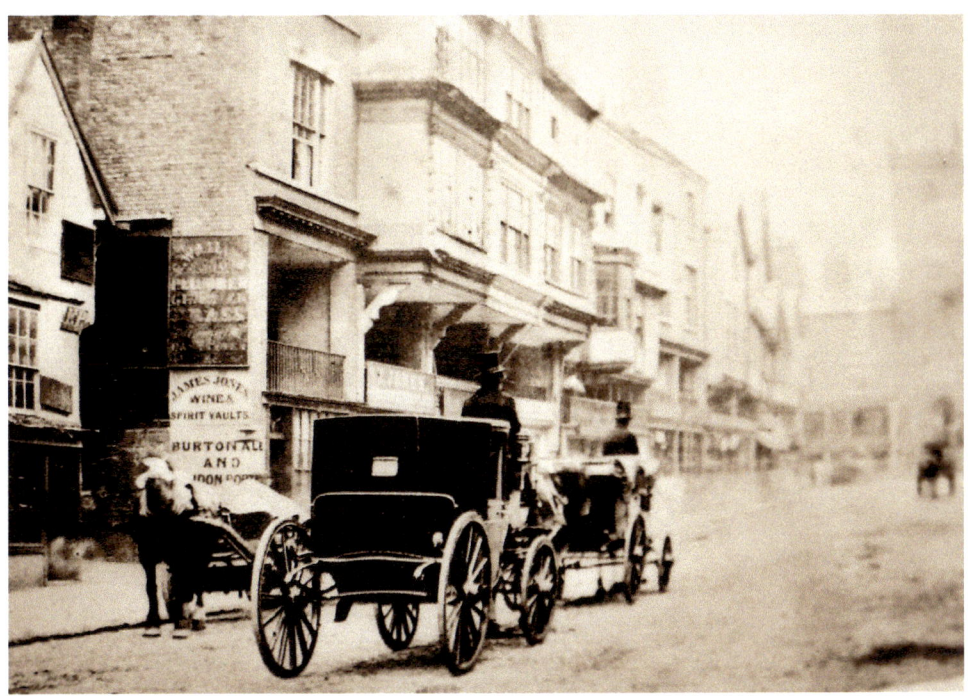

Bridge Street 1875 and 2009
The buildings above row level in the centre are known as 'The Dutch Houses' and are mid seventeenth century. St Peter's Church is at the top and little has been altered over the years other than cosmetically. Most of the alterations and re-modelling of the city was the work of John Douglas, probably one of Cheshire's most famous architects.

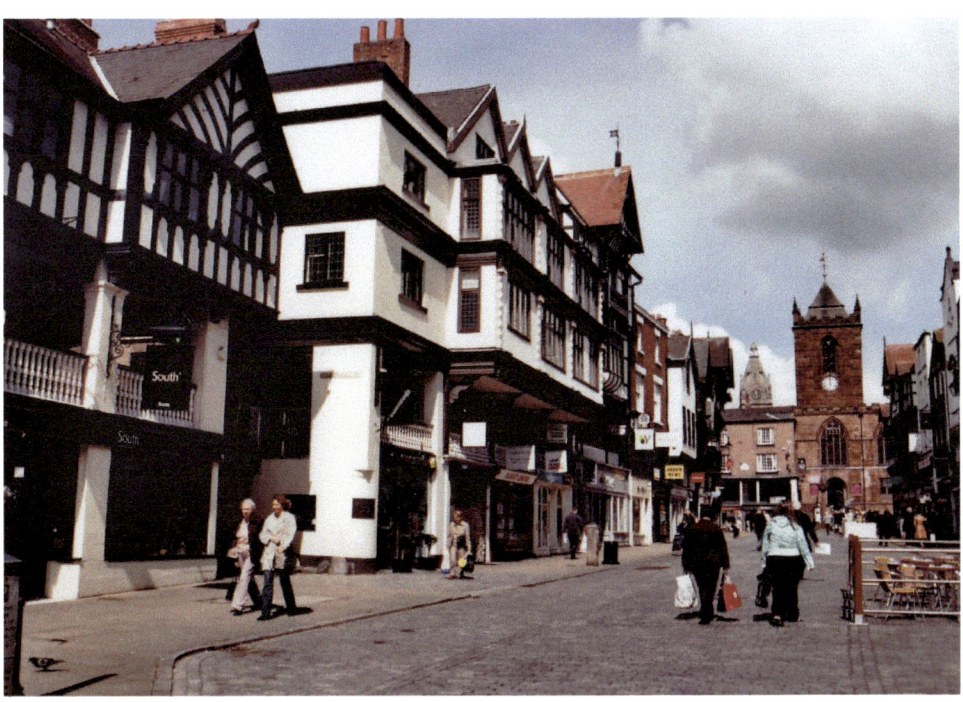

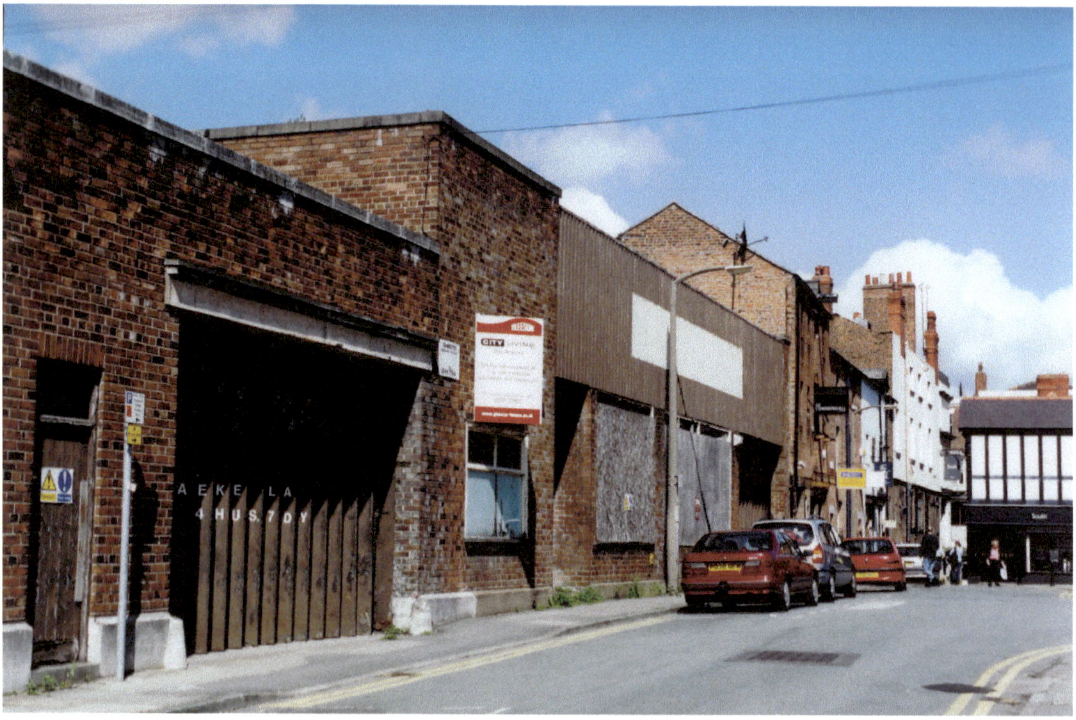

Commonhall Street 2003 and 2009

Here we see another example of good planning in modern architecture. Commonhall Street as mentioned earlier went through quite a transformation in 2003 and this is another example of the result.

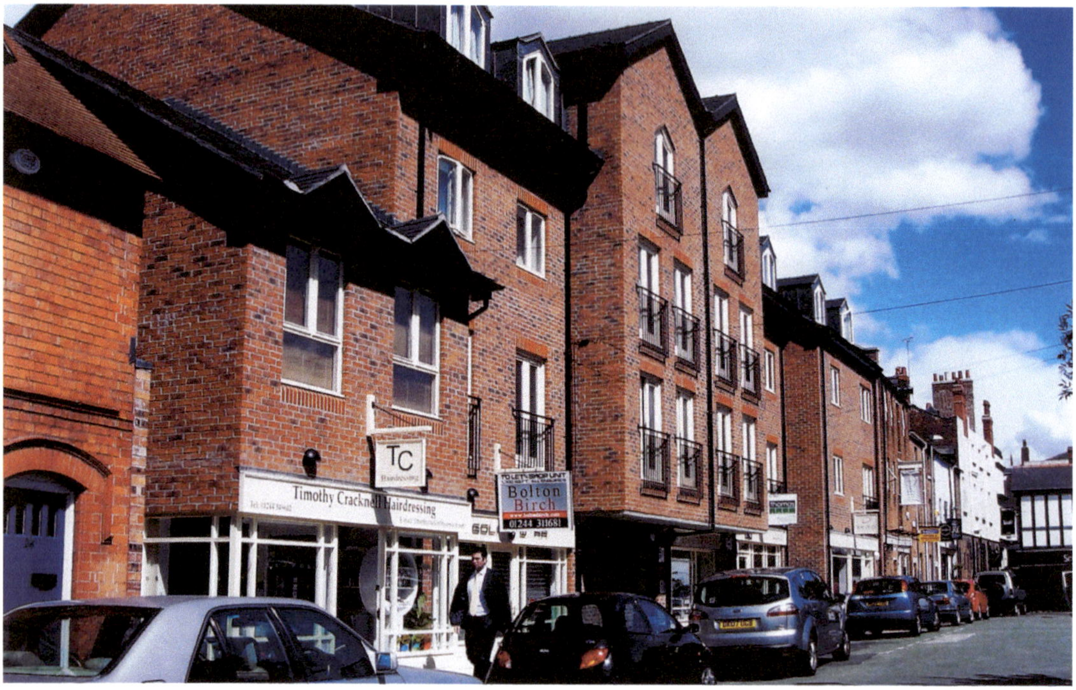

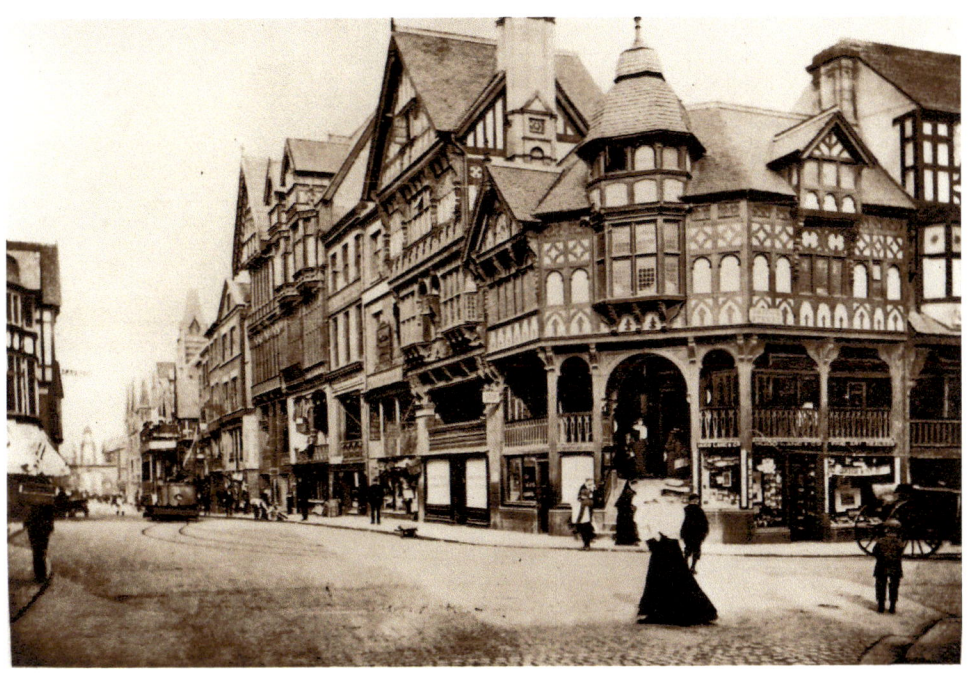

The Cross and Eastgate Street 1905 and 2010

What photograph of Chester is more iconic than of this building that stands on the corner of Bridge Street? We will see later what used to stand in its place and just how sympathetically the change has been made. It was actually built in 1888 having been designed by Thomas Lockwood. The electric tram in the old photograph has taken over the duties of the horse-drawn transport and this one is wending its way to Saltney.

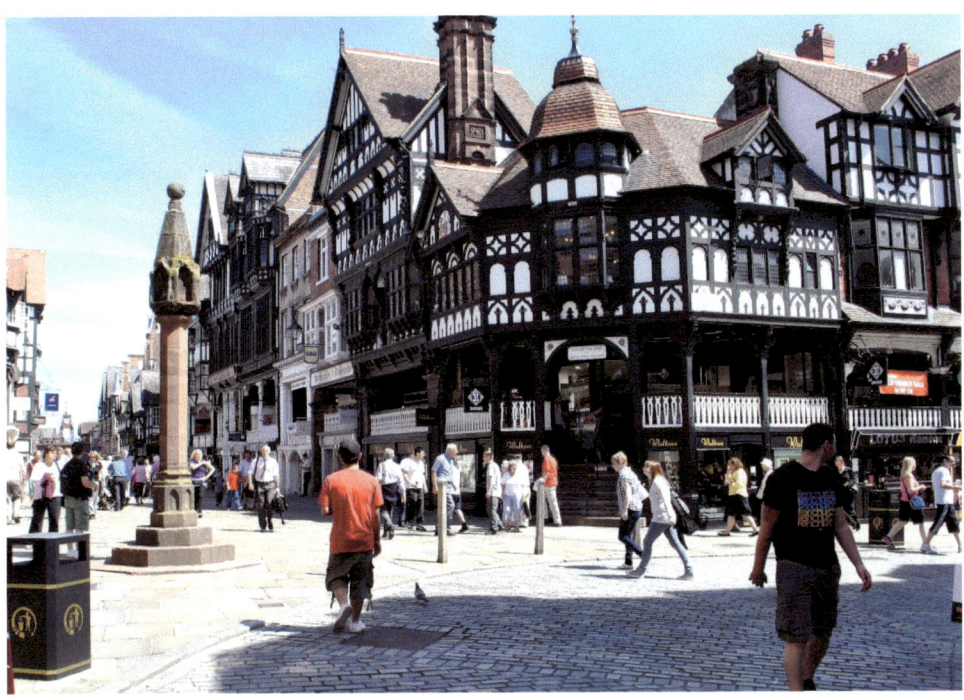

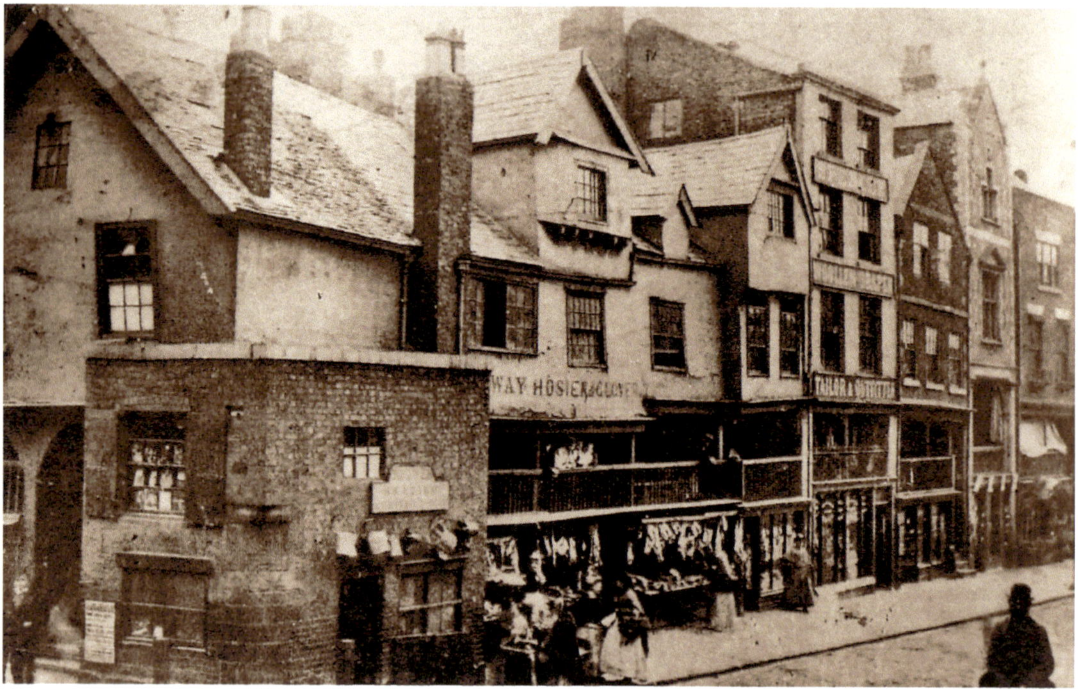

The Cross 1860 and 2010

This ancient photograph is quite poor as you would expect it to be. It depicts one of the rarest views of what is known as the Chester Cross area and shows a building in a very poor state. By 1888 it had gone and in its place was built the beautiful black and white building shown on the last page. As can be seen in the new photograph, some of the buildings further down Bridge Street are still standing.

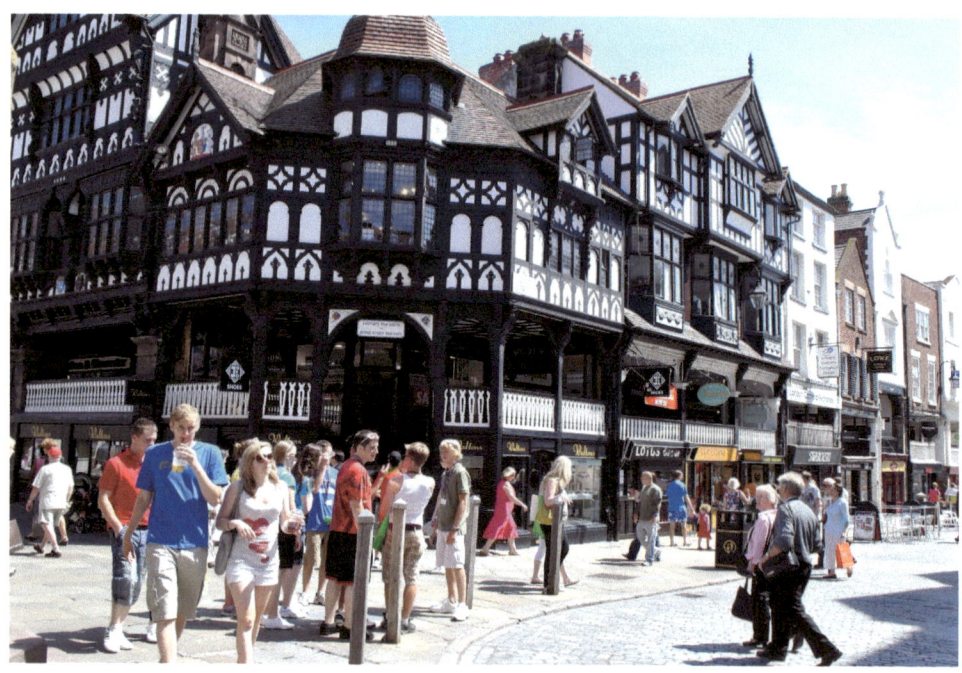

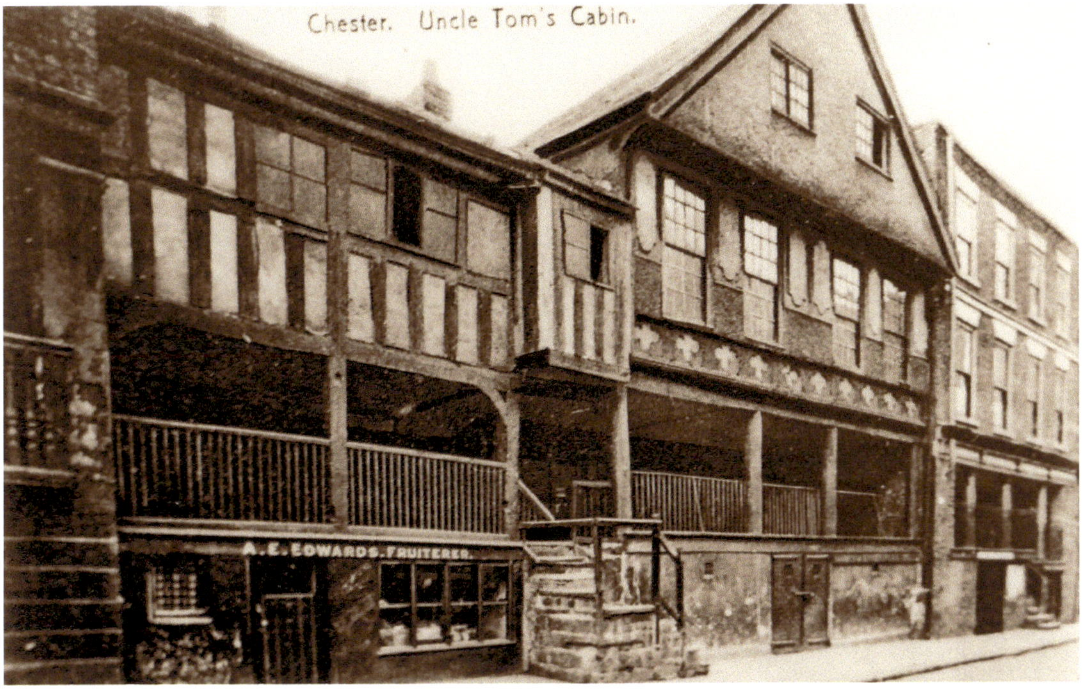

Watergate Street Uncle Tom's Cabin 1905 and 2009

This building was known as Uncle Tom's Cabin as it shows on the front of the old photograph but where that name came from seems to be lost in the mists of time. I suppose it looks a bit like a cabin? The shop at the side was the premises of Amy Elizabeth Edwards who traded as greengrocers at this premises, number 55. The old buildings were demolished in the 1950s and a hole was left in the row until the concrete eyesore was built a short while later.

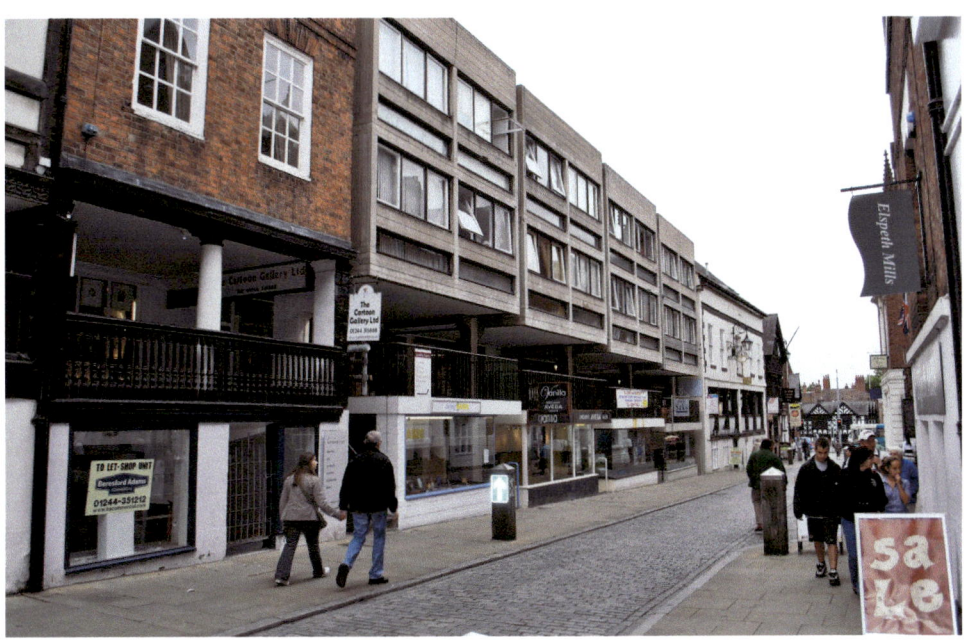

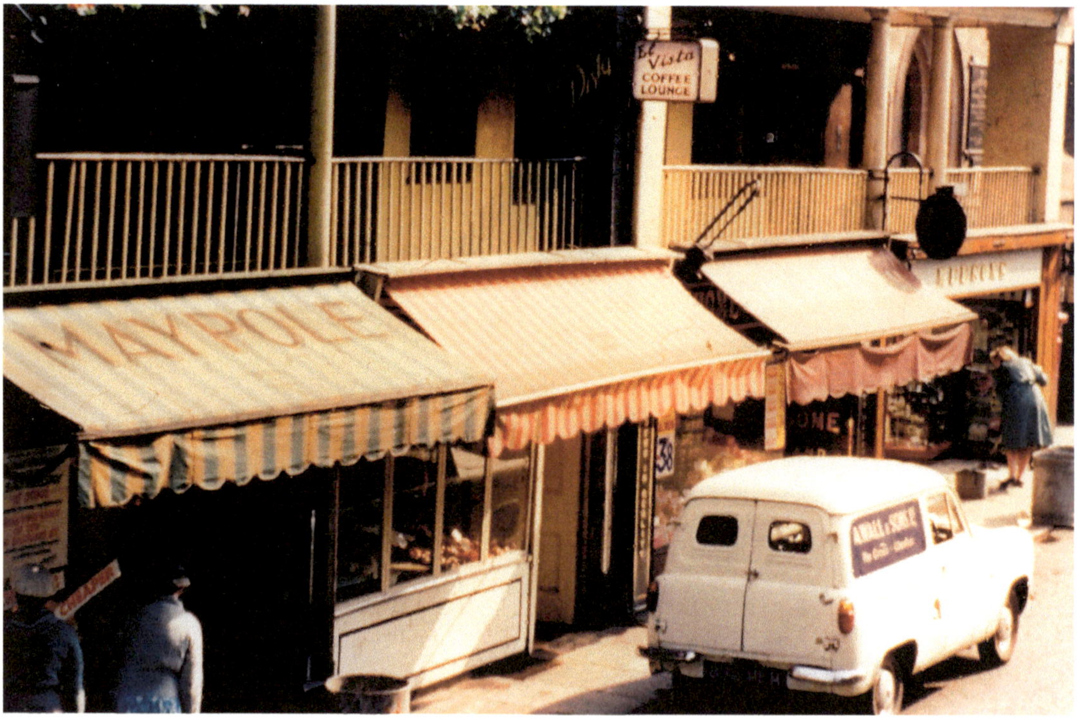

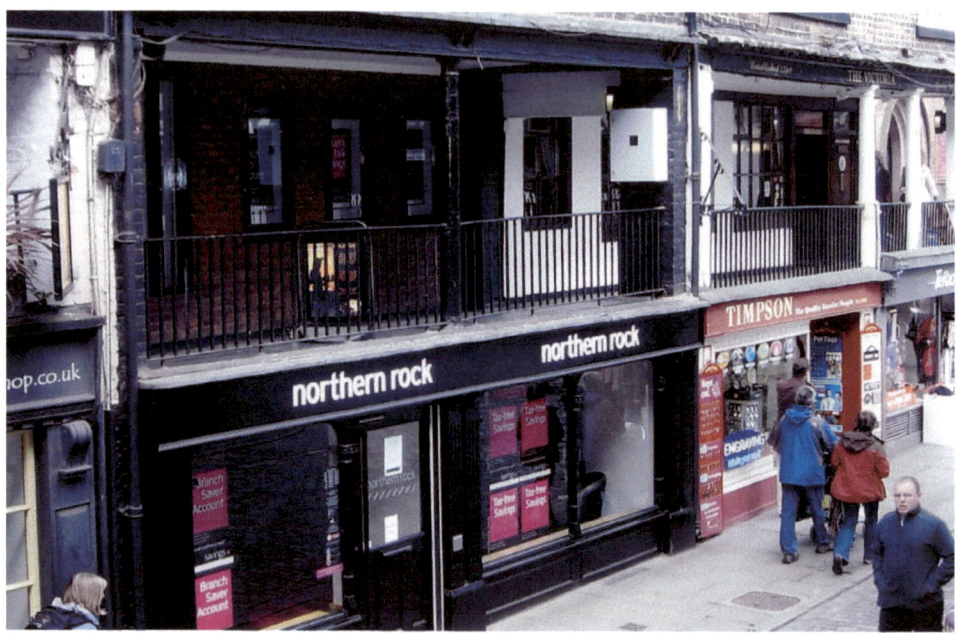

Watergate Street 1953 and 2009
These shops situated near to the cross show the Chester Rows quite clearly with upper and lower shops, Chester is the only city in the world with such a configuration. The Victoria pub can be seen in the modern shot and in the 1953 photograph the Maypole grocer's is there. This was part of a chain of grocer's known as the Maypole Dairy Company and the first shop in the chain was opened in 1887 in Wolverhampton.

Custom House Watergate Street 1905 and 2010

This building, now the Old Custom House Inn was built originally as a town house in 1637 for Thomas and Anne Weaver, the lane at the side is called Weaver Street after them. You can still see their initials carved on the front and it later became a pub. It obtained its name from the real custom house building across the street when goods brought ashore at the Chester Port would be brought up the street to be sold in the city centre. In the 1950s when Wales was 'dry' on a Sunday this was the only pub in Chester selling Border Ales from Wrexham. On Sunday night it was packed!

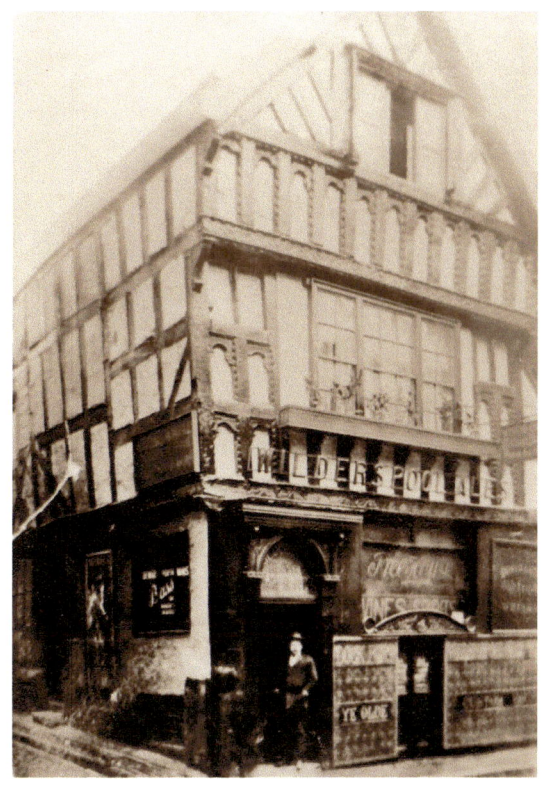

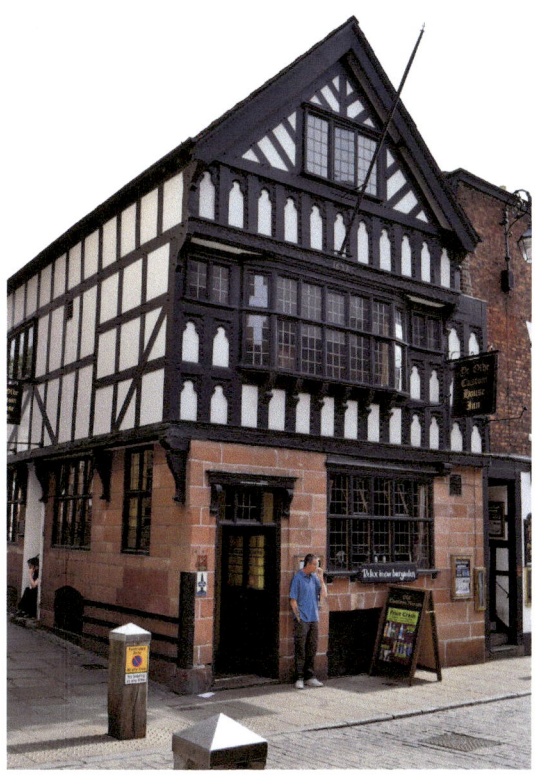

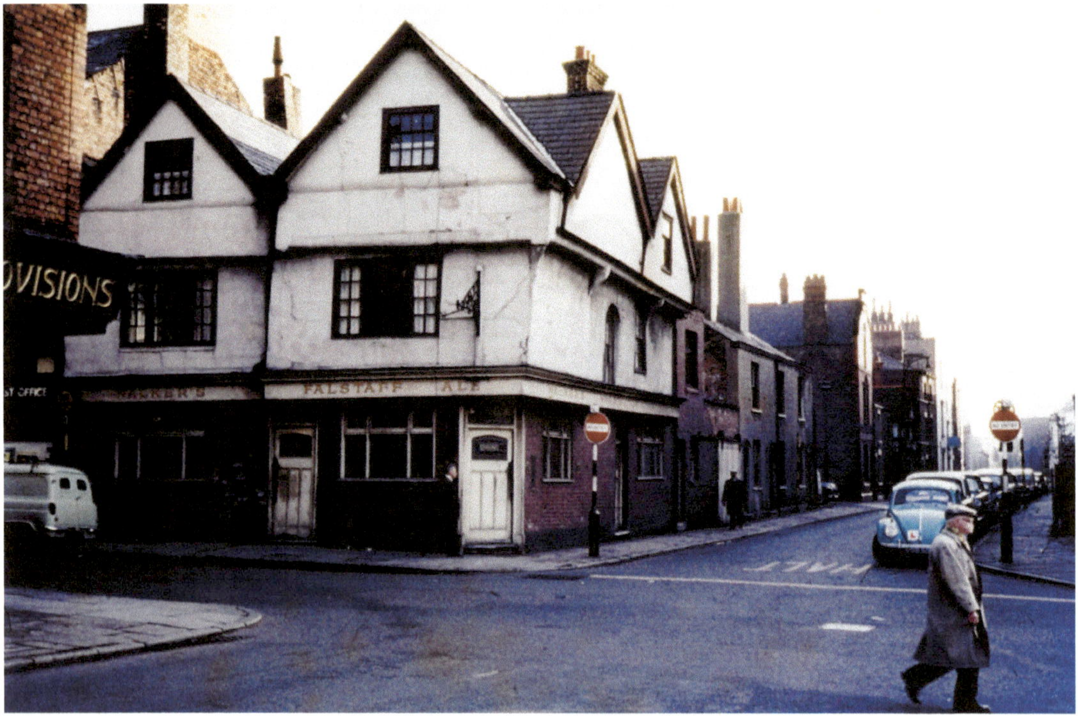

Junction Nicholas Street and Watergate Street 1963 and 2006
This is a view down Nicholas Street towards the Grosvenor roundabout showing the buildings that have all gone to make the ring road. This is now a busy crossroads and The Bar Lounge pub is on the corner.

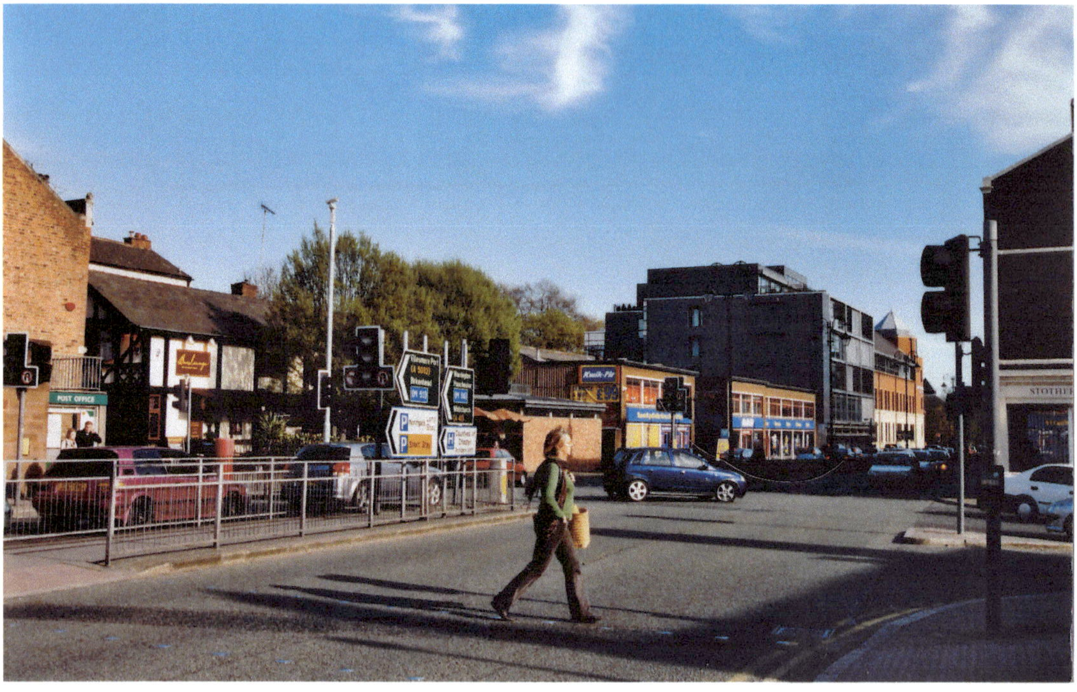

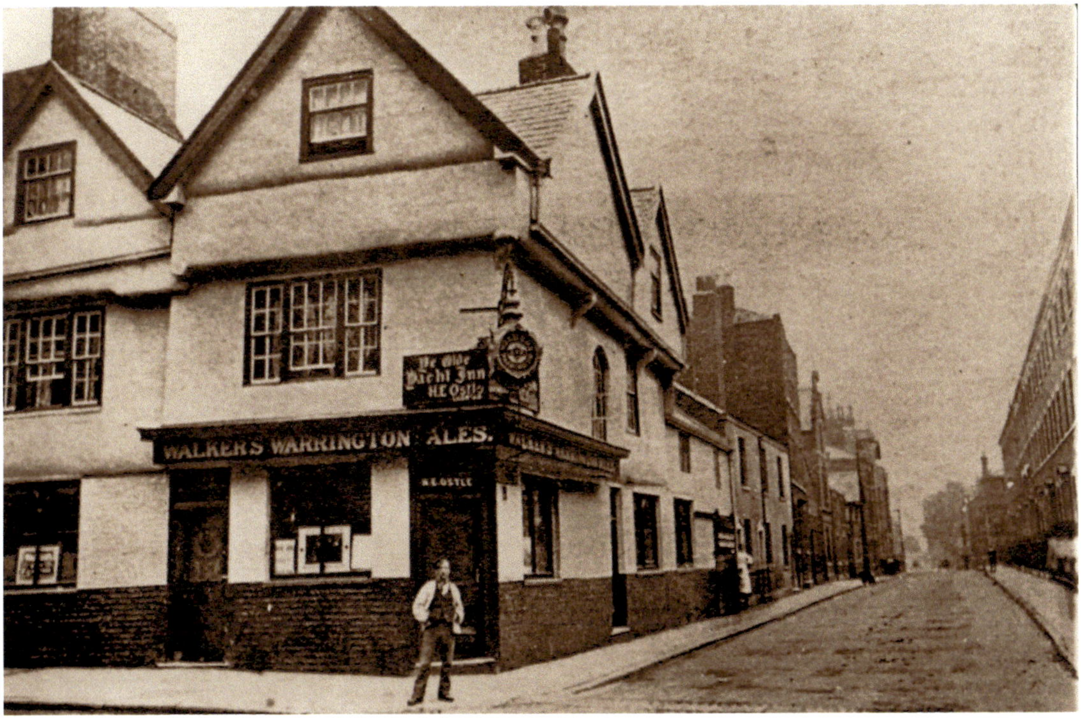

The Yacht Inn 1900 and 2010
In the 1900 photograph we see an older view of the Yacht Inn on the corner; it was named after The Yacht Field upon which it was built. This pub was once described as 'The premier hostelry in the city on its most important street. This was a coaching inn and served the coaches to London and Ireland where feasts, entertainment and good accommodation could be had. It was demolished in 1964.

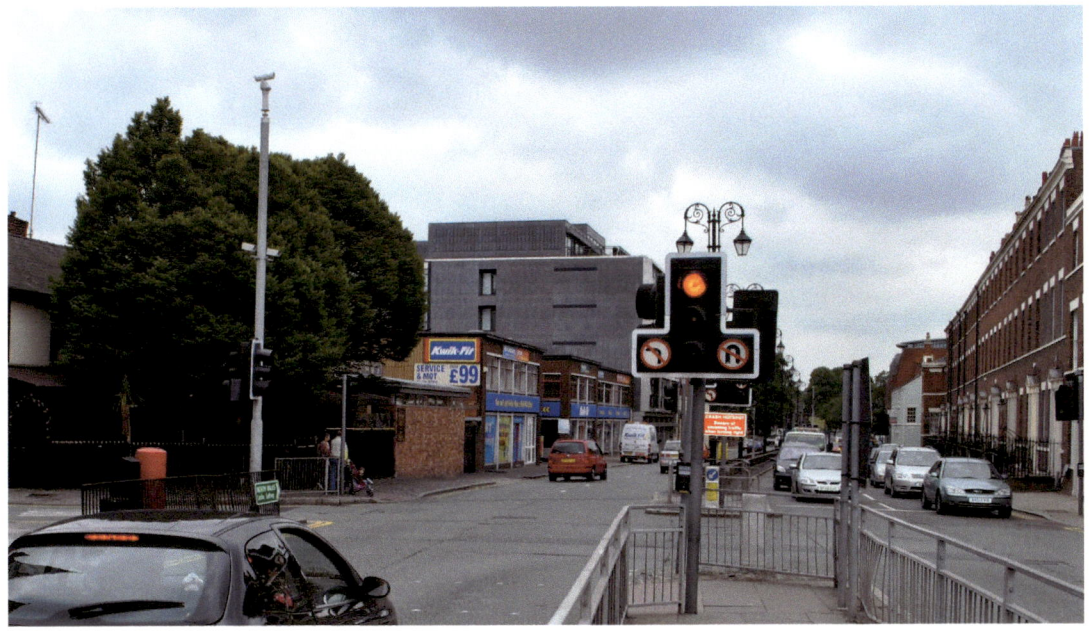

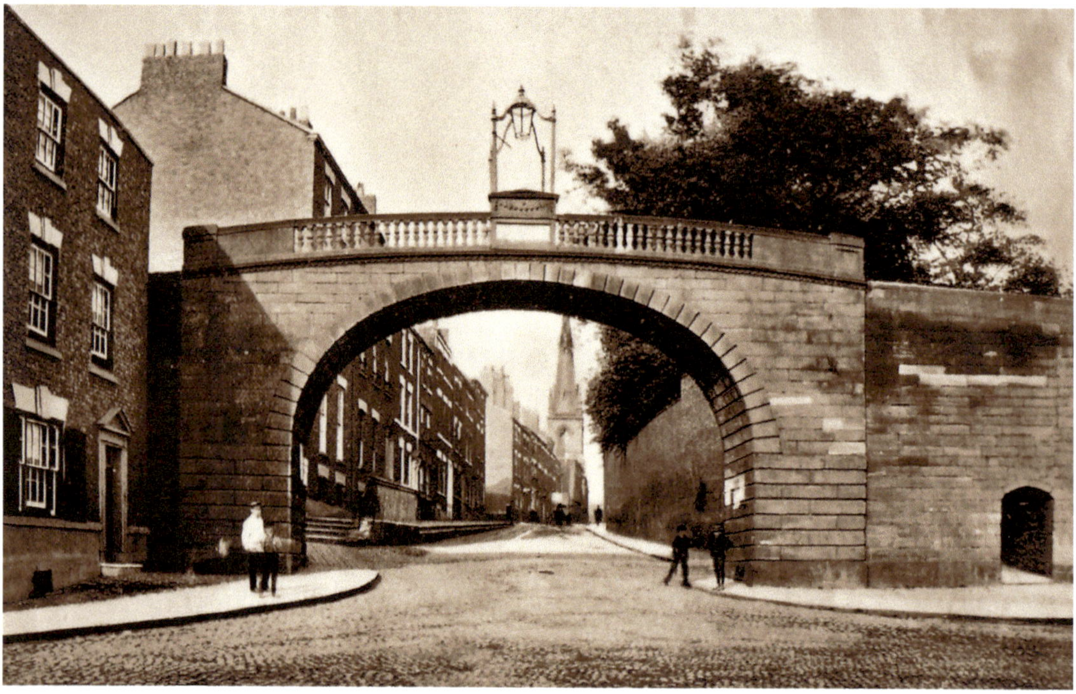

Watergate 1902 and 2010

The Watergate Arch designed by Joseph Turner was built in 1788 to replace a medieval archway which, in its heyday, was the main route from the city to the port of Chester. At that time, the present Roodee which is at the rear of the camera was under water and formed part of the port of Chester. Later it silted up and has for many years been Chester racecourse.

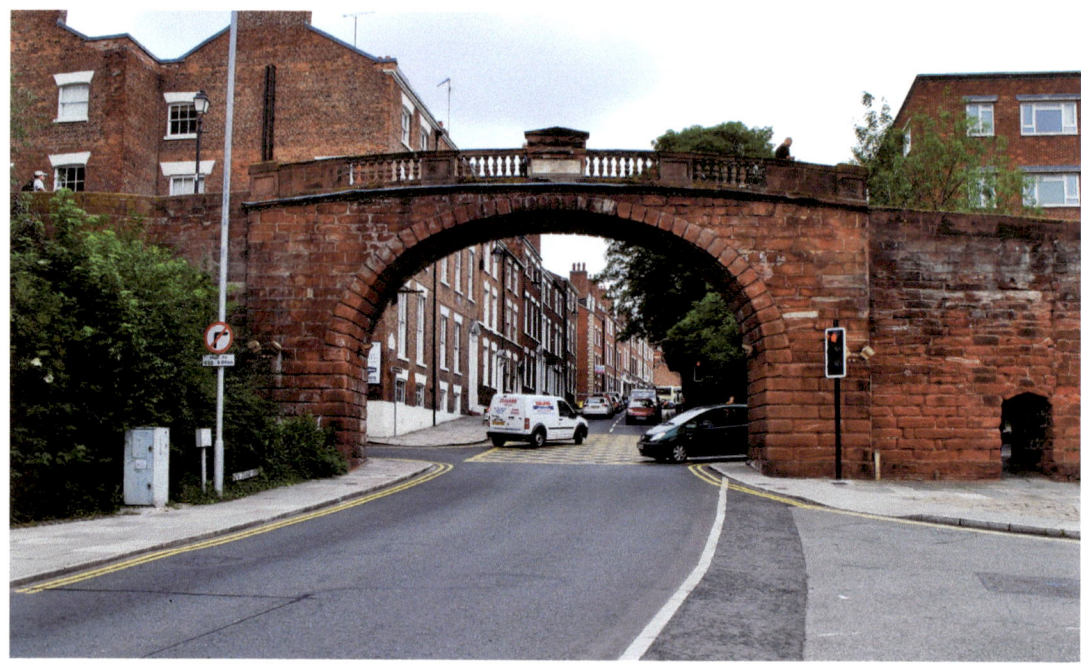

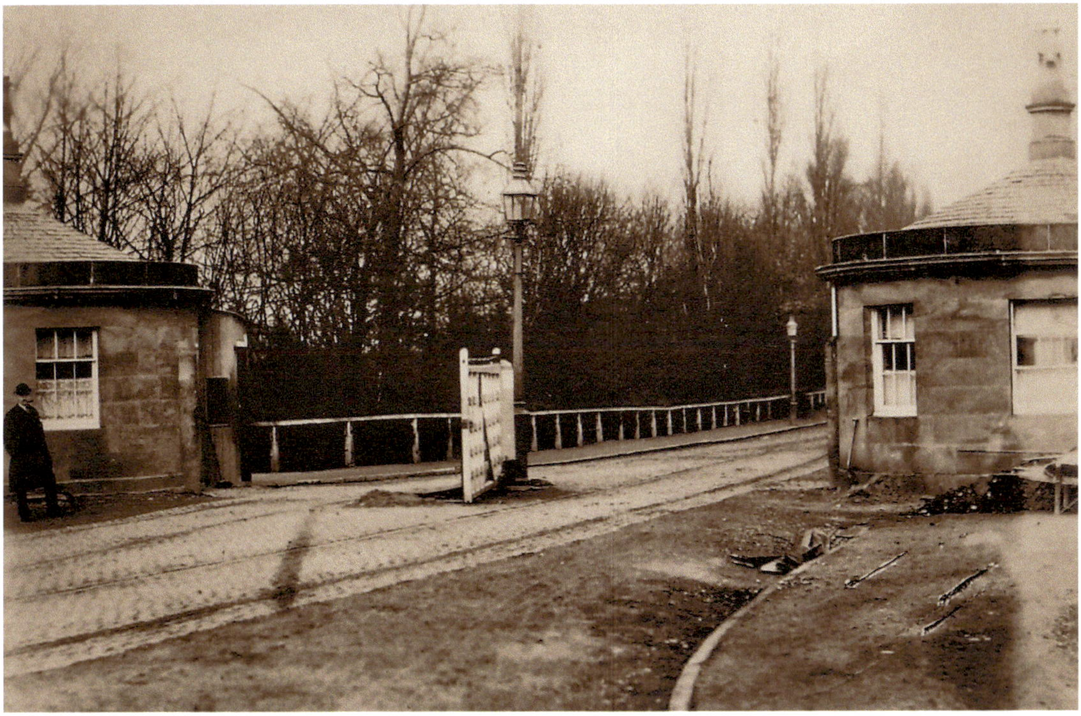

Grosvenor Road 1885 and 2010

This was once the scene of a tollbooth leading onto the Grosvenor Bridge and in the old photograph from 1885 the toll booths and gate are still there. That road leads to what is now the Grosvenor roundabout and thence Grosvenor Street and the city. The traffic in this busy area is now controlled by sets of traffic lights

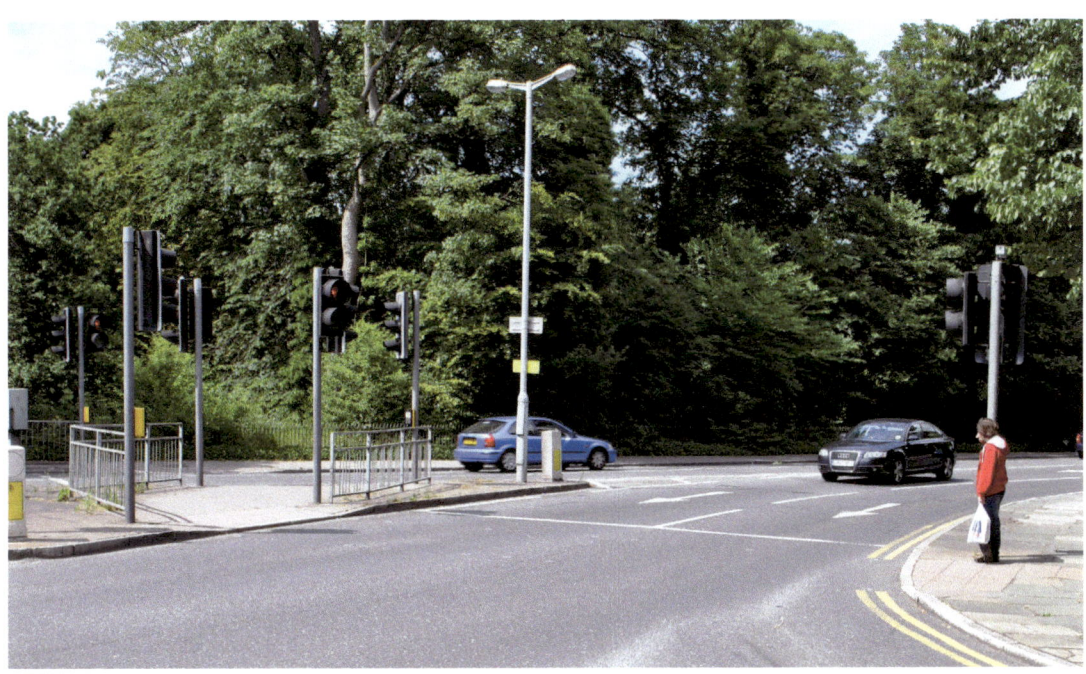

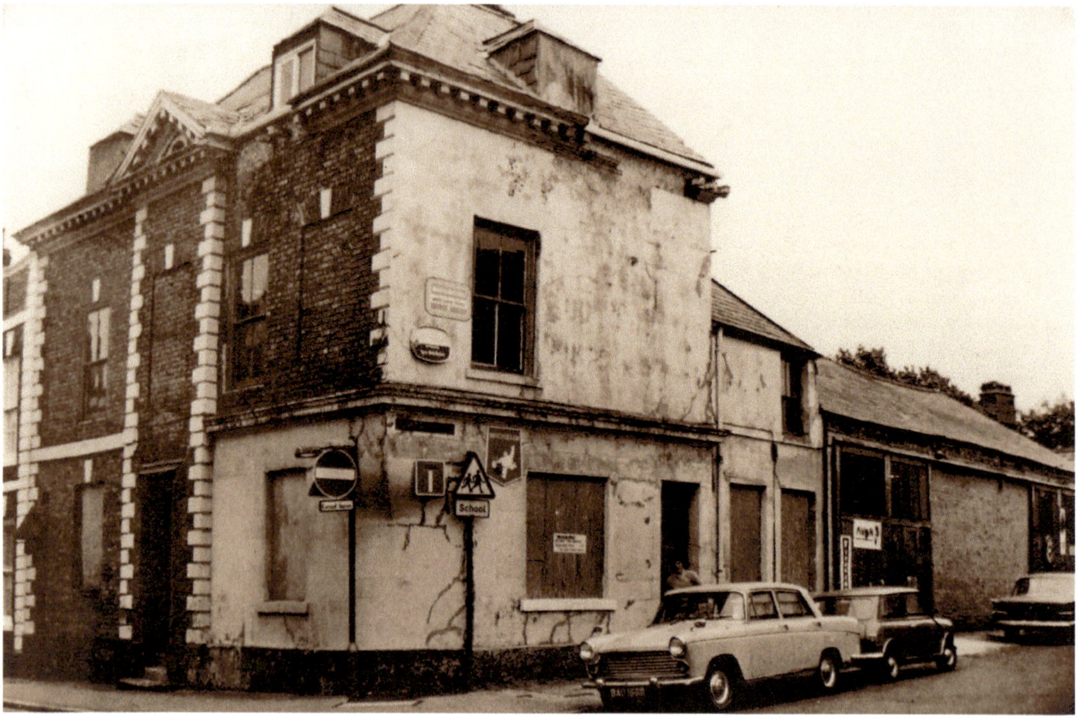

Castle Street former Golden Cock 1965 and 2009
This view taken at the top of Castle Street is of the old Golden Cock hotel. This was later converted into a garage and has now been well restored with a new block of flats alongside. Castle Street can be found off the Grosvenor roundabout.

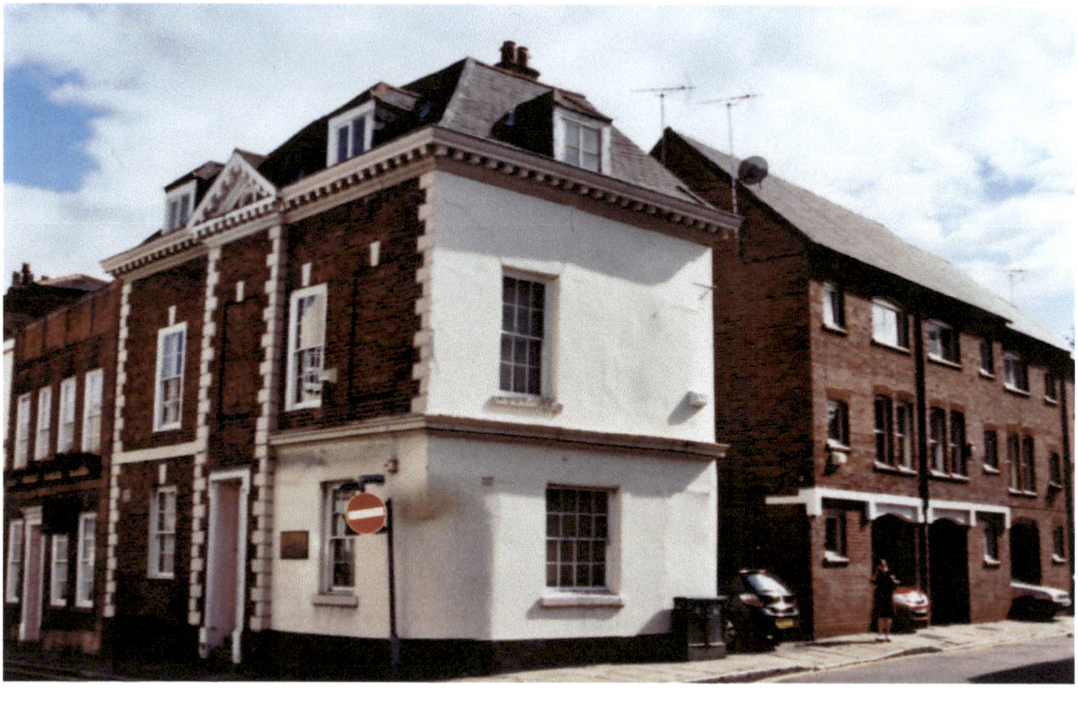

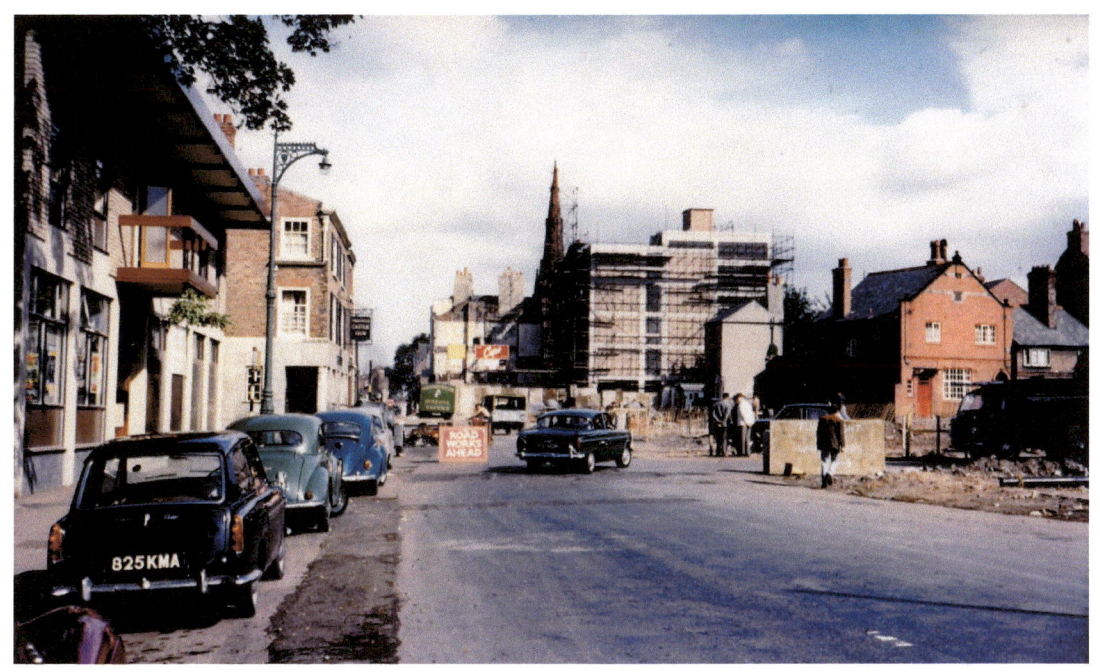

Nicholas Street 1964 and 2010

Nicholas Street is now part of the ring road and starts at the Grosvenor roundabout. The 1964 photograph was taken as building work was in progress to both widen the street and replace most of the buildings. Still intact however is the former church of The Holy Trinity with its spire showing in both photographs. No longer used as a church it is now the Guildhall of the Freemen and Guilds of Chester. On the west side a row of Georgian houses still stand known as Pill-Box Promenade because most were occupied by doctors.

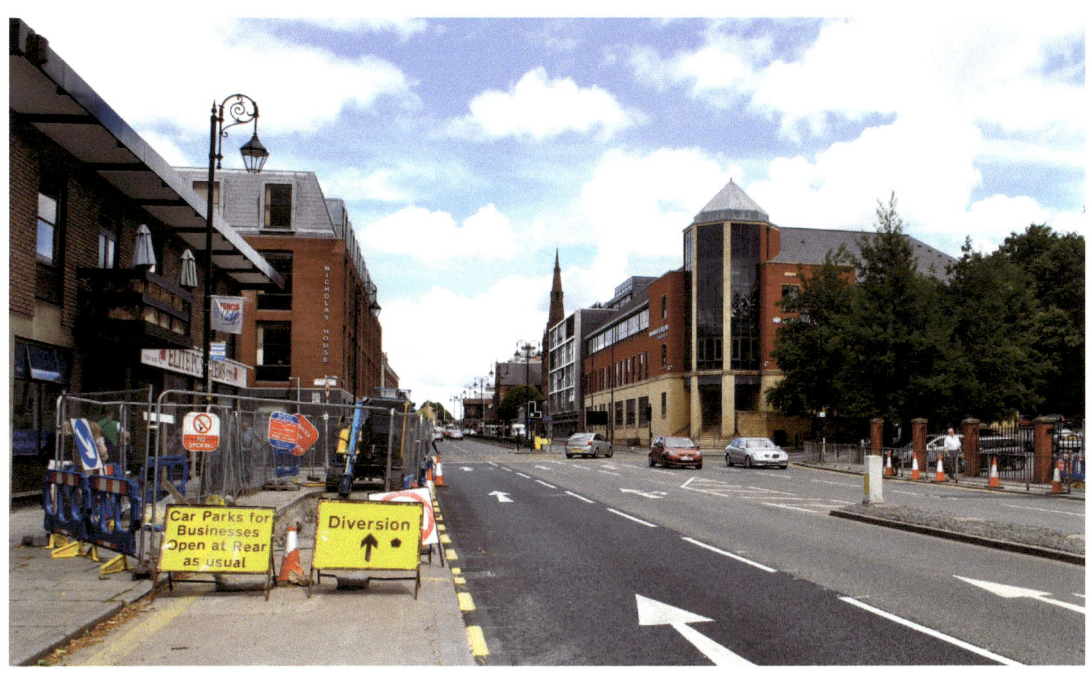

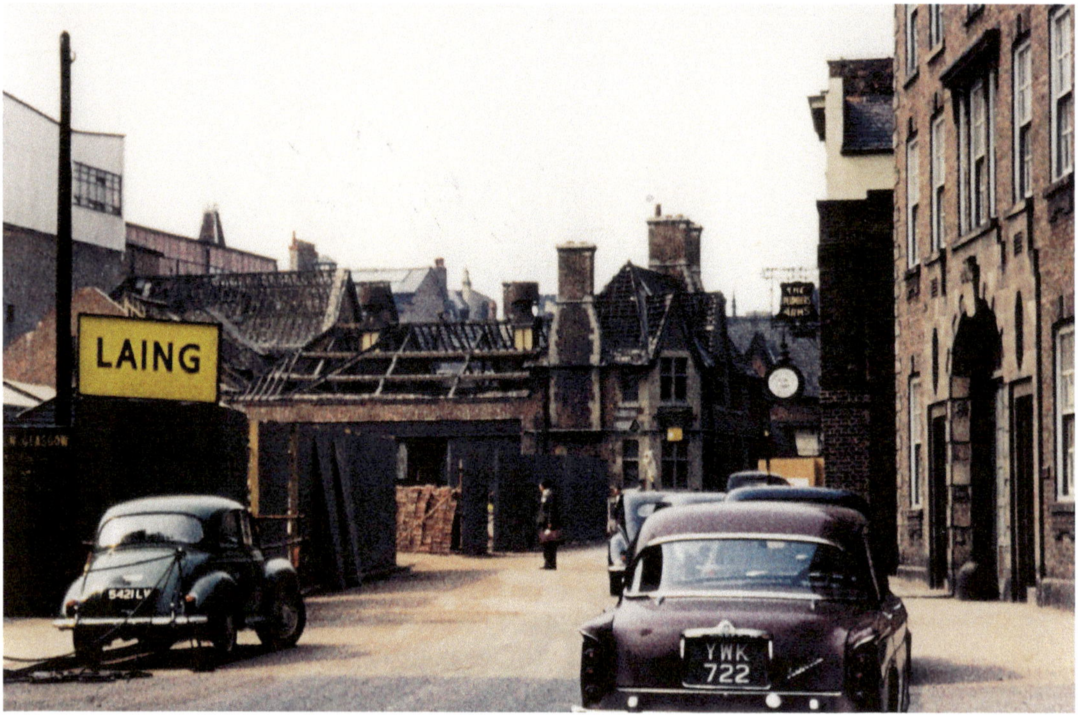

Newgate Street 1964 and 2010

This much-altered street in the middle of the city is seen in 1964 at the time of the start of the demolition. It used to lead from Pepper Street into Eastgate Street but has now become the entrance to the car park for the shops and the Grosvenor Hotel. The large and prestigious building with its impressive portico that can be seen on the right has thankfully been retained.

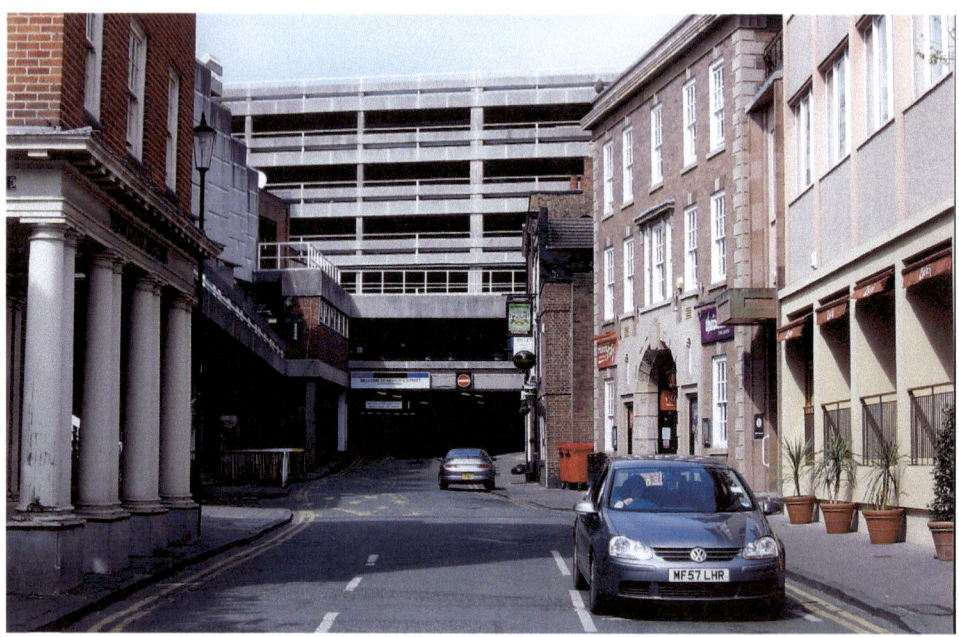

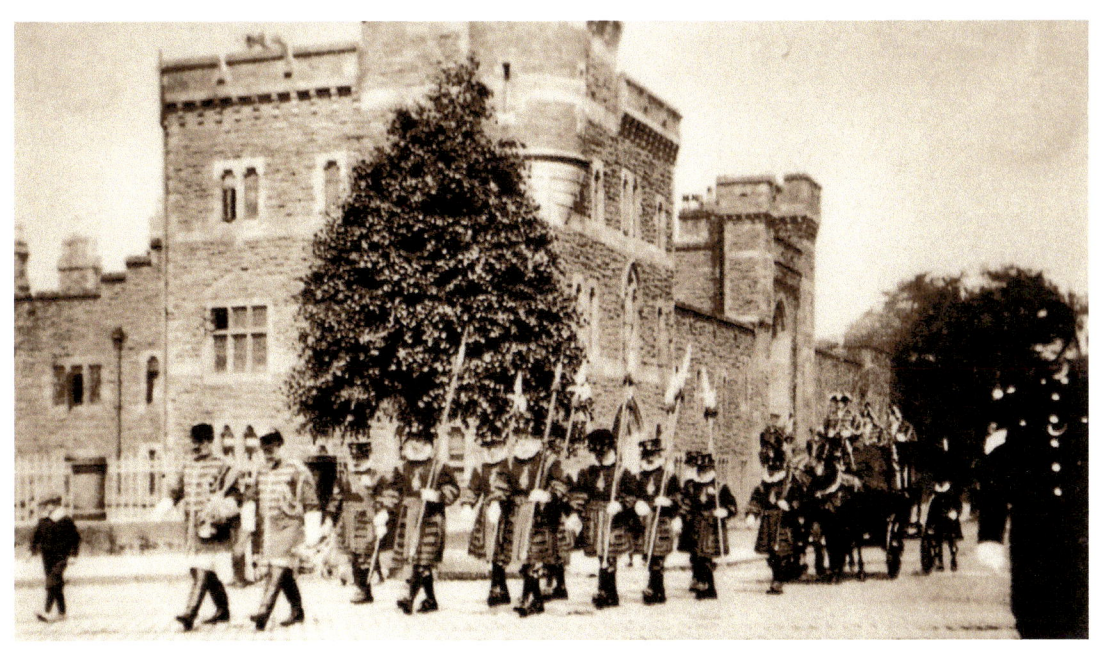

Site of Cheshire Regiment HQ 1900 and 2010
The buildings in the old photograph were built in 1858 for the Cheshire Regiment and where situated just off the Grosvenor Roundabout and into Nicholas Street. The men marching in the photograph are Chester's Javelin Men who escorted the Judge in his carriage to the Assizes. The buildings were eventually demolished to make way for the police headquarters. Just like the Militia Buildings, the Cheshire Regiment is also now defunct having been incorporated into the Mercian Regiment.

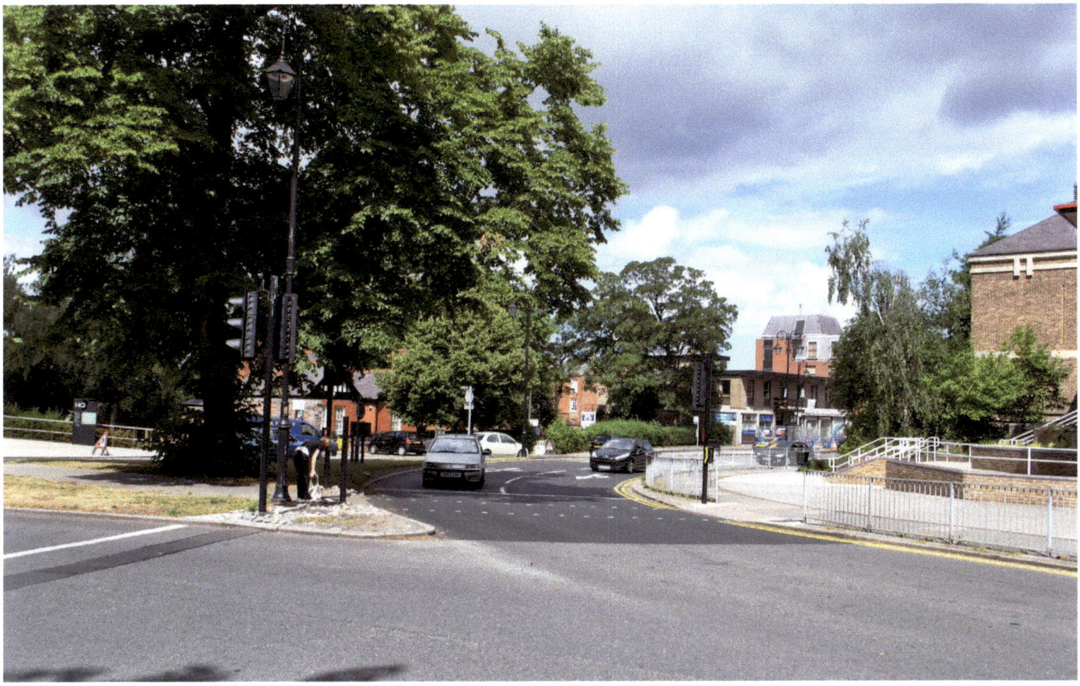

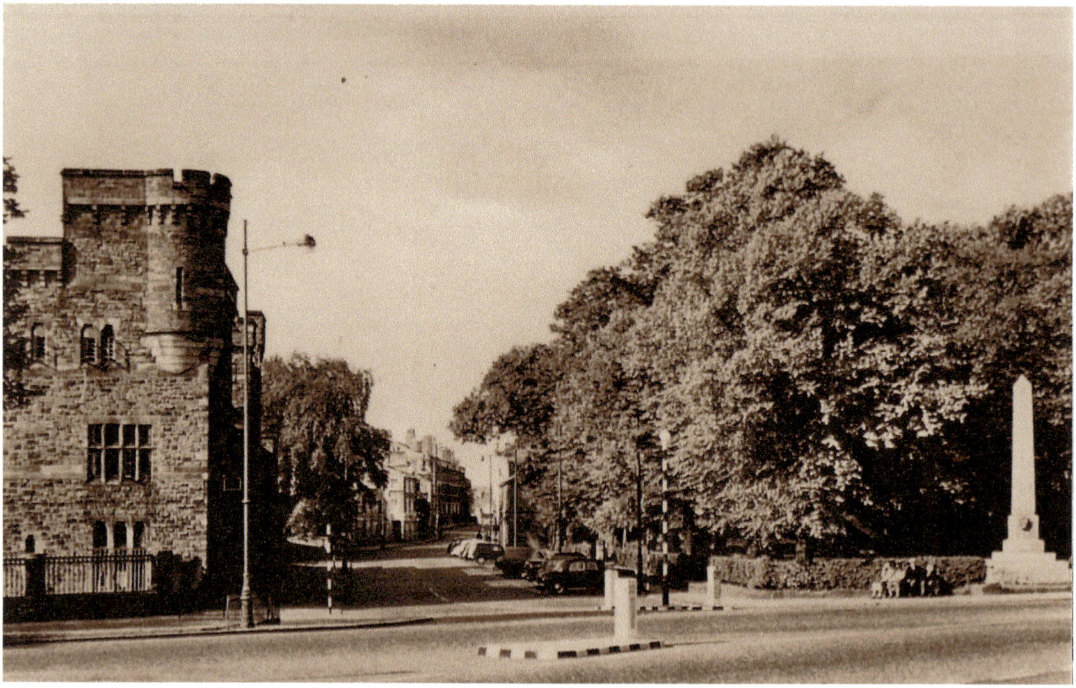

A view up Nicholas Street 1952 and 2010

This photograph looks again at the old Militia Building. This was used as married quarters for the troops based at the castle. I'm told that the living conditions for the soldier's families were extremely poor. The obelisk was at one time standing in the cemetery of St Bridget's church which stood here. It commemorates Mathew Henry who was a Presbyterian minister, like part of the old graveyard it is in the centre of the Grosvenor roundabout.

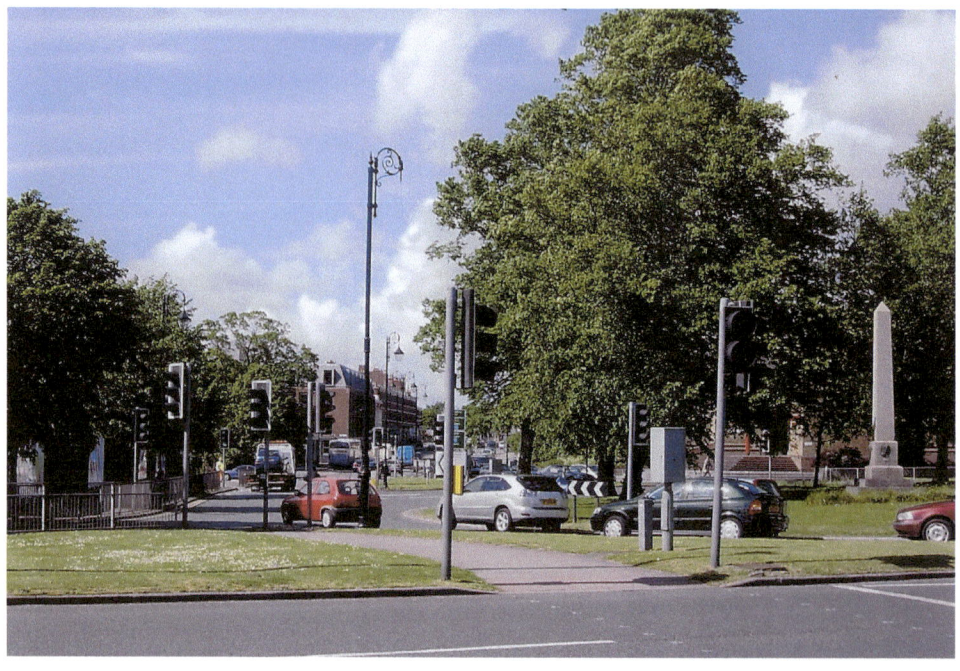

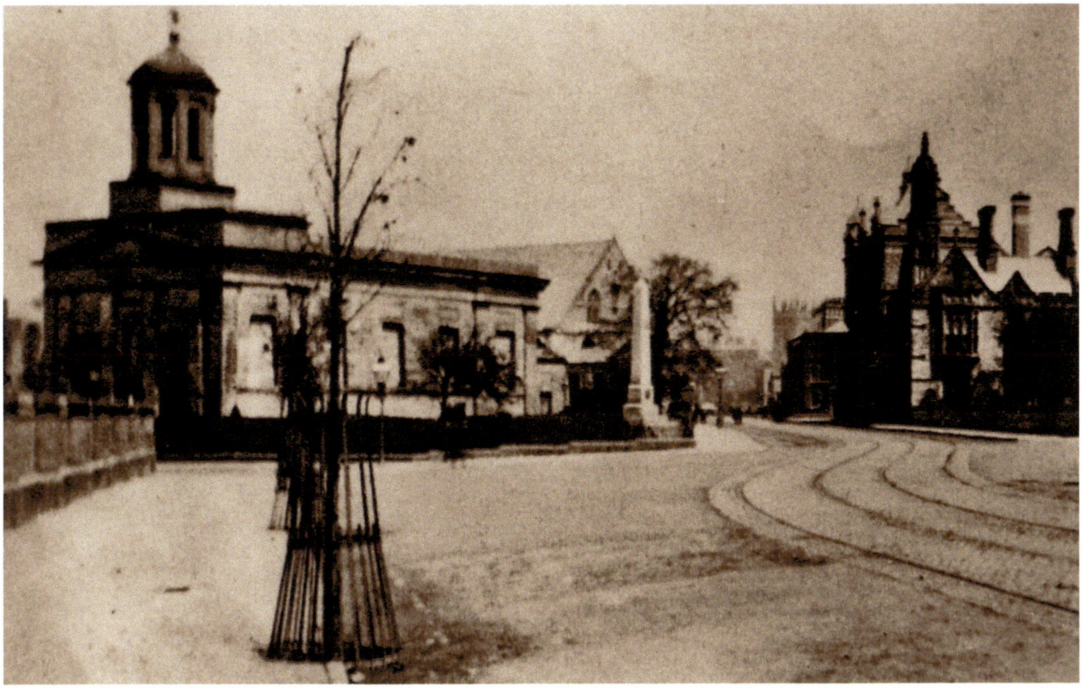

St Bridget's Church 1889 and 2010

A poor old photograph from 1889 of St Bridget's Church but shows the area where the ring road now starts, it was demolished in 1892. This church was built in 1828 to replace another St Bridget's that was inaugurated in the reign of King Offa *c.* 797 and was demolished to make way for the Grosvenor Bridge approach road. The statue is of Field Marshall Viscount Combermere.

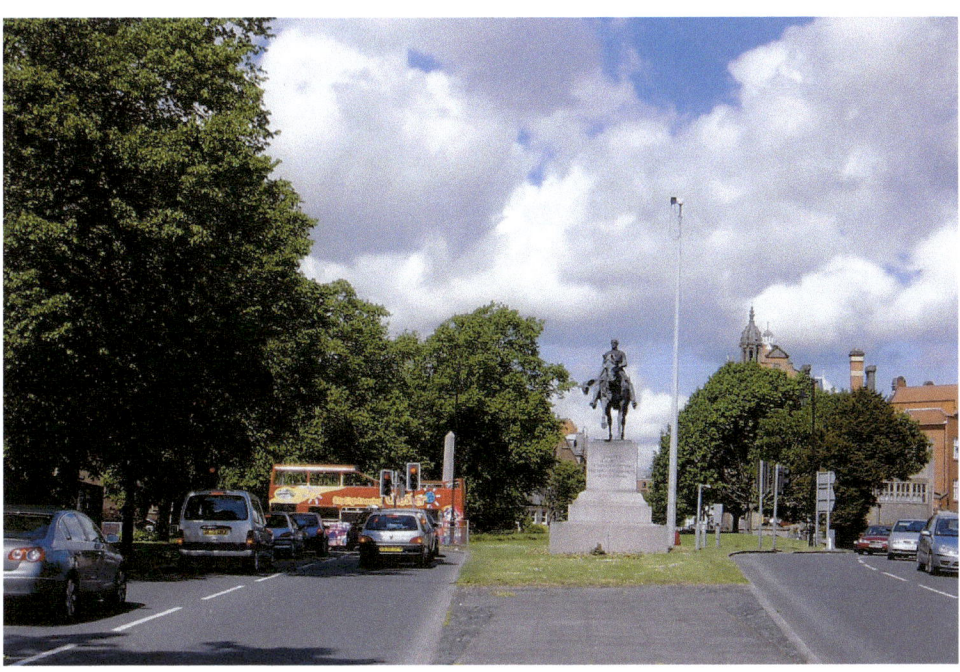

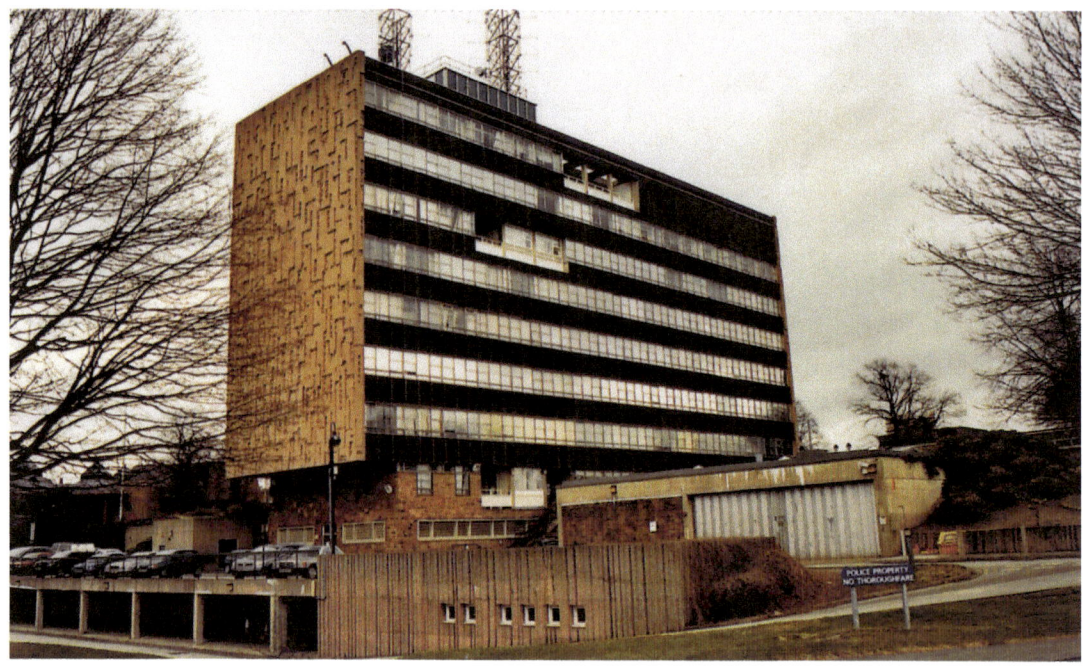

Old Police Headquarters 1990s and 2010
This ugly building was only built in 1966, the artwork on the ends of the building won an award in 1969 but the small area of land that it stood on soon meant that it was too small. In 2006 the building finally closed and the Police Headquarters were transferred to Winsford. A plan that would perhaps have been better in 1966! It has now been demolished and replaced by the aptly named HQ building which incorporates, Council offices, a hotel and luxury flats.

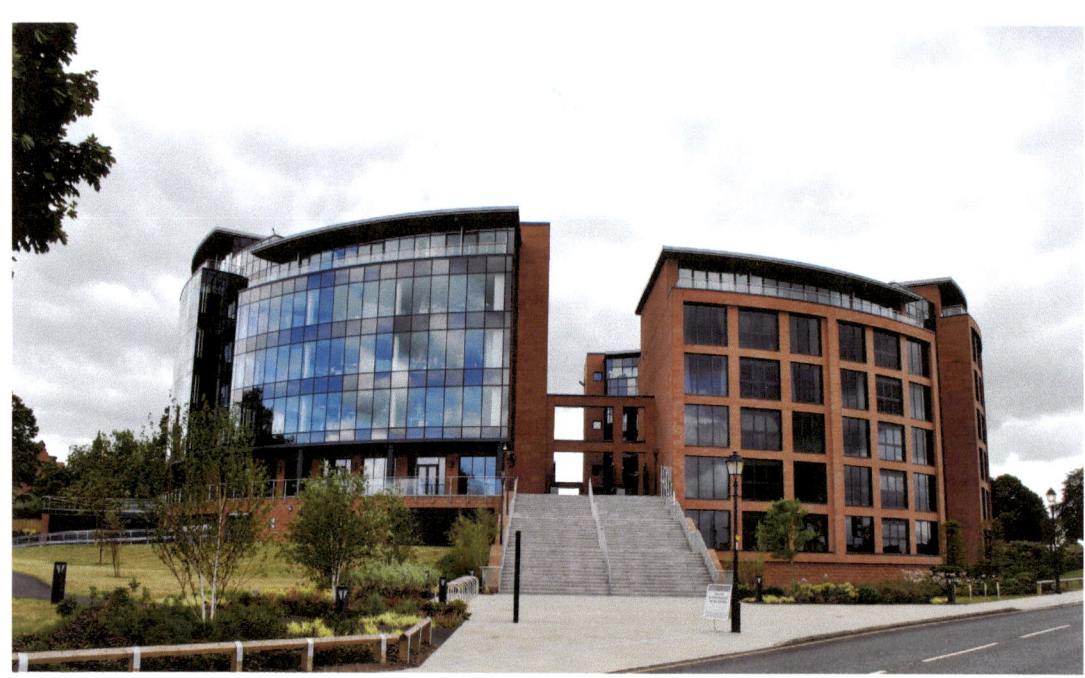

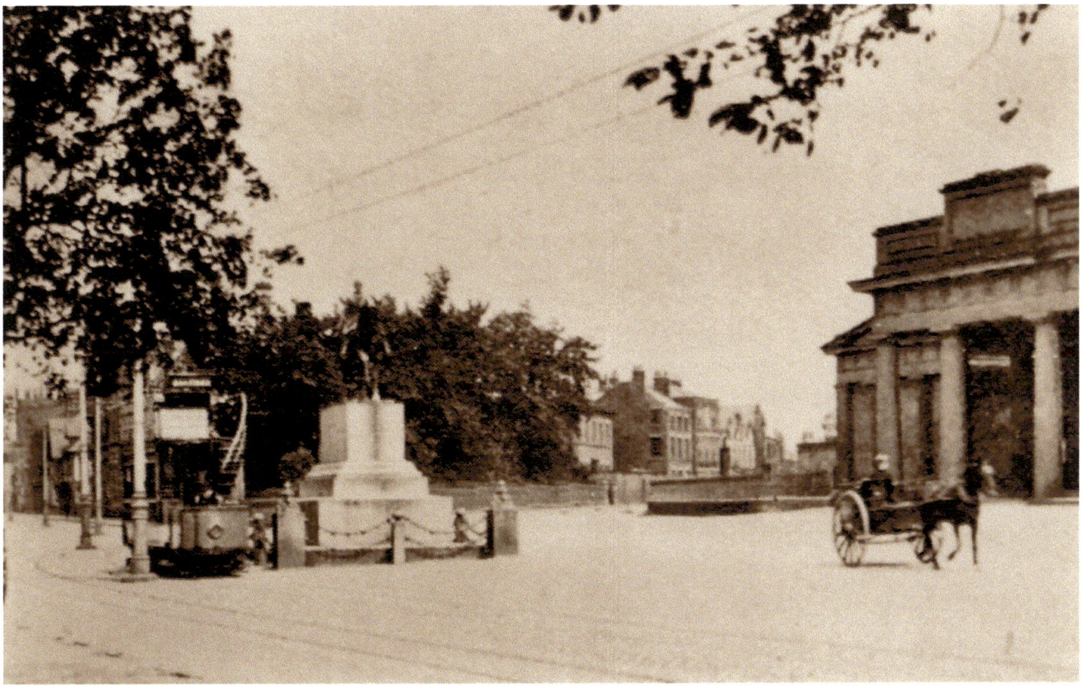

Castle Gates 1905 and 2010
The large gateway with its massive Doric columns forms the entrance to Chester Castle. It was designed by the architect Thomas Harrison and building works were carried out from 1788 to 1822. The castle itself was built in 1070 by Hugh Lupus, the first Earl of Chester and the Chester Crown Court is now housed here. Also to be found within the courtyard is the Cheshire Military Museum which is well worth a visit. Note the tramcar that the Field Marshall once looked down on and if he could talk, the changes that he has seen!

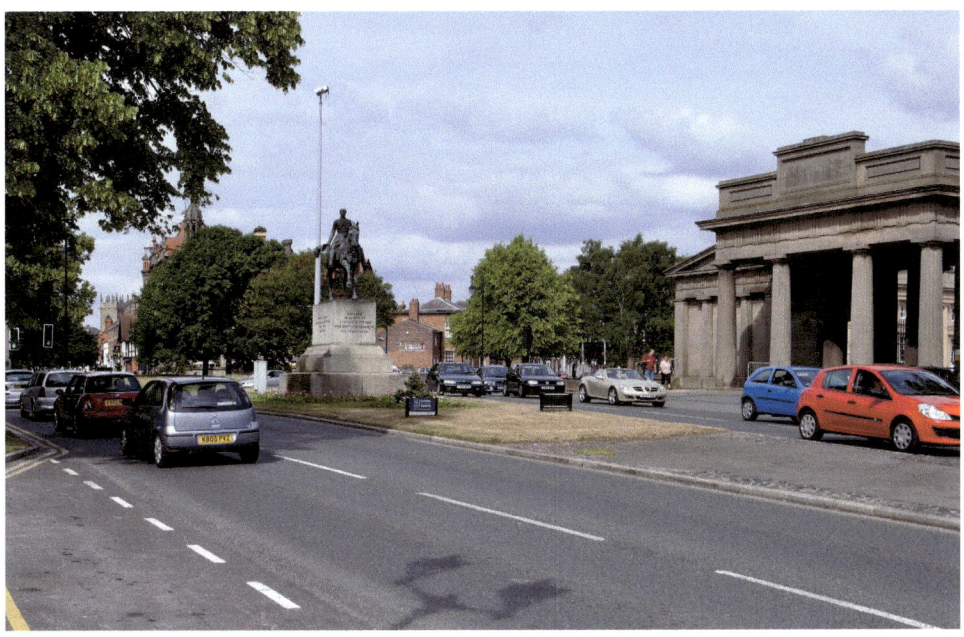

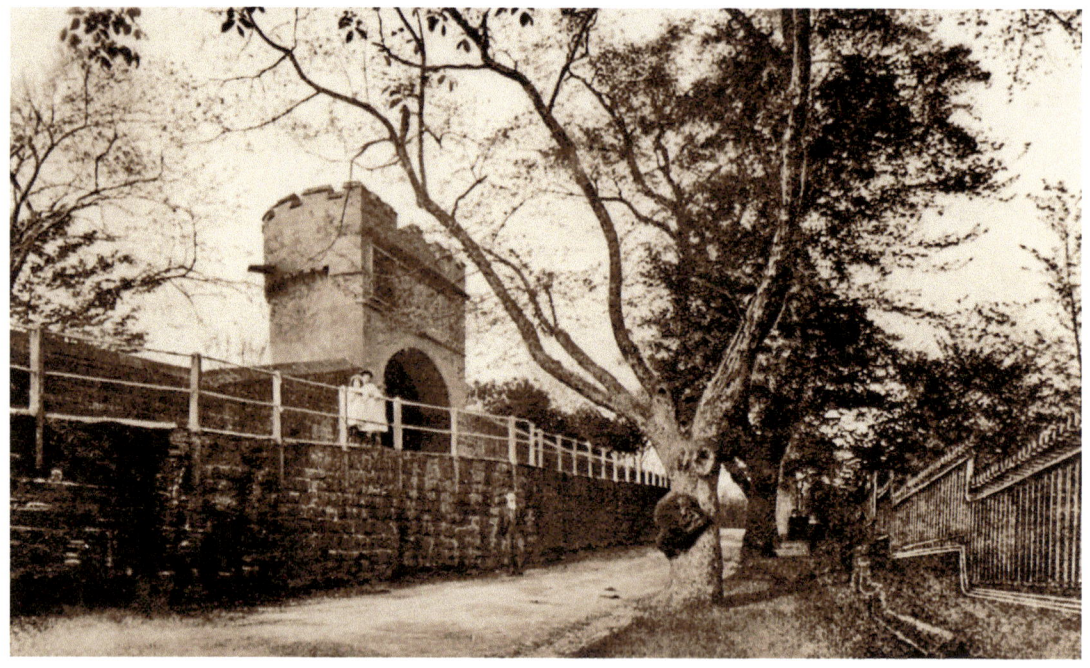

Goblin Tower on the City Walls 1908 and 2010
This unusual half tower is situated on the North Wall and was originally called Goblin Tower, a name that can still be seen at the top of it together with its rebuild date of 1894. It also bears the name Pemberton's Parlour after John Pemberton, a rope maker and Mayor of Chester in 1730. It has a well-worn sandstone tablet naming the mayors and the men responsible for repairing the wall in days long gone. The modern houses in the new photograph are on the site of the old Chester Royal Infirmary.

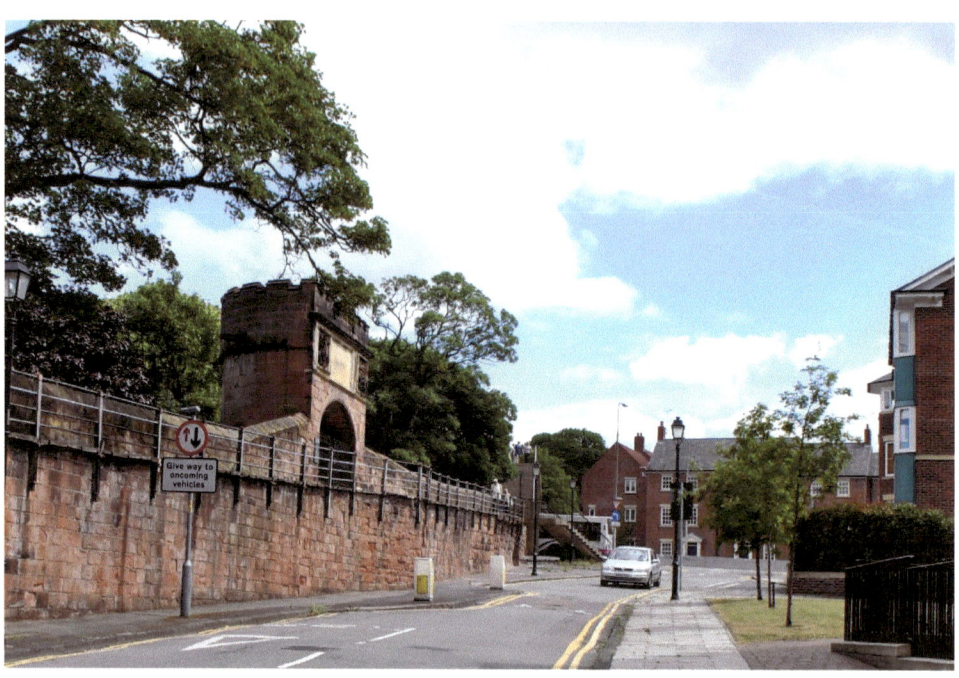

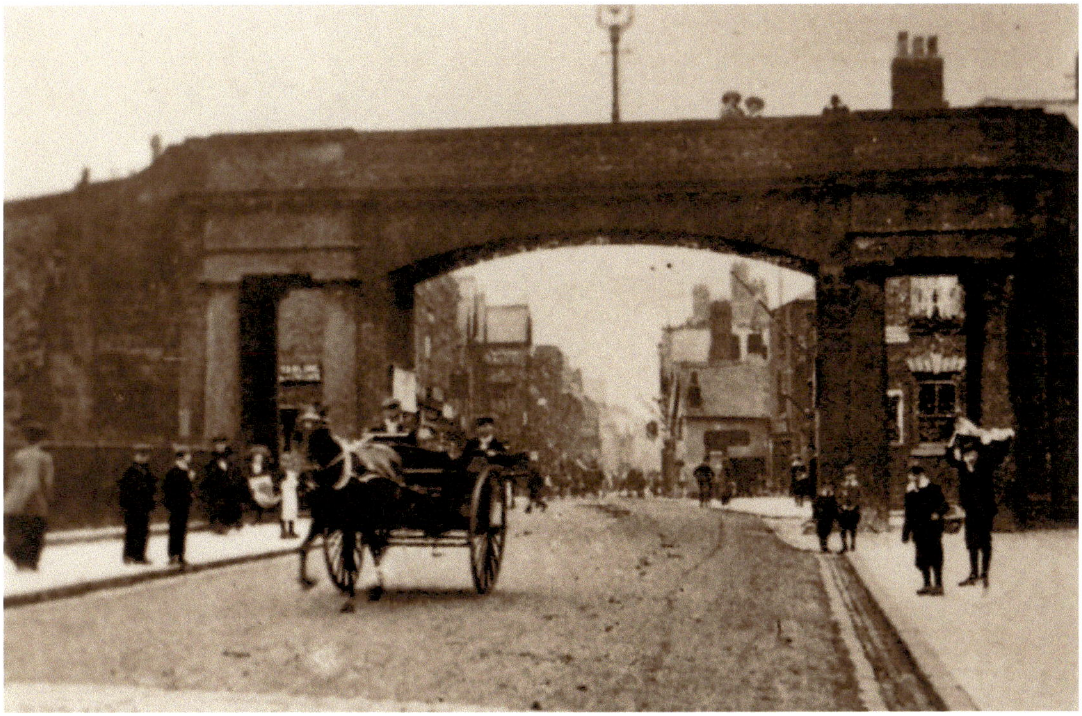

Northgate 1905 and 2010
The Northgate was re-built in 1810 to replace a much smaller gateway which until 1807 housed the city gaol. The new gaol was built on the site of the present Queen's School in 1807 but closed in 1872. The school is by the City Walls located through the gate and immediate right.

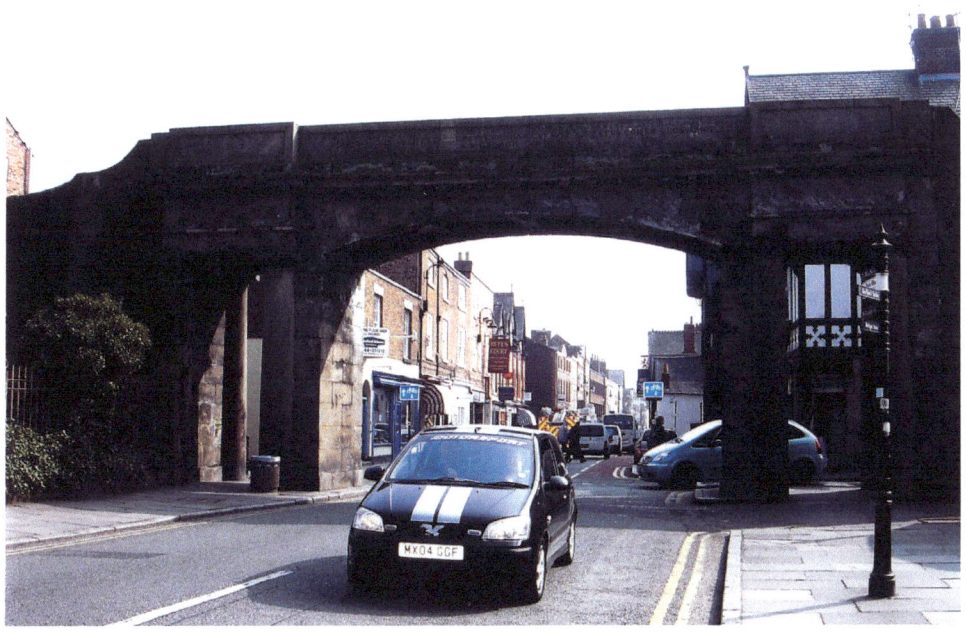

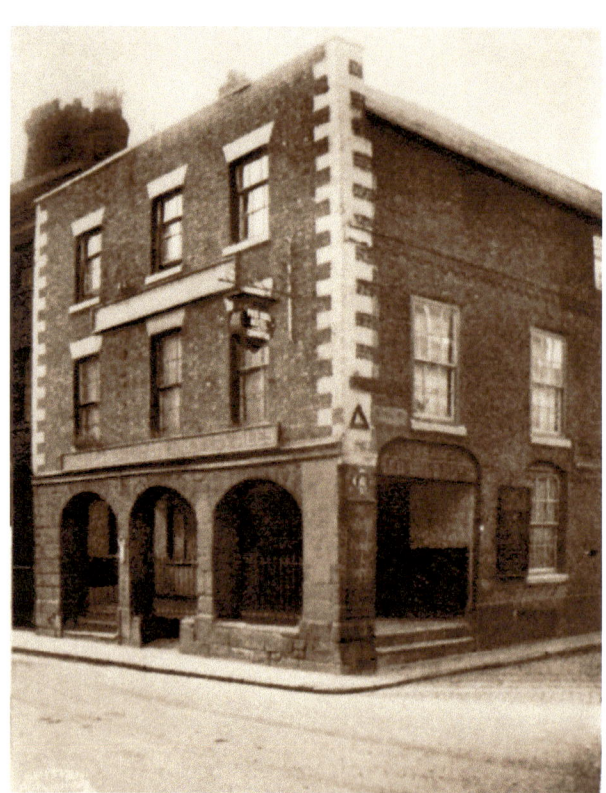
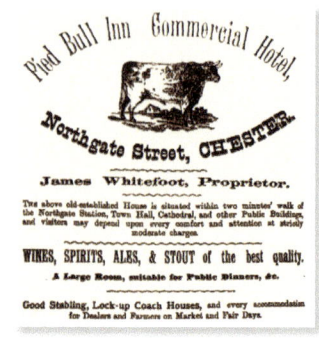

The Pied Bull Hotel early 1900s and 2010

The Pied Bull Hotel still stands in Northgate Street and is another well known Chester coaching inn. On the wall in the old photograph is a board giving mileage to various destinations by coach. This is believed to be the longest continually licensed public house in Chester. The Cycle Storage sign is still on the side wall in the 2010 photograph and the inset shows an 1860s advert.

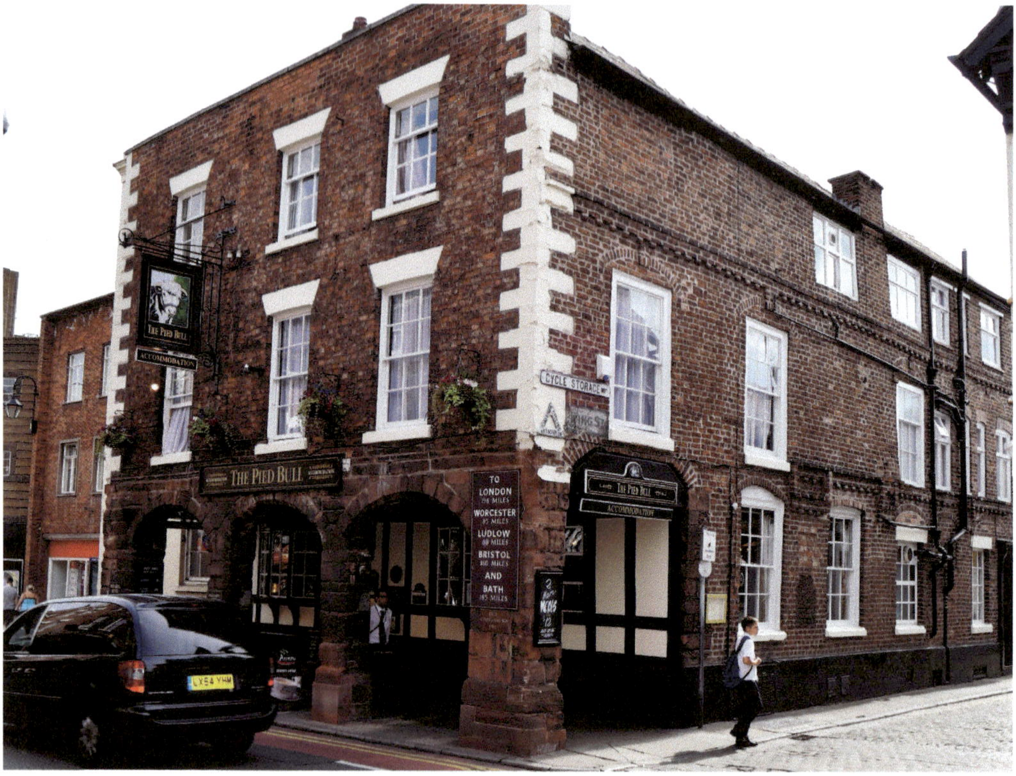

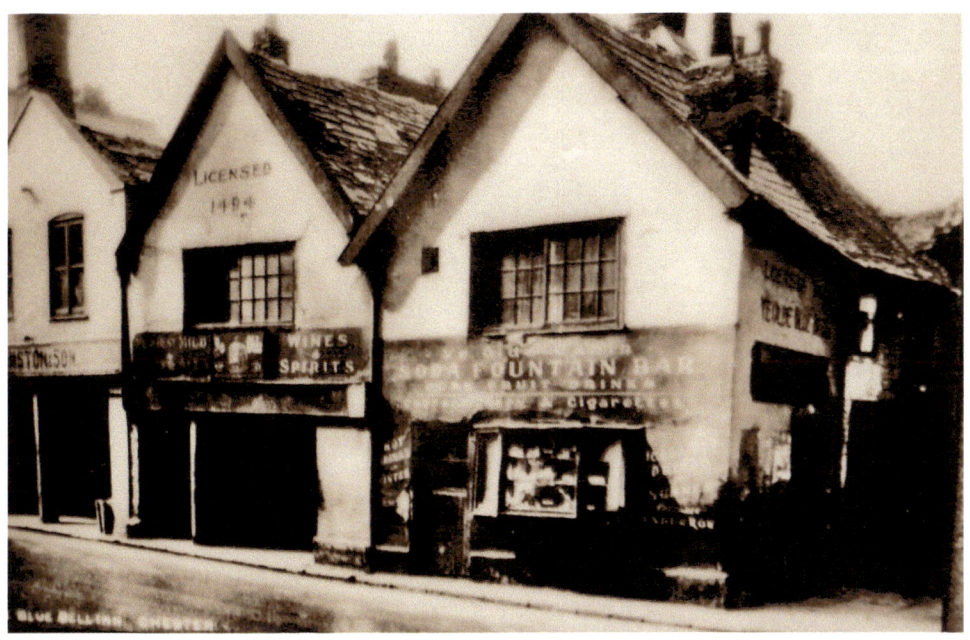

The Blue Bell Inn 1912 and 2009
The Blue Bell Inn is situated in Northgate Street and is the oldest domestic buildings to survive outside the Row system. They were built during the mid fifteenth to sixteenth centuries as two houses; they became a single property in the eighteenth century. For most of its life, the Blue Bell has been an inn, claiming to have received its first licence in 1494. In the 1930s it was threatened by plans to widen Northgate Street and closed as an inn, It opened as an antique shop in 1948 but was very run down and had to be rescued by the Chester Civic Trust and restored in 1960. It is now a restaurant.

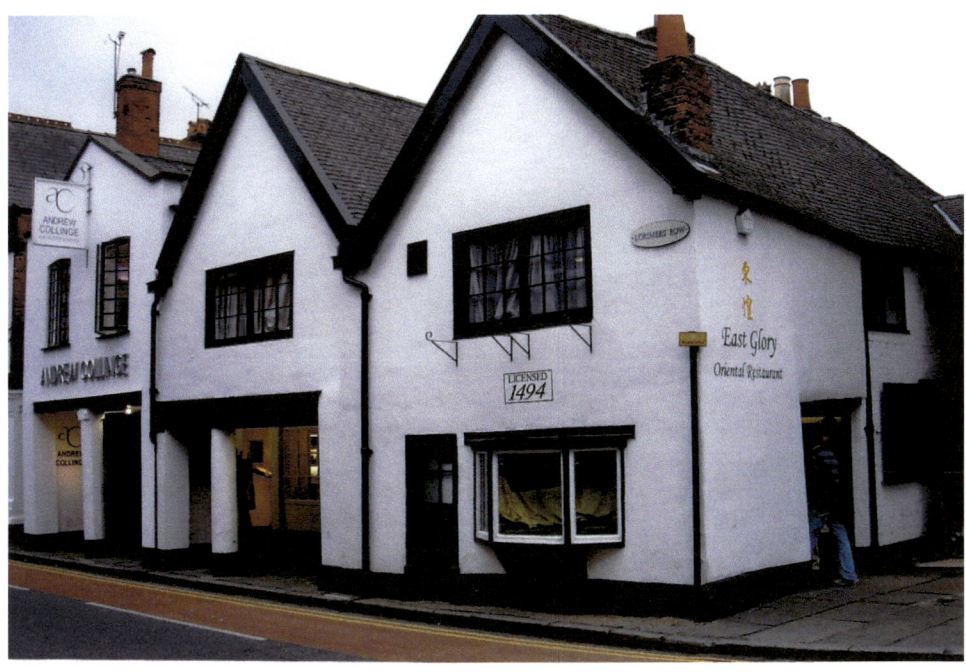

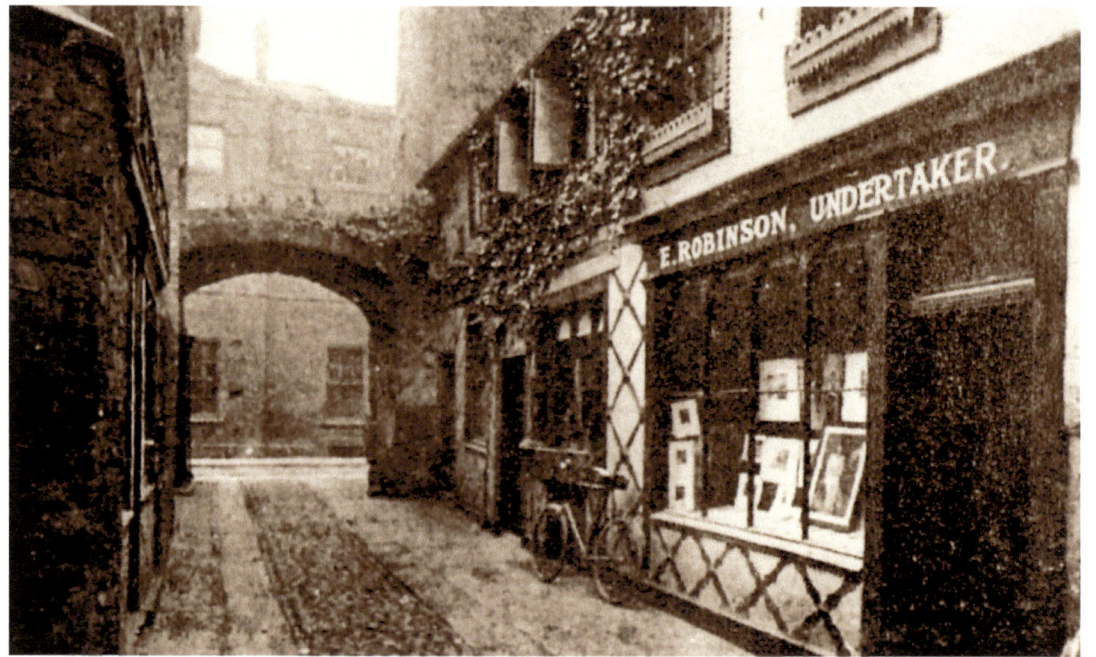

Little Abbey Gateway 1920s and 2010
This gate arch and part of precinct wall is to the former Abbey of St Werburgh (now Cathedral Church of Christ & the Blessed Virgin Mary, St Werburgh Street). This ancient gateway leads from Northgate Street to Abbey Square. It was once lined with business premises but now houses a car park and the outline of the buildings shown in the old photograph can be seen.

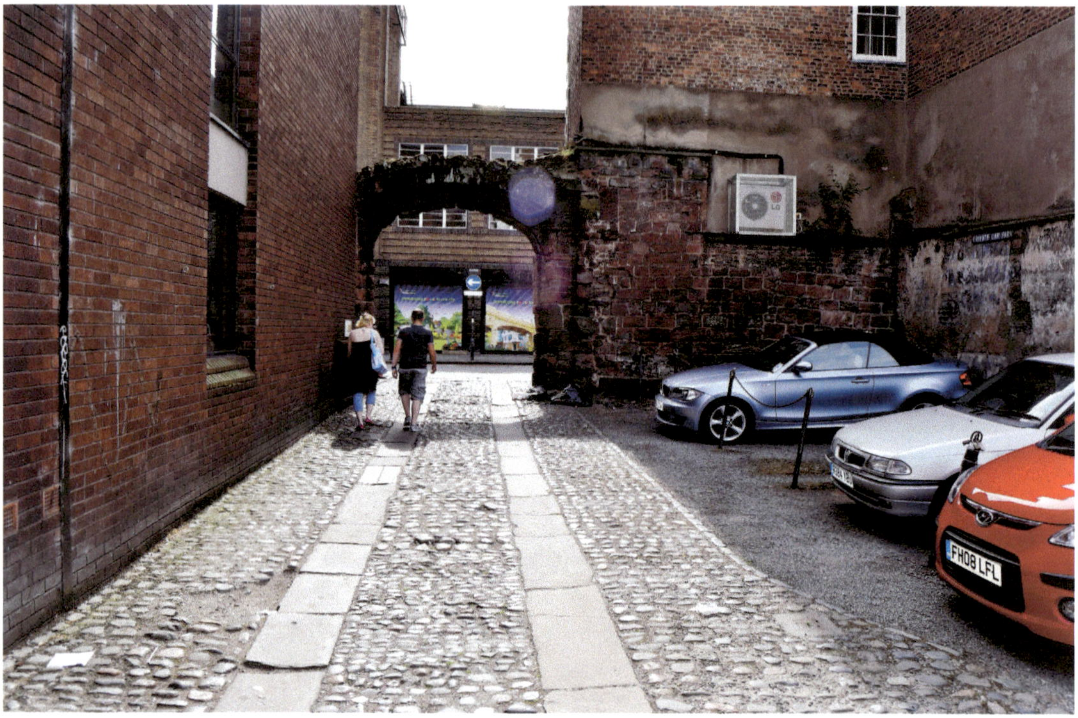

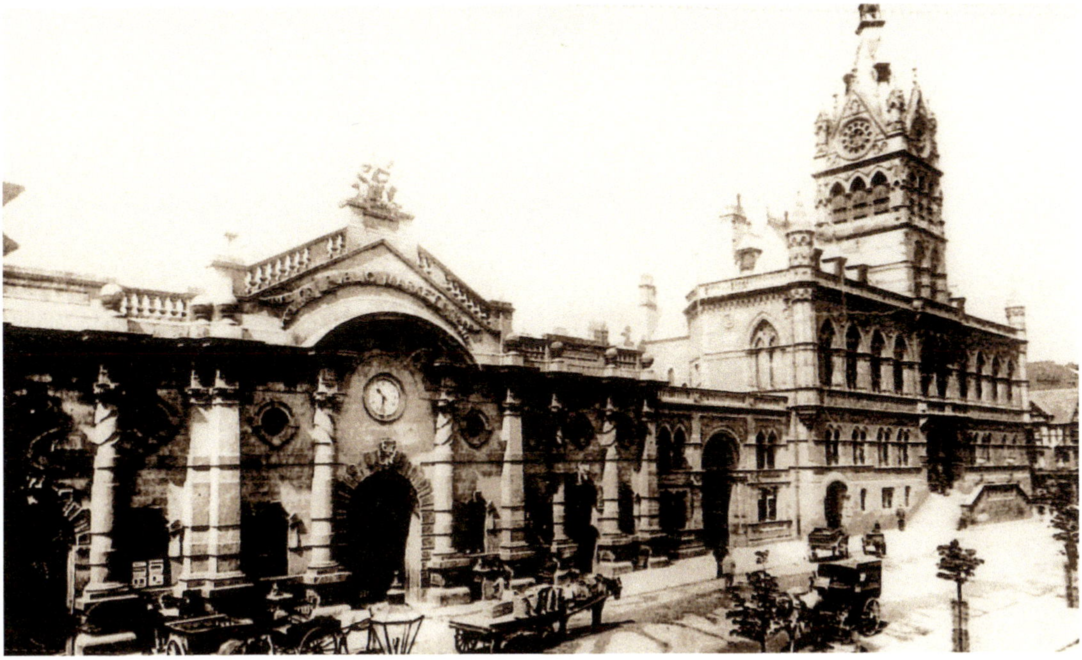

Old Market Hall 1890s and 2010
This is Town Hall Square in Northgate Street and the Market Hall was built in 1863 with an ornate baroque façade. Sadly it was demolished in 1967 and replaced with a brick box like frontage. Then in 1995 it was replaced again with a mainly glass and stone frontage. As can be seen in the new photograph, a tree masks this new addition.

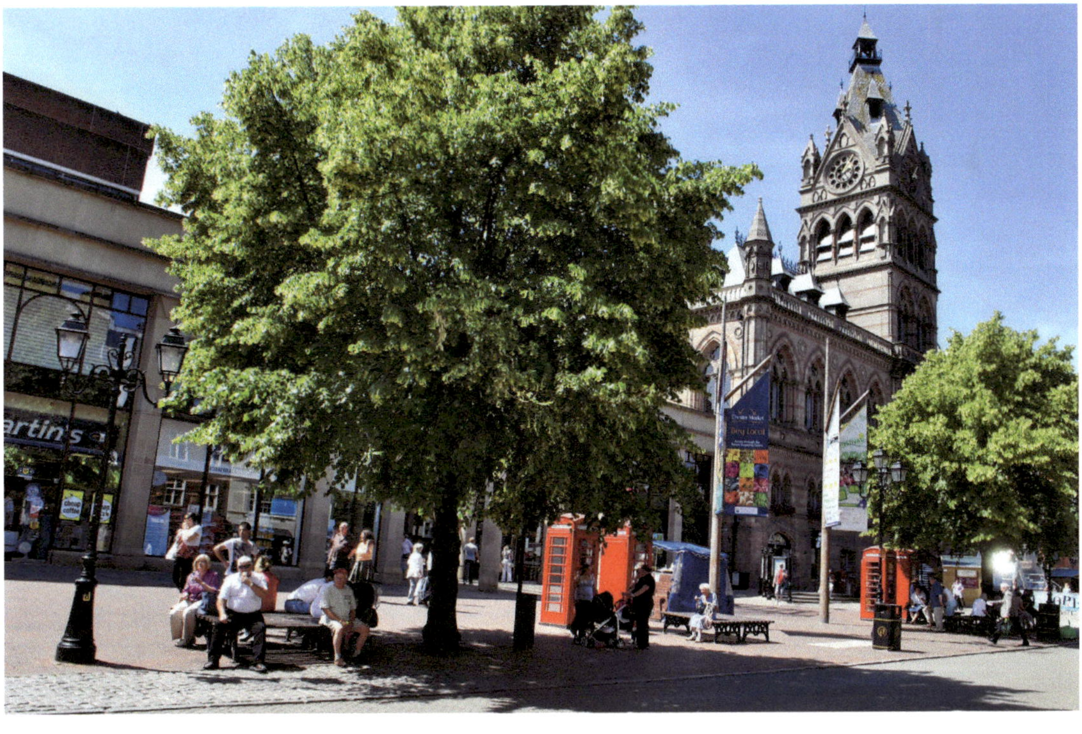

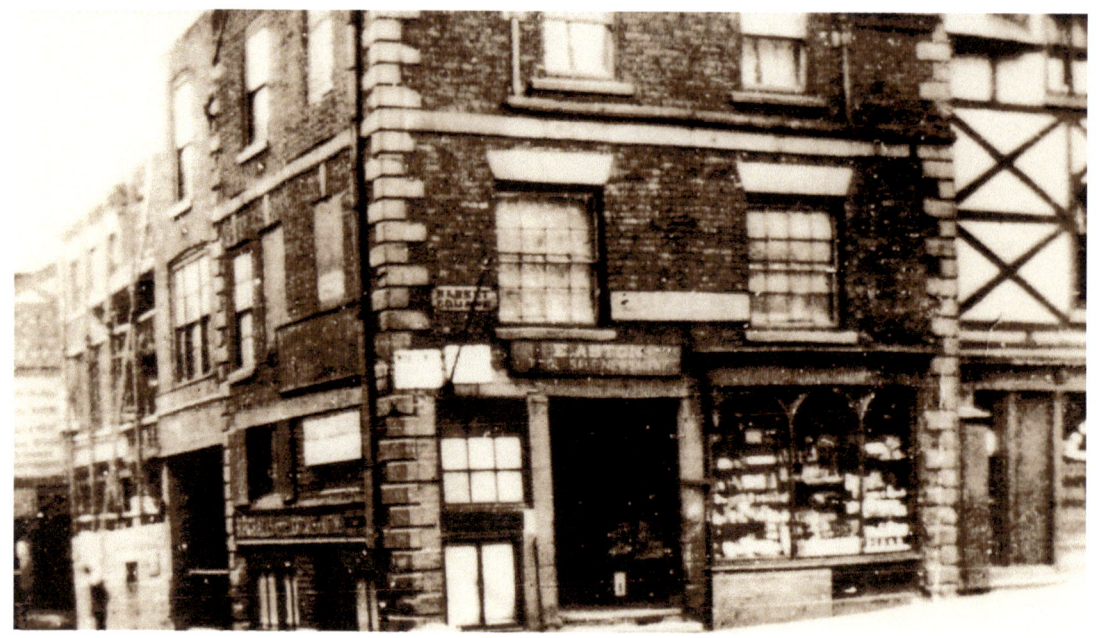

Northgate Street west 1897 and 2010

This side of the street at one time had two tier shops with rows as in Bridge Street and Eastgate Street but it was demolished in the 1890s soon after the old photograph was taken. The buildings from St Peters church up to the Dublin Packet which is just around the corner went and were re-built with the upper floors built over the pavement to form an arcade known as Shoemakers' Row. Once again, I don't think we can complain about the quality of the replacement buildings!

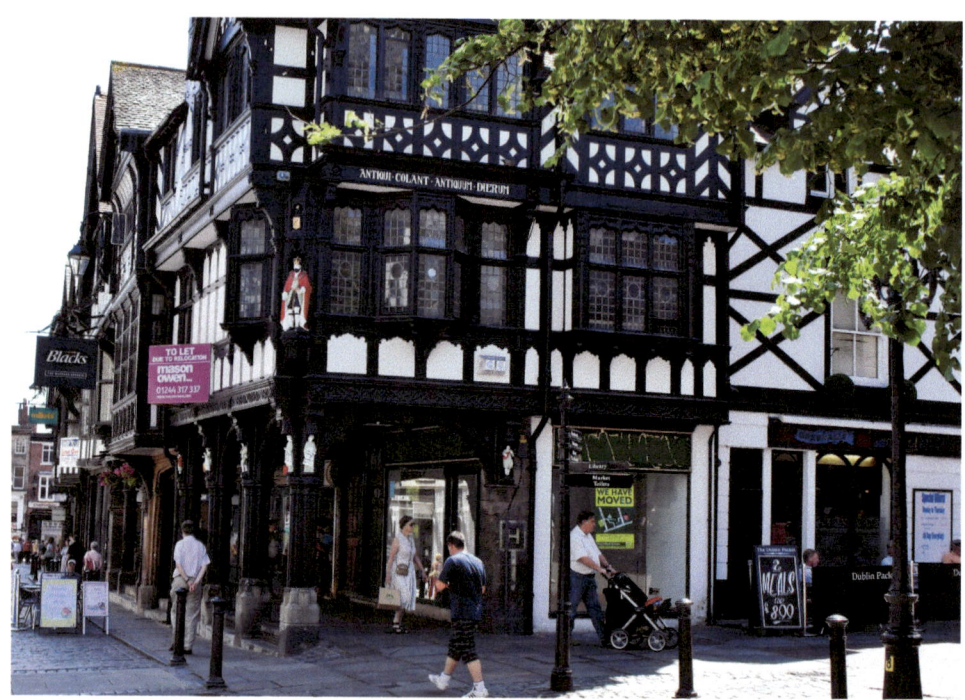

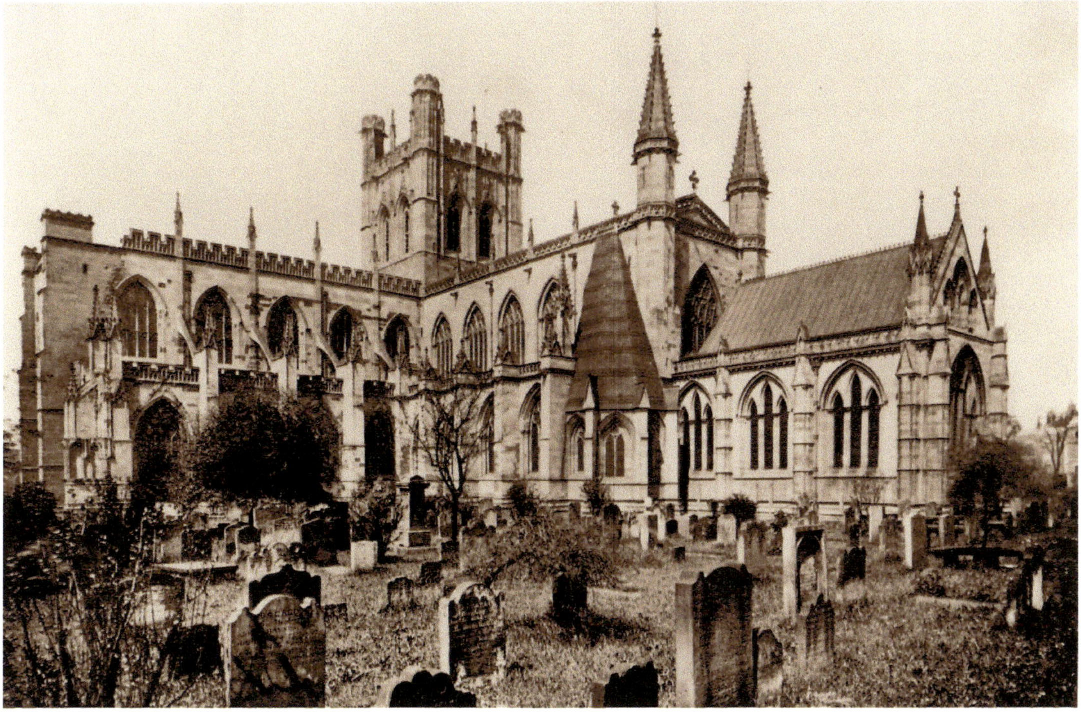

Chester Cathedral 1902 and undated

All the gravestones have been removed as can be seen by comparing the two photographs and the whole area has been transformed into a garden of remembrance for the Cheshire Regiment, now The Mercian Regiment. The flowerbeds are laid out in the form of a medal and its ribbon. They are shown off at their best in the modern undated photograph.

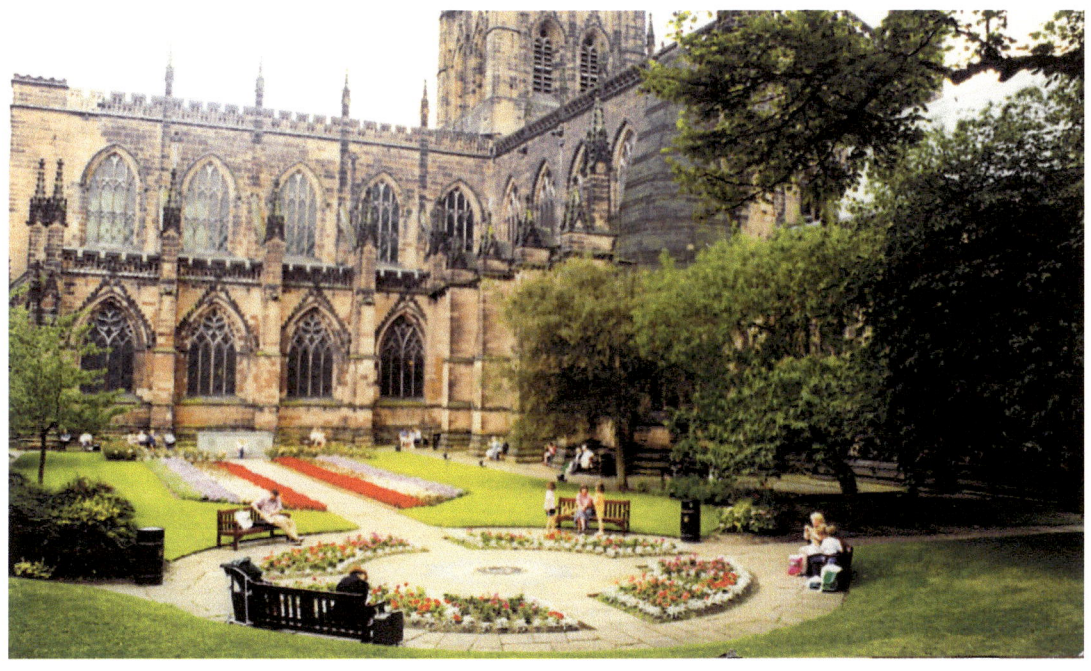

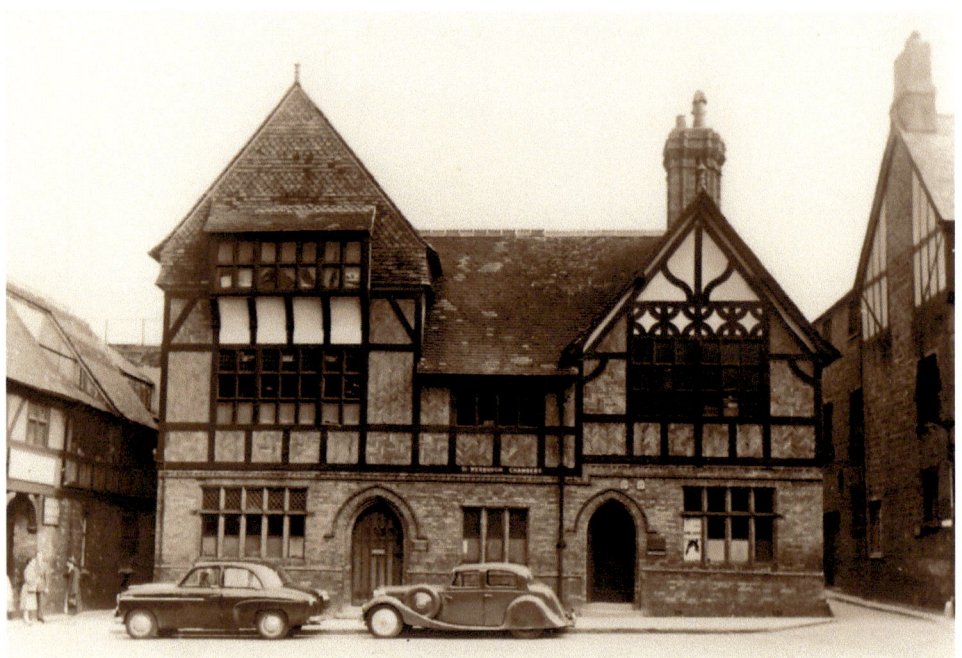

St Werburgh Street 1964 and 2010
The building here is St Werburgh Chambers and it stands opposite the cathedral. The openings that can be seen in the 1955 photograph on either side of the building are two of the remaining four medieval lanes within the city. Left is Godstall Lane and right is Leen Lane. The whole character of the building is lost since its conversion to shop premises.

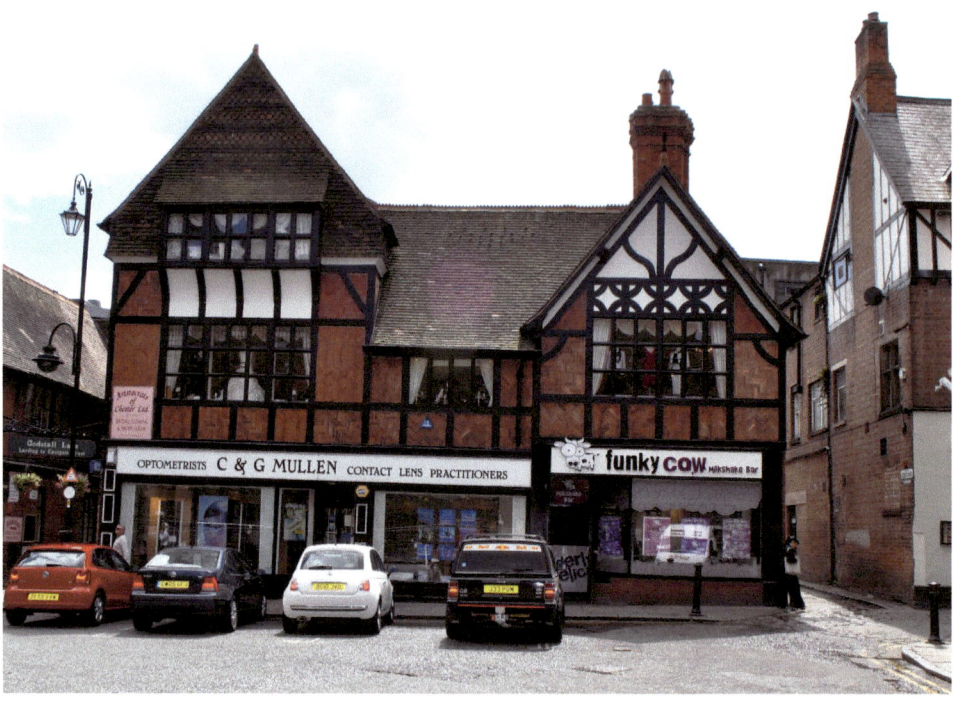

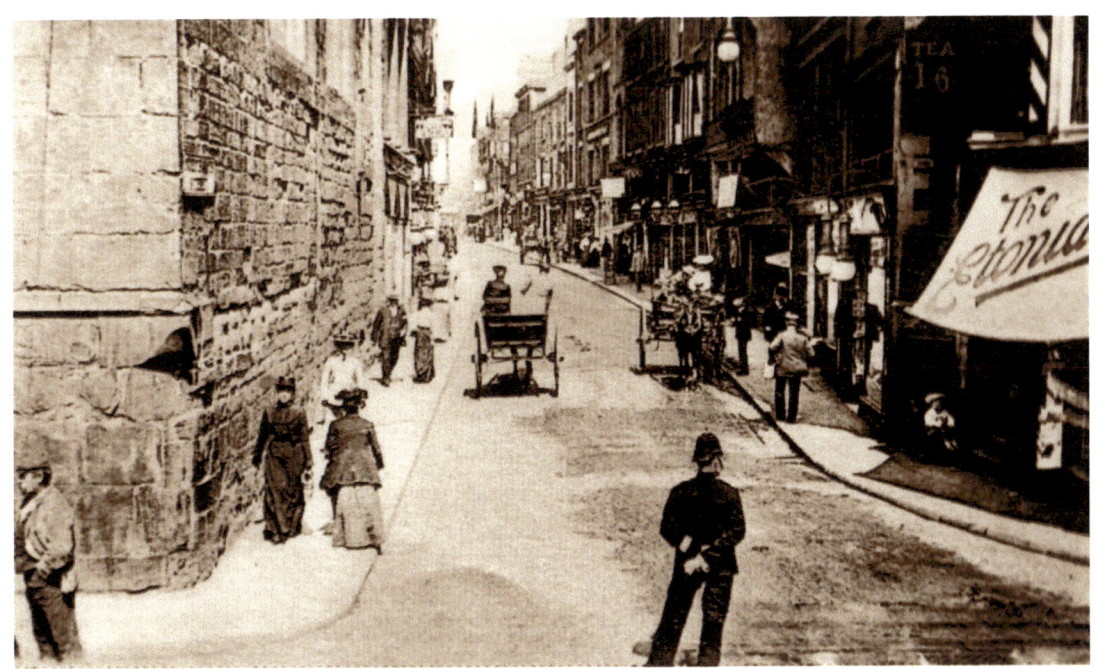

Northgate Street 1908 and 2010
The ancient church at the junction with Eastgate Street and Northgate Street, St Peter's church seen on the left of the photographs was built by Aethelflaed, the daughter of King Alfred in AD 907 so is one of the oldest in the county. The policeman in the old photograph has rather an easy job directing traffic!

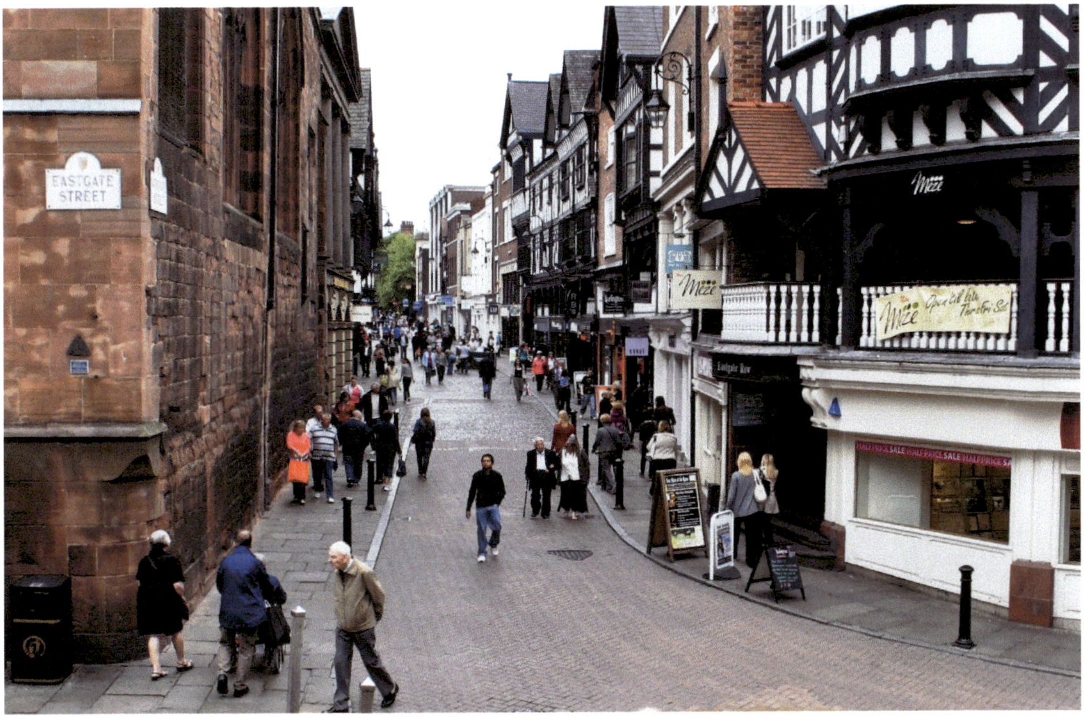

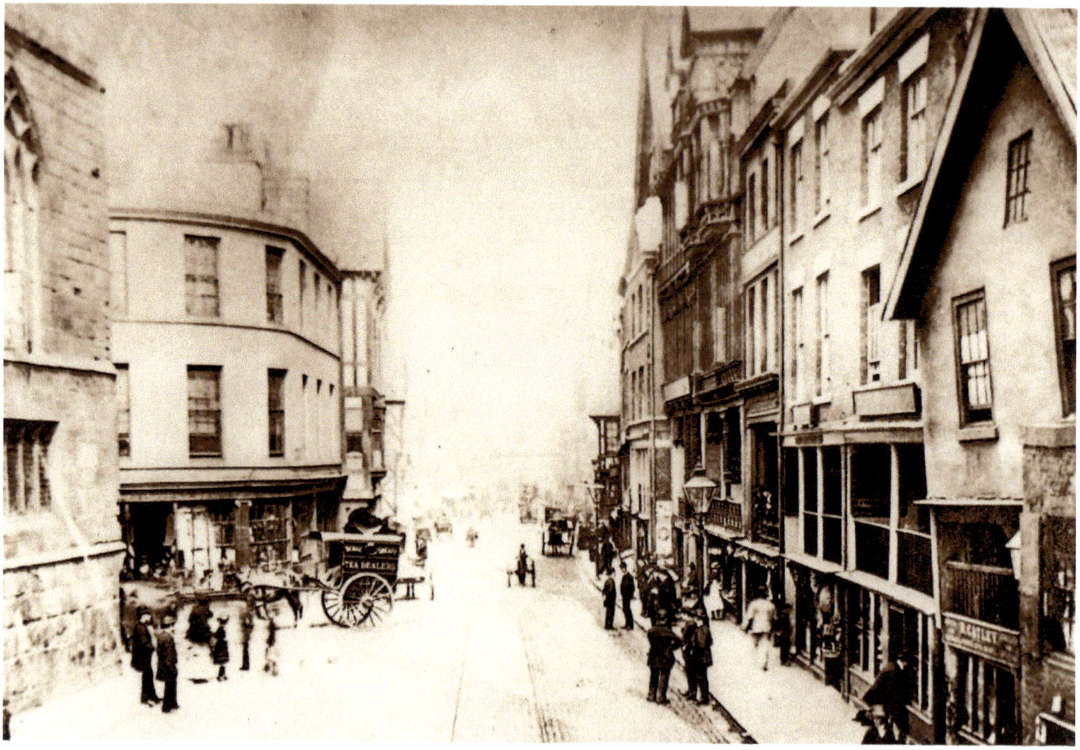

Eastgate Street 1800s and 2010
The old photograph is quite poor but filled with period interest. The tea delivery van is turning into Northgate Street, a veritable snapshot in time.

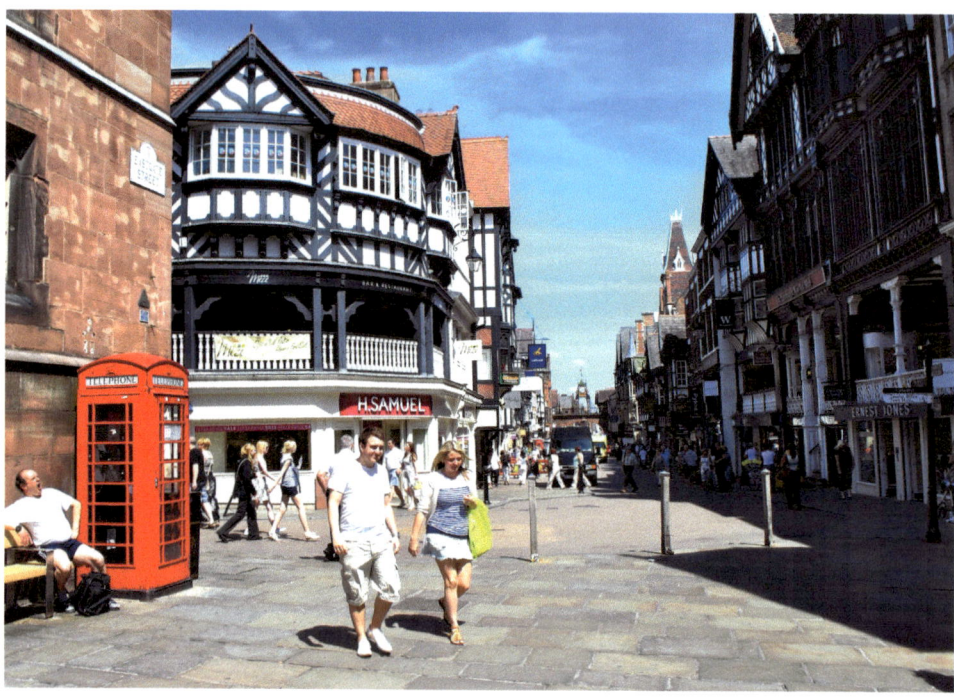

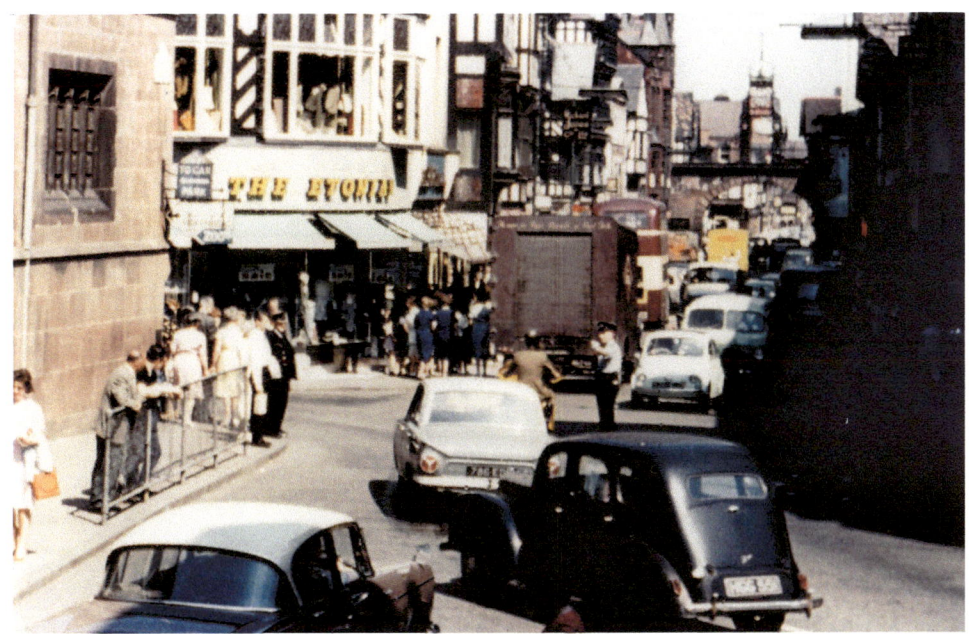

Eastgate Street 1963 and 2010
Back now for a later view of Eastgate Street and The Cross, as you can see, The Cross is not there in the 1963 photograph but is in the 2010 one. The Cross was first mentioned in the City Records in 1377. It was demolished by Parliamentary forces at the end of the Civil War. The base is at Plas Newydd in Llangollen, the rest was hidden under the steps of St Peters Church where it remained until 1820. After spending time in a churchwarden's garden and the Grosvenor Museum it was erected on its original site by the City Council in 1974.

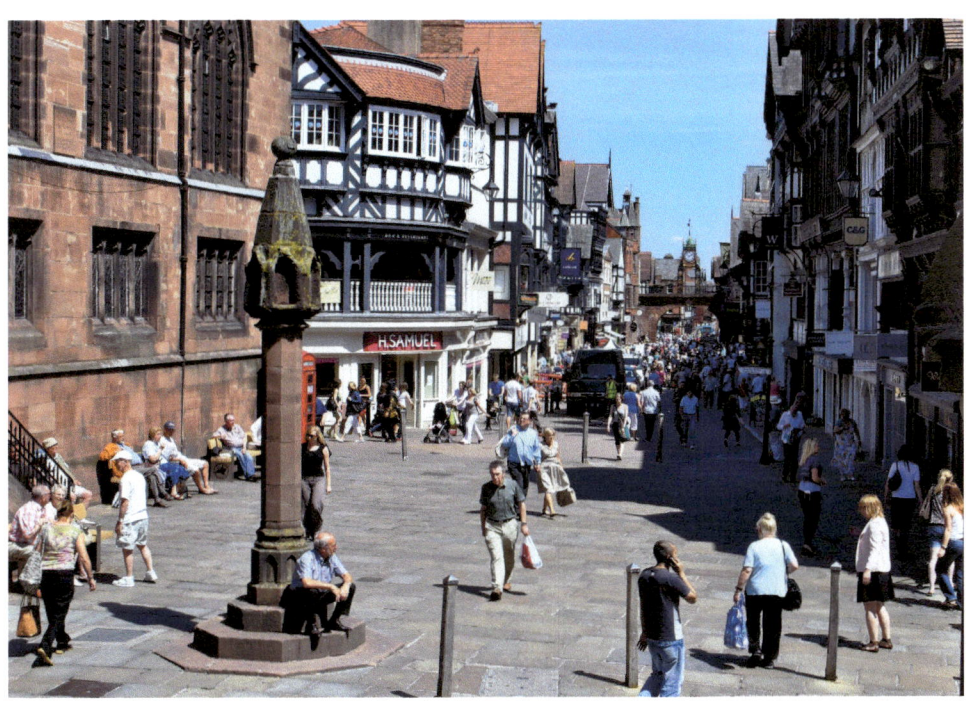

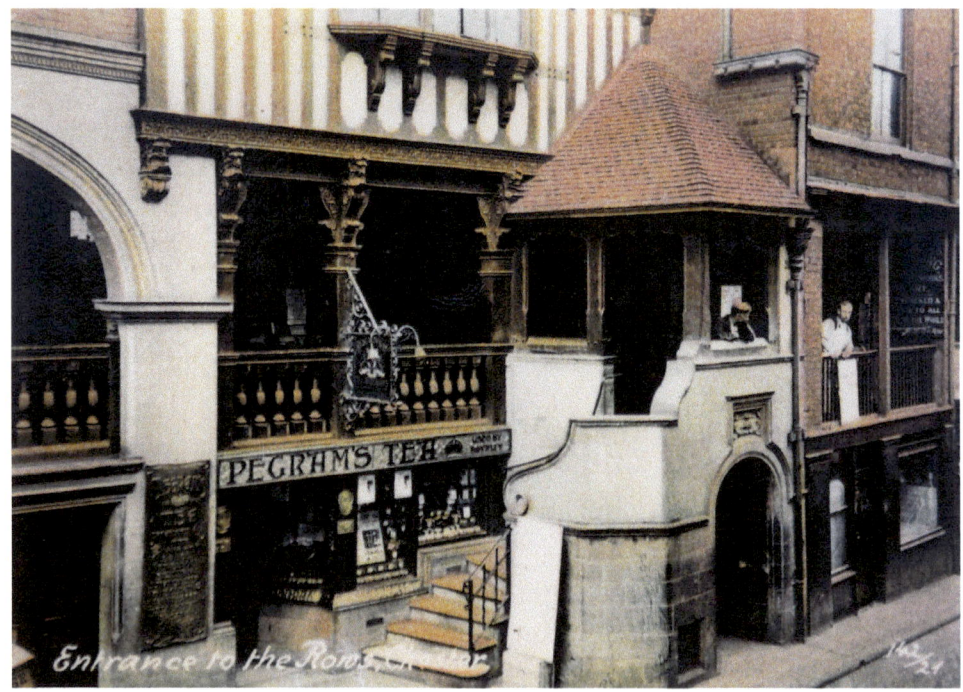

Shops in Watergate Street 1912 and 2009

Back now to Watergate Street and near to The Cross we find this set of steps leading up to the rows. This corner section was designed by Thomas Lockwood and built in 1892. Over the years many different types of shops have come and gone. Pegram's was a well-known grocery chain with shops throughout the country and on the far right in the old photograph is number 5 Bradshaw's Tripe Shop selling a delicacy that we do not enjoy quite as much today!

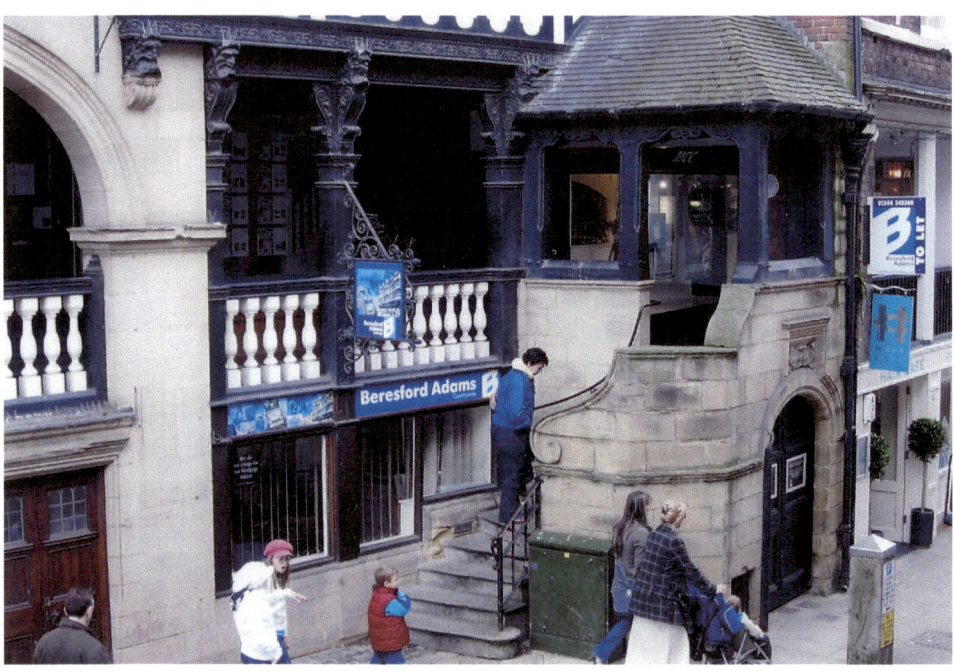

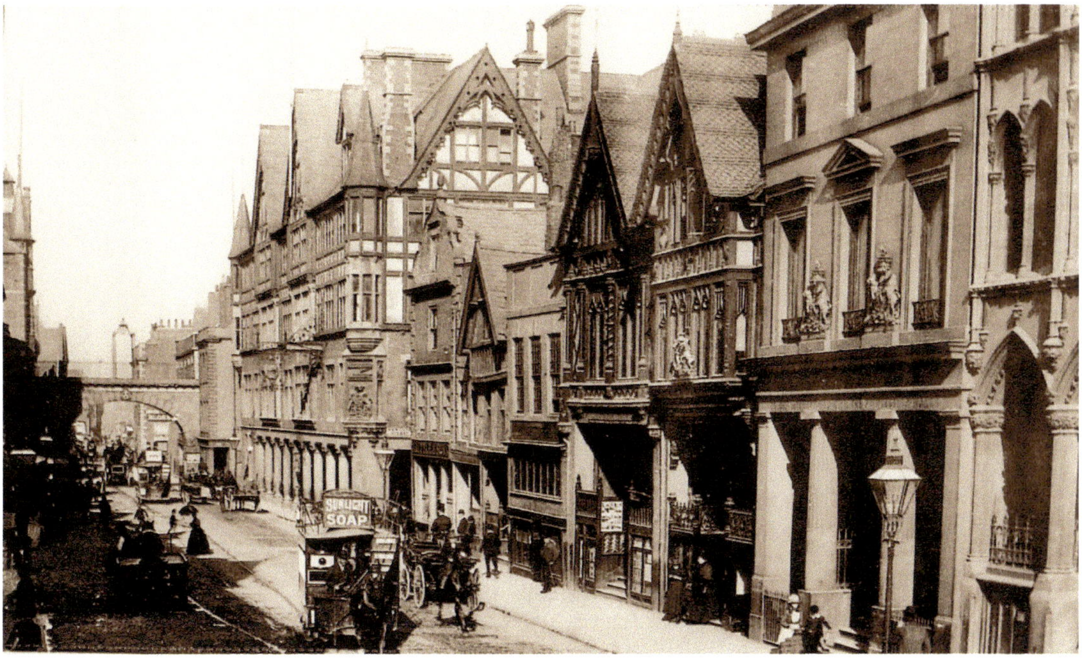

Eastgate Street 1897 and 2010
Here we have quite a unique photograph as it shows the famous Chester Clock which straddles the City Walls over Eastgate Street. This old photograph was taken as the clock was under construction and was to celebrate Queen Victoria's Diamond Jubilee in that year. This photograph as absolutely filled with period charm with horse trams and many other forms of horse-drawn transport. There have been some alterations to the buildings but in the main little has changed architecturally.

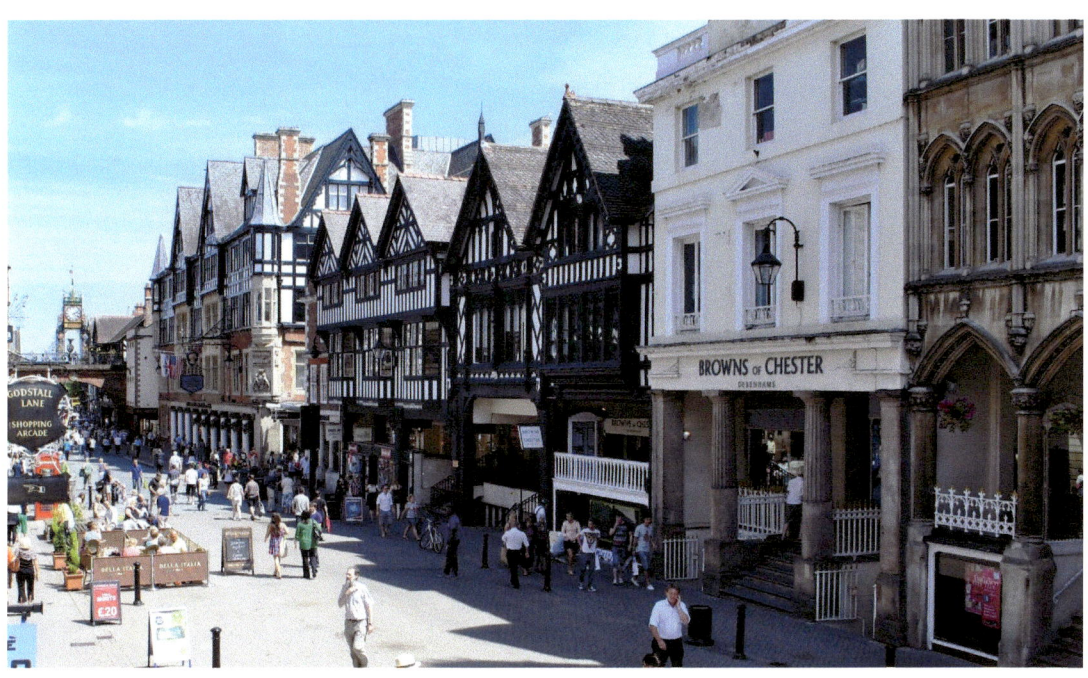

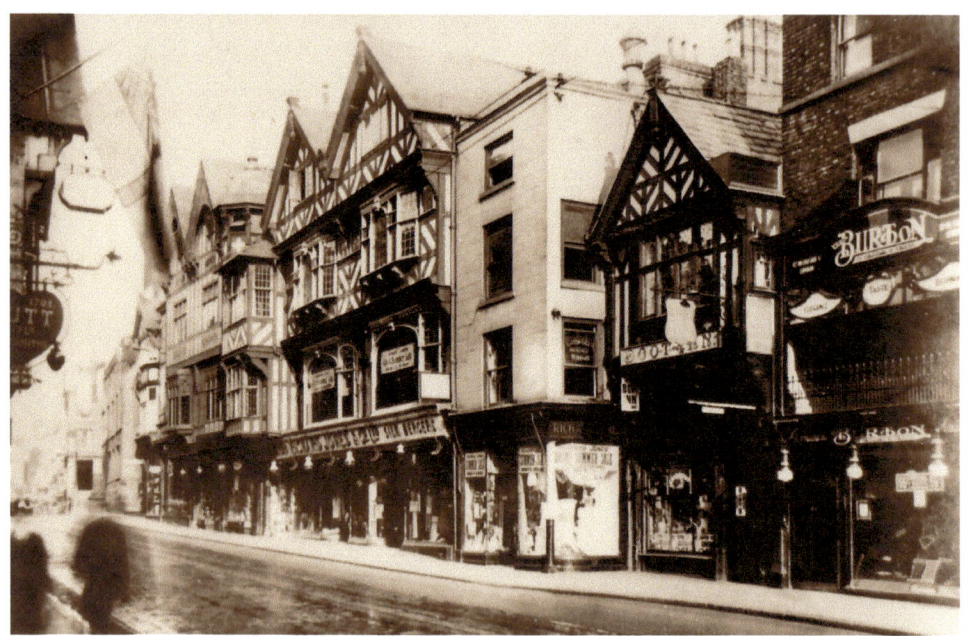

Eastgate Street 1908 and 2010
Eastgate Street and a look towards The Cross, some cosmetic changes have taken place over the years. The Boot Inn shown in the 1908 photograph has become Ye Olde Boot in the modern one; it also shows its date as 1643. One of the vibrantly-painted Rhinos can be seen, these were launched on the 5 July 2010 as Rhino Mania. 170 of these statues have been placed in Chester's streets and it is all in aid of a good cause.

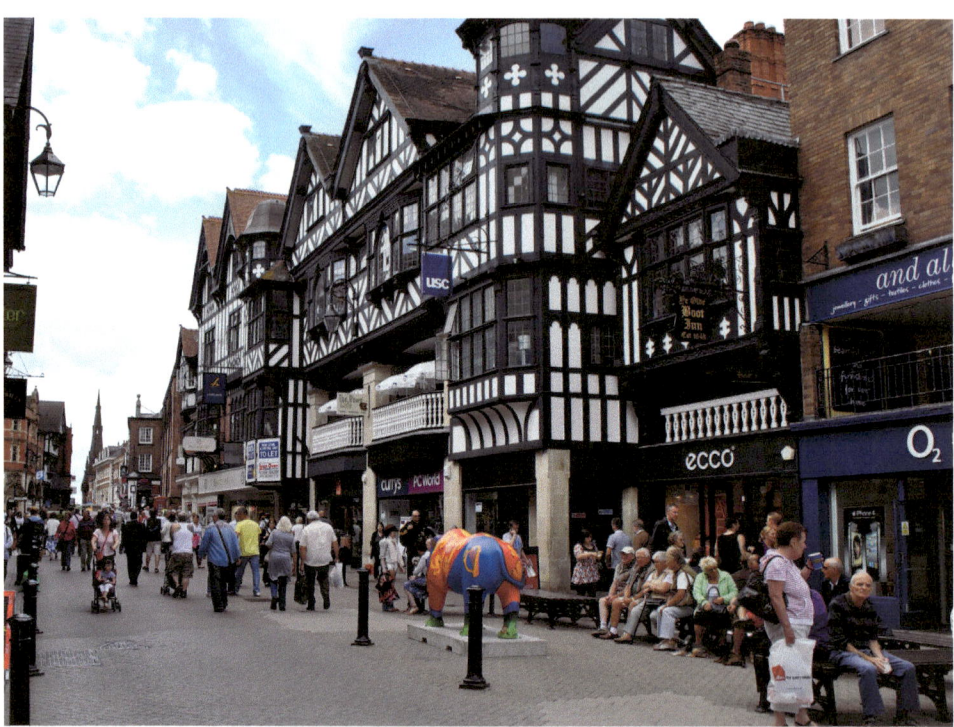

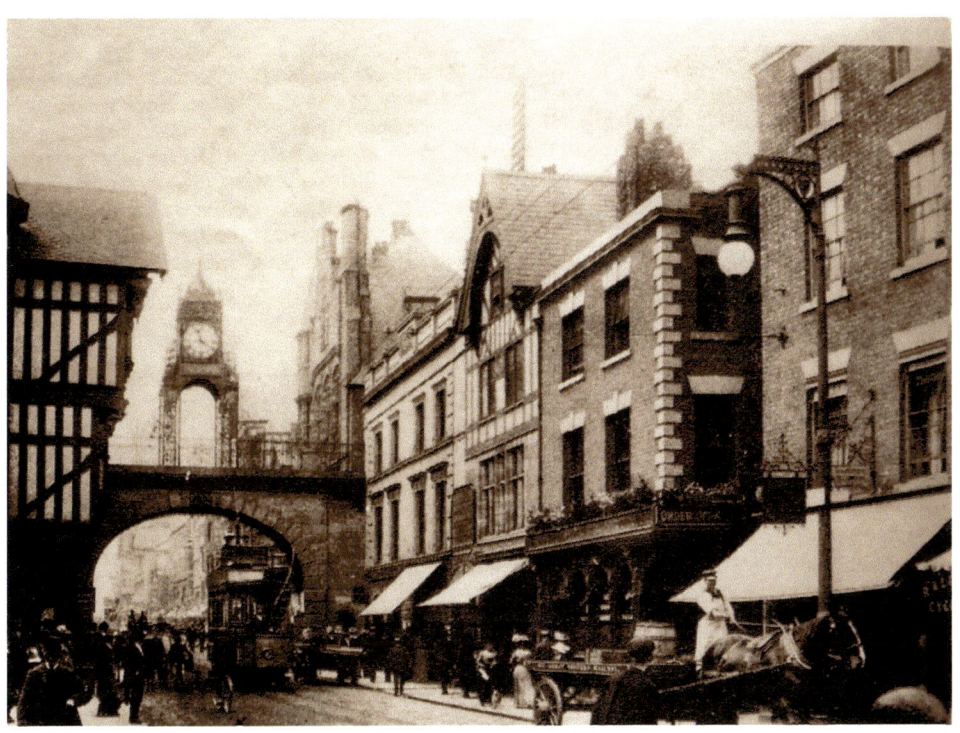

Eastgate Street 1906 and 2010
A look now towards the clock in the direction of The Cross, we will look at the clock a little closer later on. The old photograph shows us a horse and dray with an electric tram passing through the gateway on its way to the railway station.

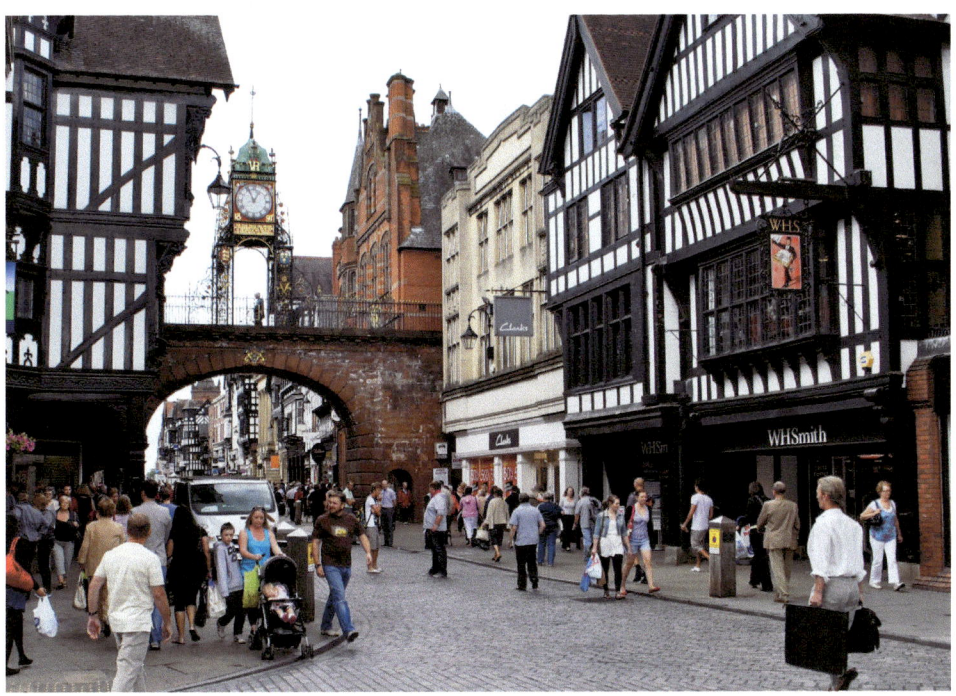

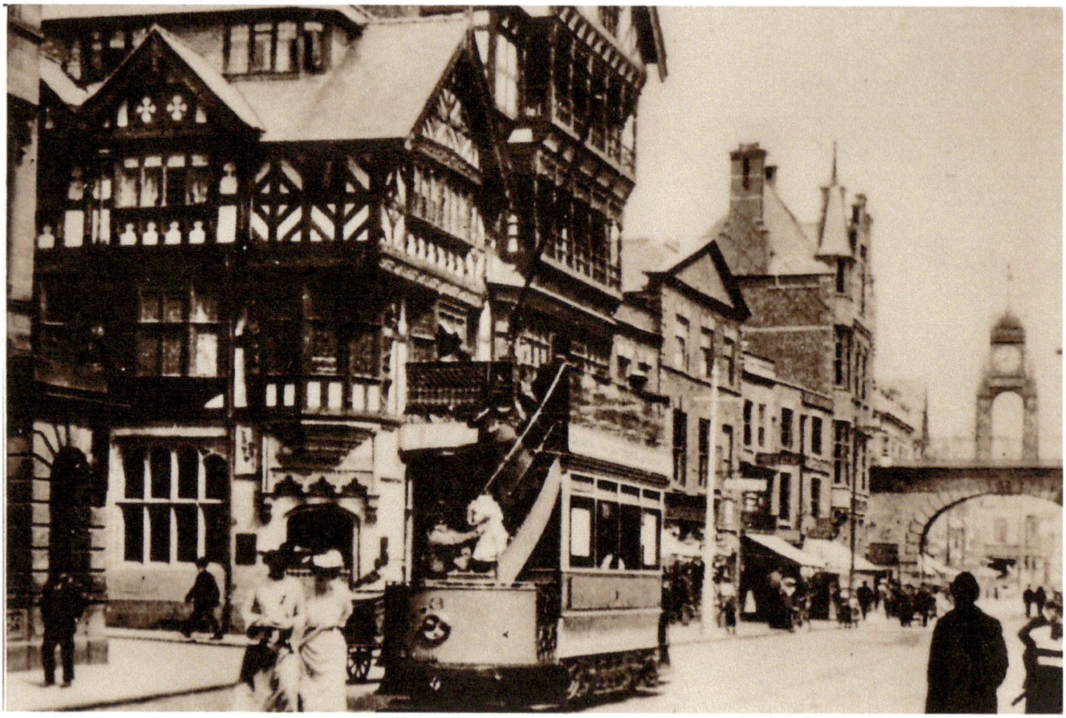

Eastgate Street junction St Werburgh Street 1905 and 2010
A look down Eastgate Street at its junction with St Werburgh's Street; very little has changed here over the intervening years. The tram conductor is helping a young girl to alight as her mother follows.

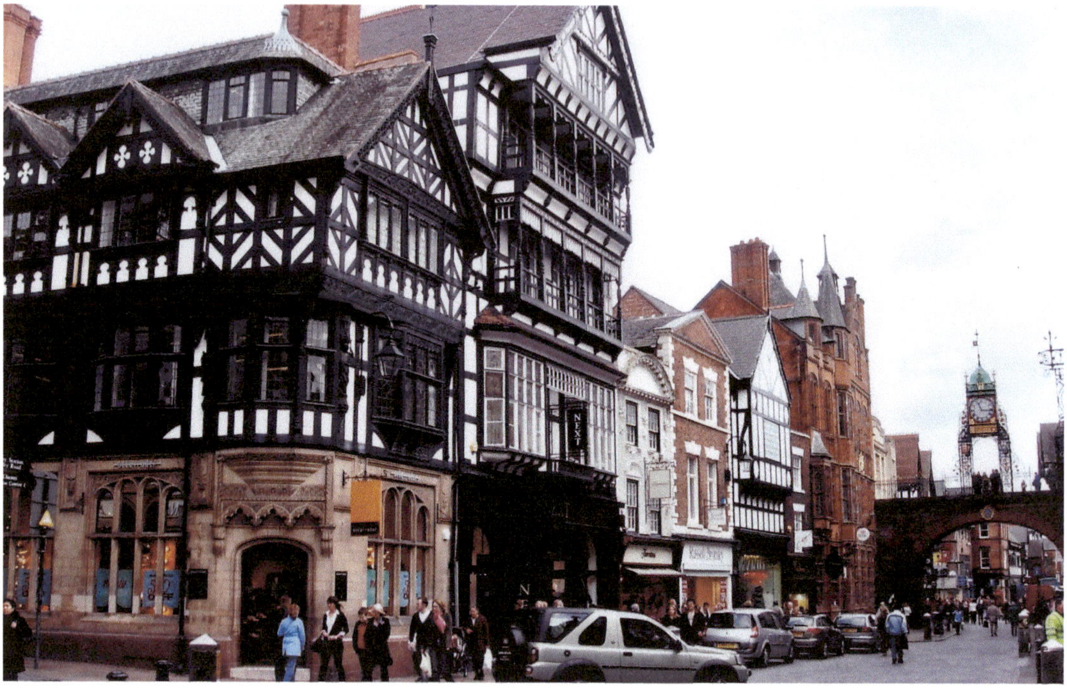

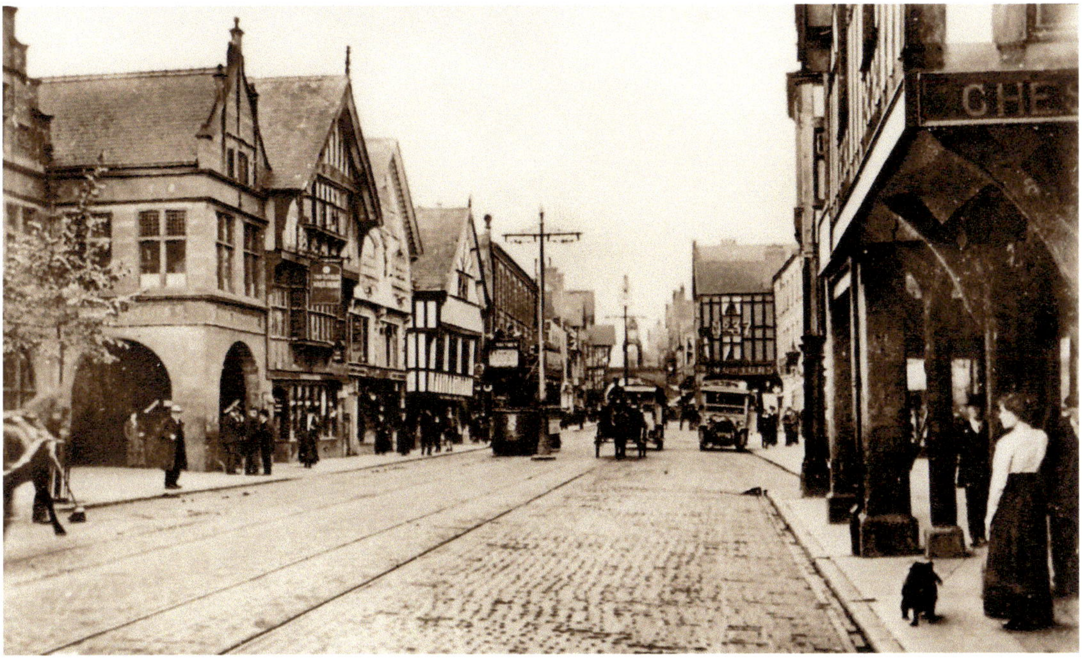

Foregate Street 1906 and 2010

We now walk down Foregate Street and stop opposite the McDonald's takeaway. Looking back towards the clock we see in the old photograph electric trams and motor buses with a horse and cart ambling down towards the camera. This area has changed quite a bit over the years and some very nice buildings have gone to make way for the not so nice. Just after the black and white building on the right is the site of the Brewers Arms pub that we will look at shortly.

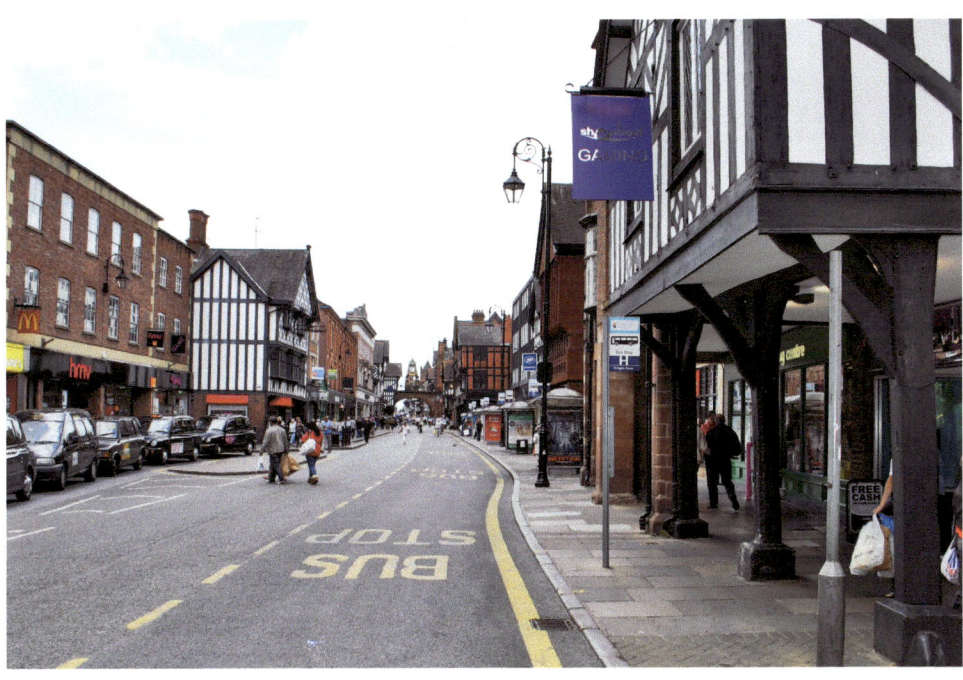

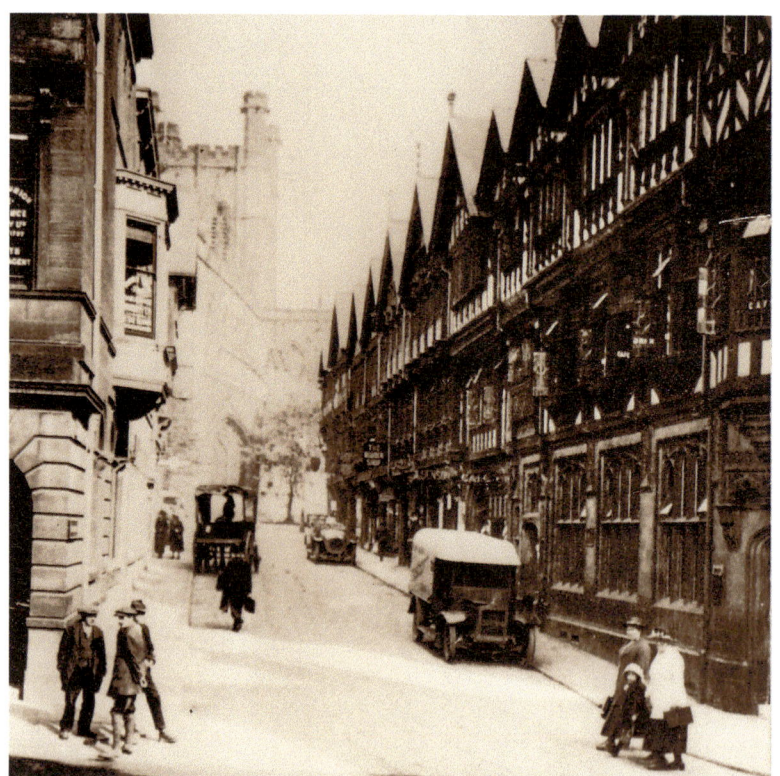

St Werburgh Street 1920s and 2010

We now a look up St Werburgh Street towards the cathedral, this street was once half the width that it was until it was widened and the east side redeveloped by the Corporation with the backing of the Duke of Westminster and the designs of architect John Douglas. A plaque was erected here in 1923 in appreciation of the work done by John Douglas.

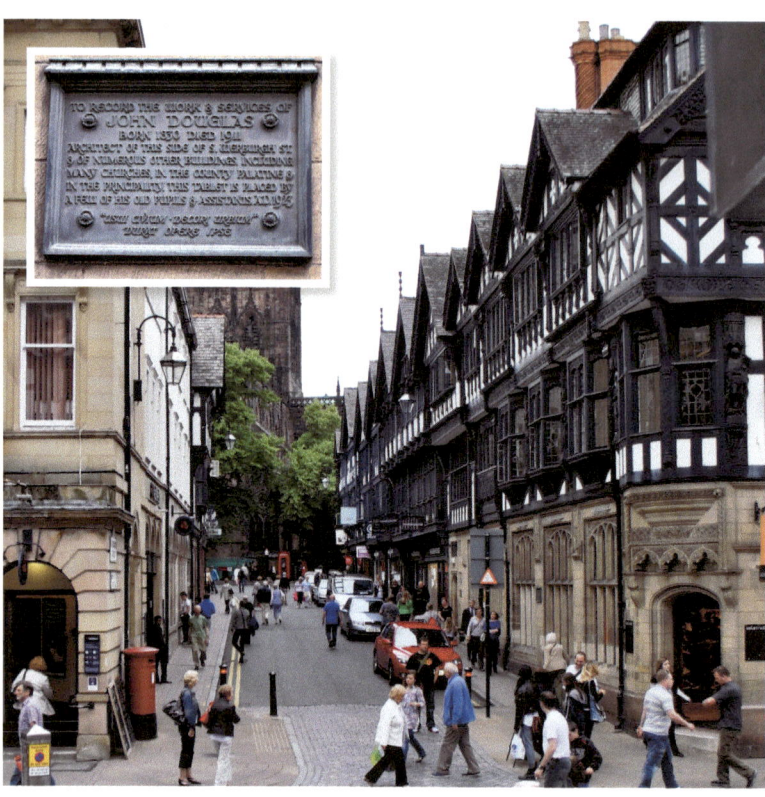

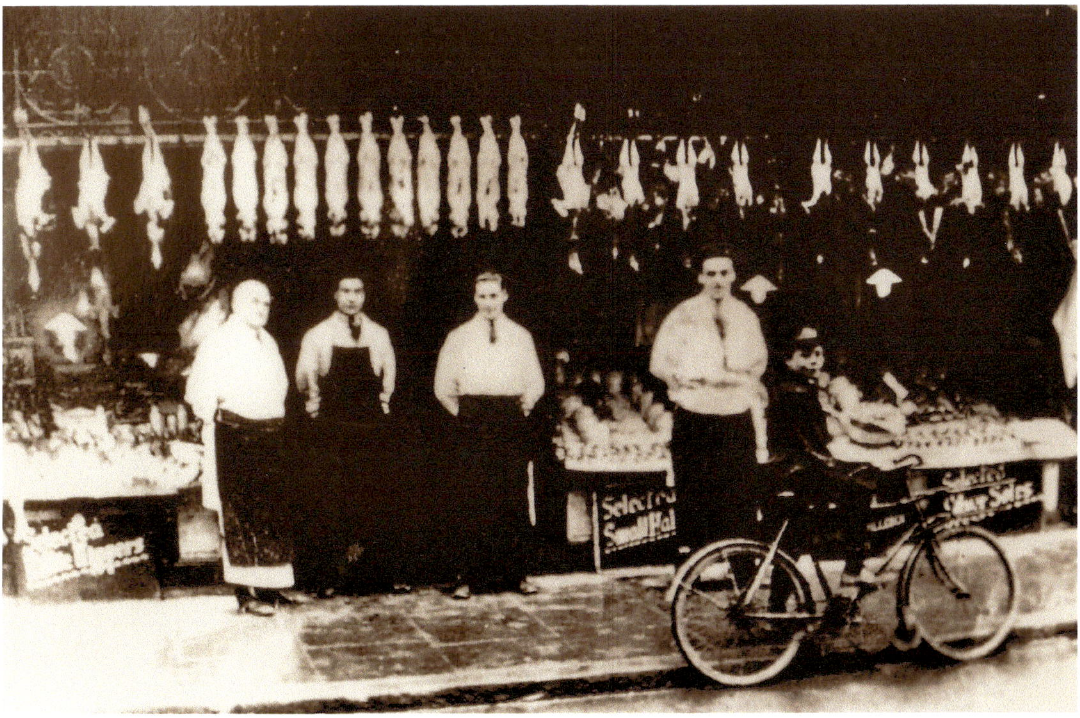

Eastgate Street shop 1930s and 2010

This shop is a good example of one of the lower shops on the Eastgate Street Row; it is situated at number 10 Eastgate Street and in the 1930s housed T. L. Wilkinson & Sons Ltd (Muirhead & Willcock Ltd) fishmonger's and butcher's. The old picture is not of the best quality but the roundels in the railing on the second row can be seen.

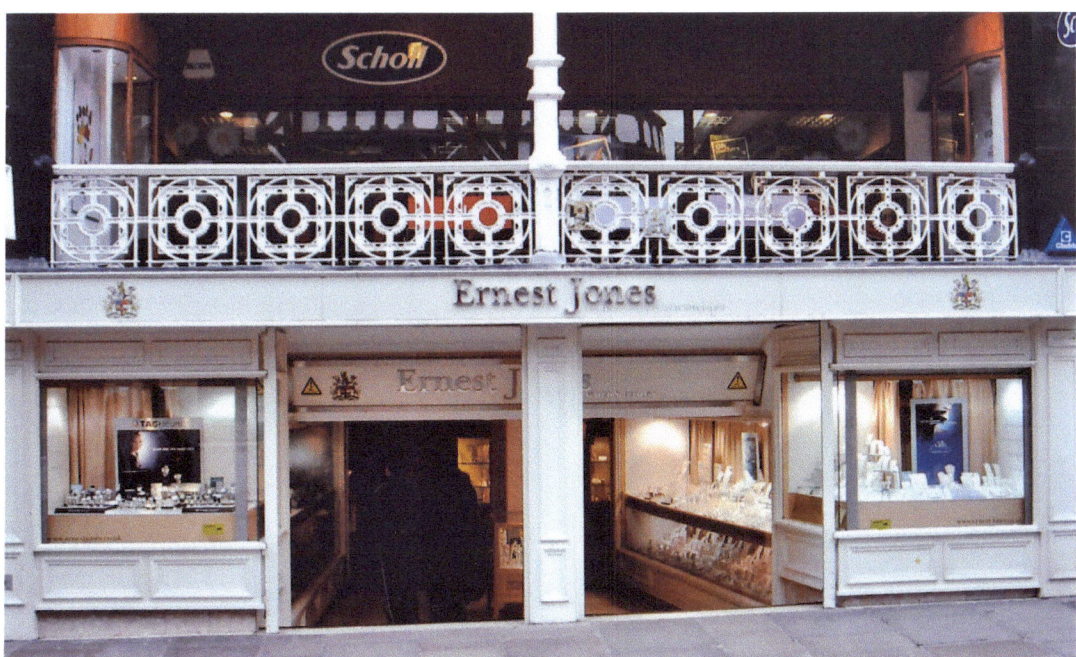

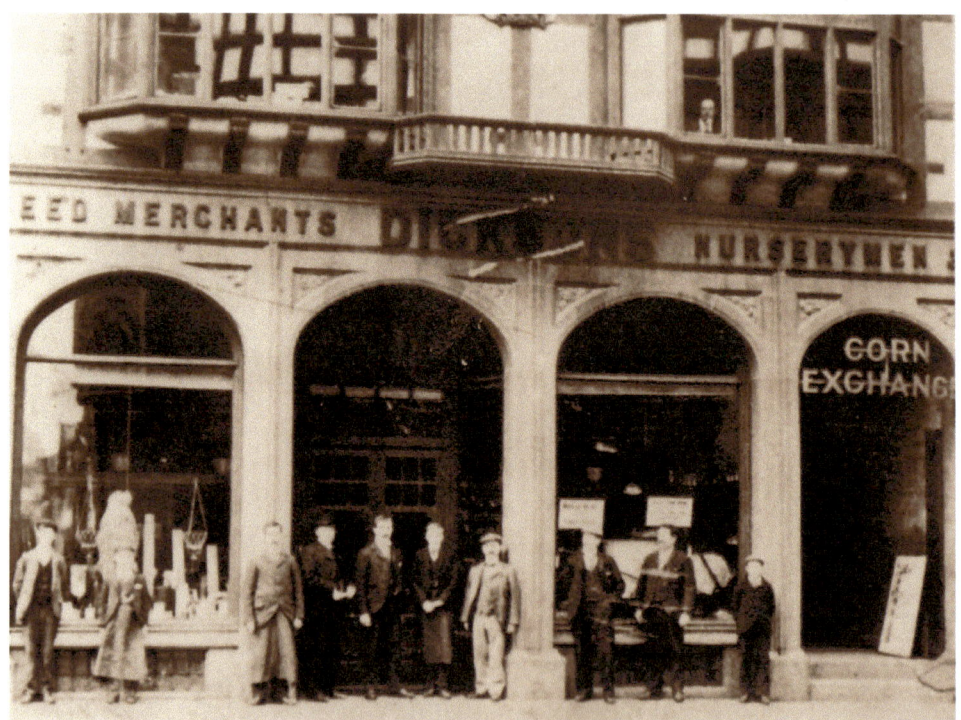

Next late Seed Merchants 1904 and 2010
This building in 1904 was the headquarters of Dickson's Seed Merchants and their seed nursery was in Dickson Drive, Newton. The entrance on the right under the Corn Exchange sign was also the entrance to Chester's first silent movie cinema called The Picturedrome opened 8 November 1909 and closed on 29 March 1924. It was a Woolworth's store for many years and is now a branch of Next.

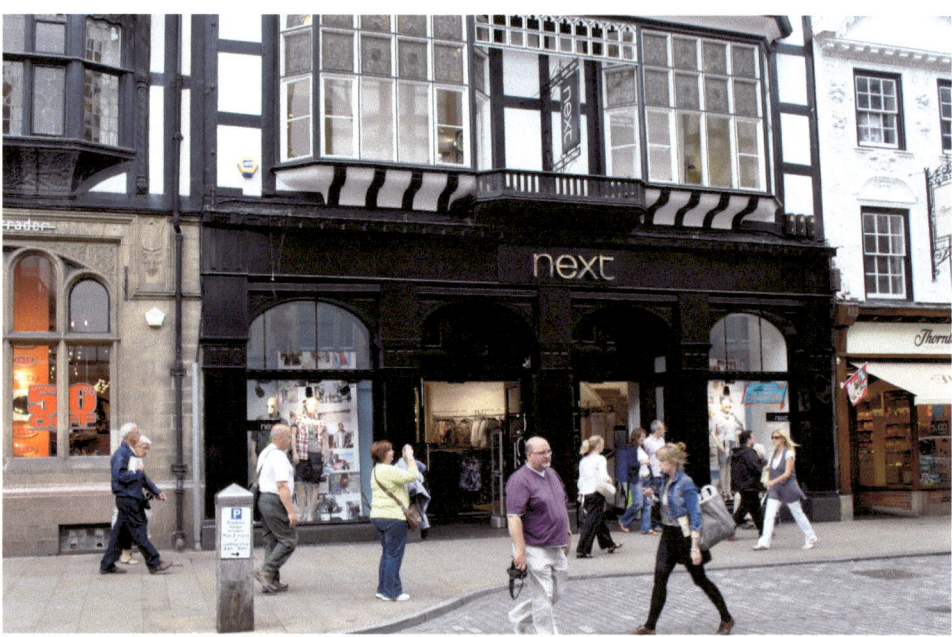

Eastgate 1955 and 2010

These photographs were taken from the walls near to the Eastgate Clock as we look down into Eastgate Street towards The Cross. A policeman can be seen on point duty at the junction with St Werburgh Street. It looks rather a thankless task with a myriad of pedestrians and motor traffic seemingly wandering about at will!

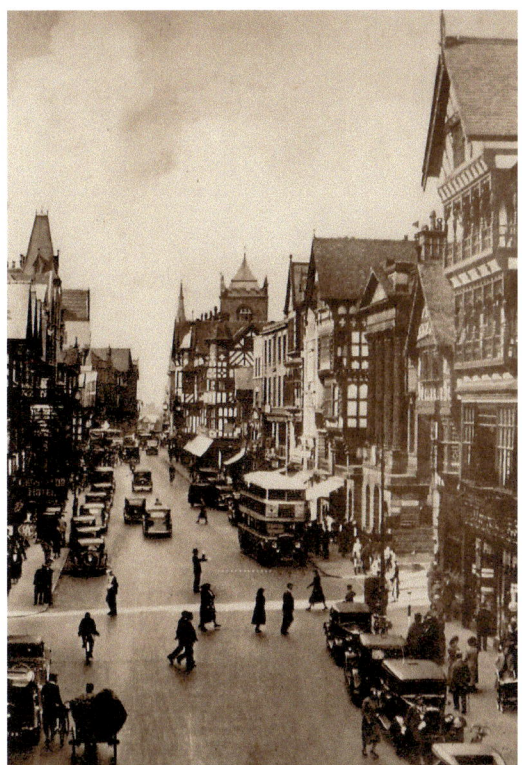

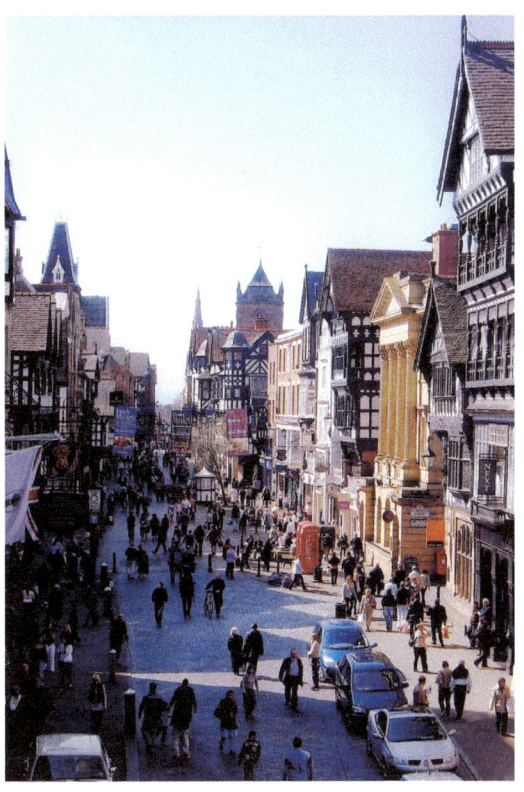

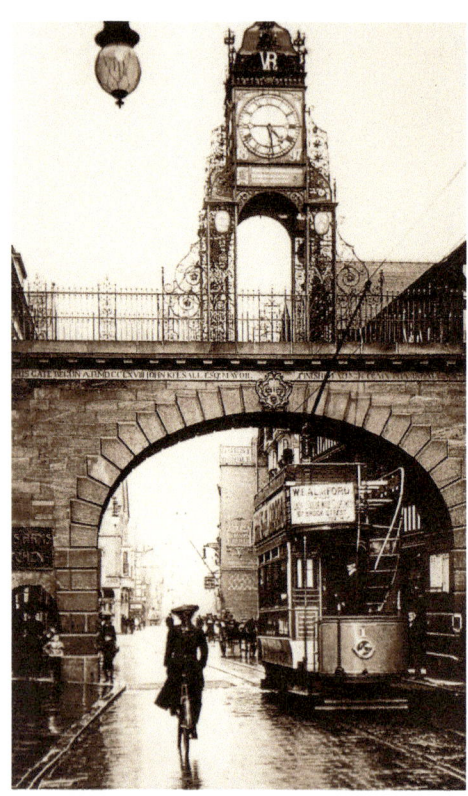

The Clock 1910 and 2010

A look at the famous clock now with a photograph taken of Eastgate Street away from the cross, the clock was designed by the Sandiway architect John Douglas to celebrate Queen Victoria's Diamond Jubilee. It was built by the cousin of John Douglas, James Swindley of Handbridge and the clock itself provided by J. B. Joyce of Whitchurch. Until 1974 it had to be wound by hand every week and is said to be the most photographed clock in the world after Big Ben.

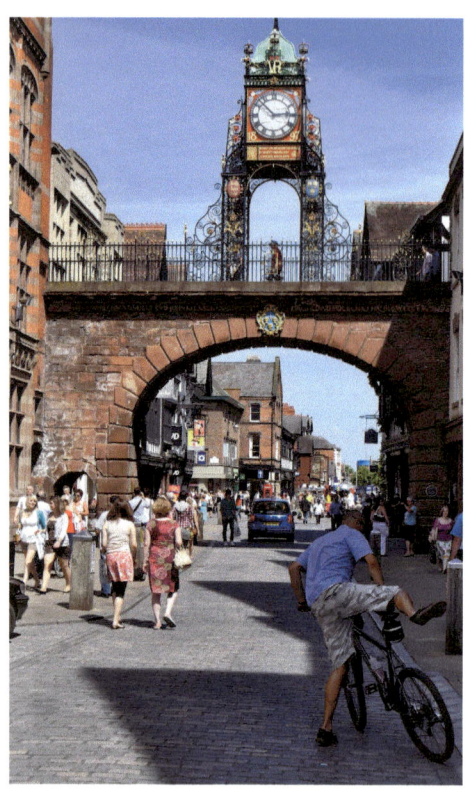

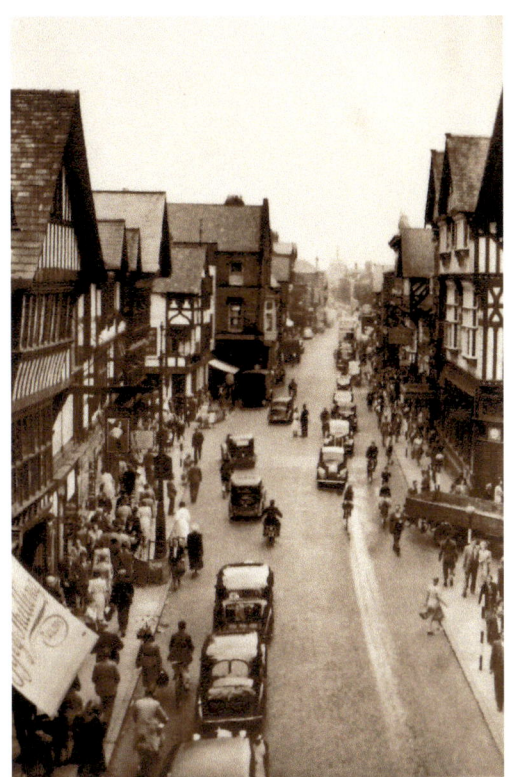

Eastgate into Foregate Street 1958 and 2010
Looking down from the Eastgate Street clock towards the water tower in the far distance, we can see that only a few changes have been made to the vista, at least from this vantage point.

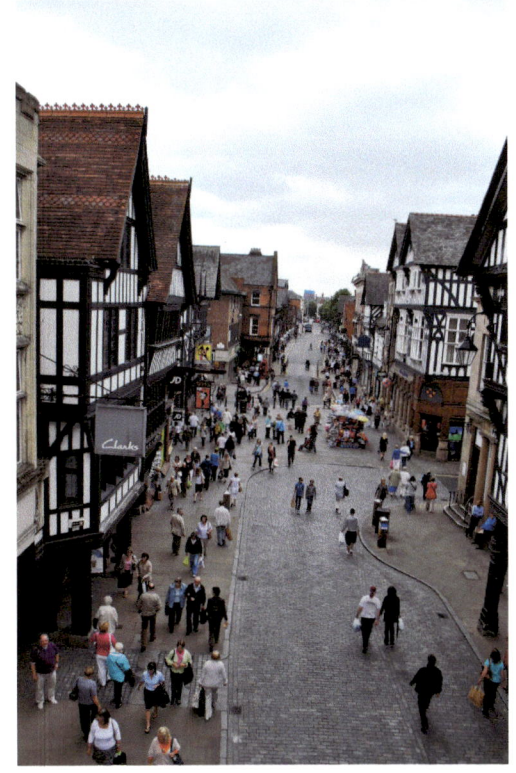

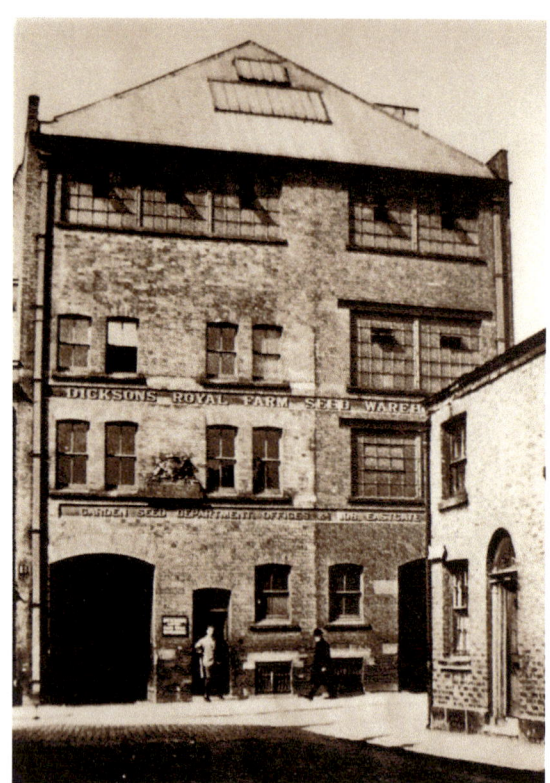

Dickson's Seed Warehouse St John Street 1930s and 2009

As seen earlier, this company traded in Eastgate Street opposite the Grosvenor Hotel and had a nursery in Dickson's Drive, Newton but their main warehouse was this one situated nearby in St John Street. It later became S. G. Mason Ltd printers and has now been completely modernised and is still vacant.

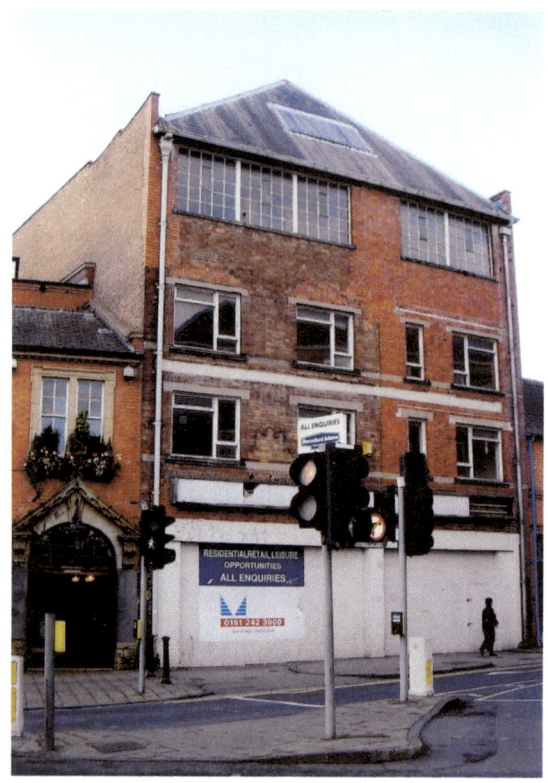

St John Street 1905 and 2010

The post office in St John Street has been in the same building for many years and the old photograph shows it in its original glory in 1905. The modern photograph shows the changes that have been made over the years. I doubt that as many postmen and telegraph boys work from there now. In 1905 people would send postcards to each other in the safe knowledge that they would arrive the following day if not on the day they were posted.

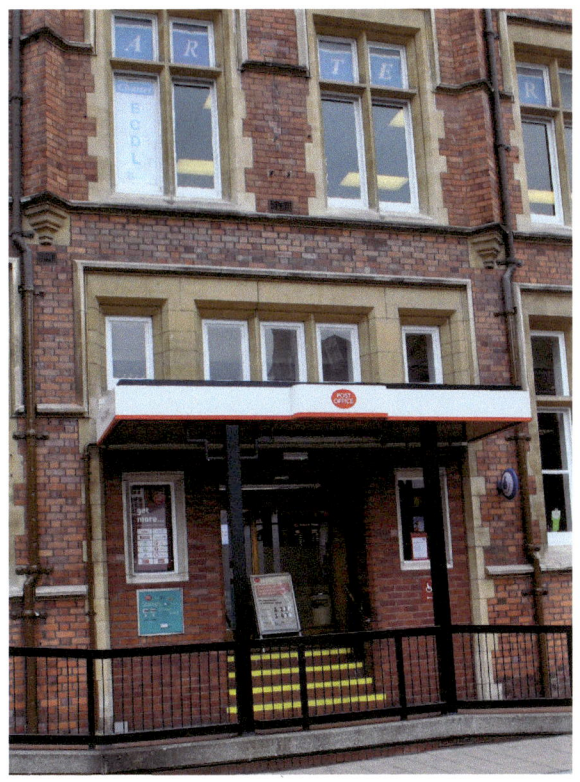

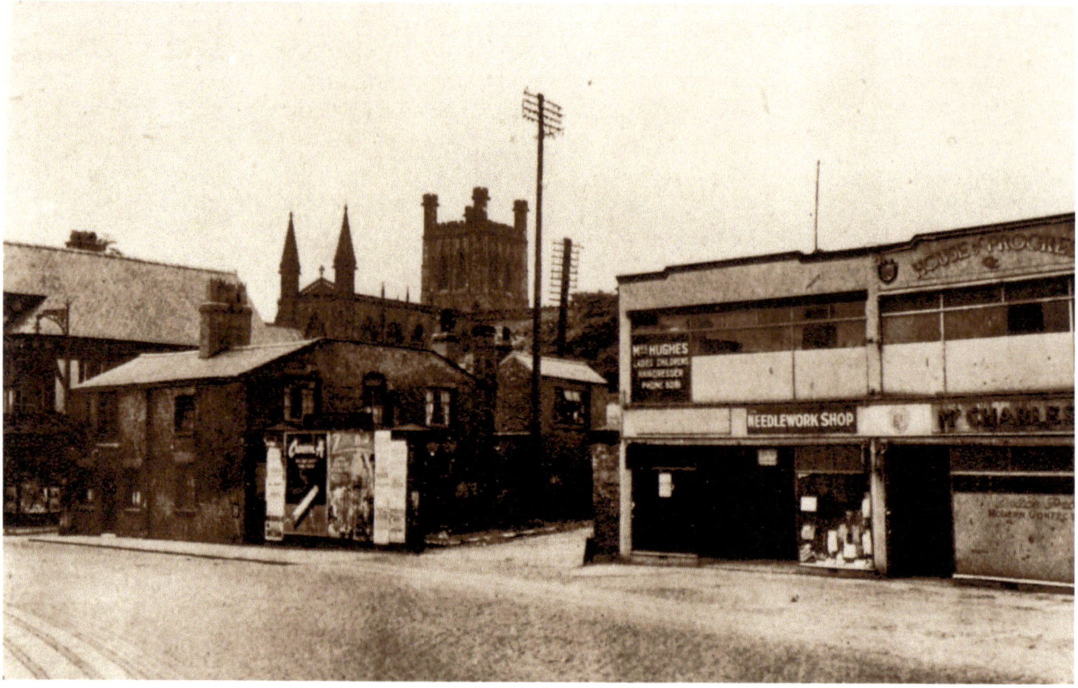

Frodsham Street from Cow Lane Bridge 1950s and 2010

The name Cow Lane no longer exists in Chester but this road, now known as Frodsham Street was once paved with granite sets and was named as it led to the former cattle market at Gorse Stacks. The bridge that crosses the canal here is still called Cow Lane Bridge and bears a plaque to commemorate its opening by Alderman E. W. Keys on the 26 January 1960 after its reconstruction.

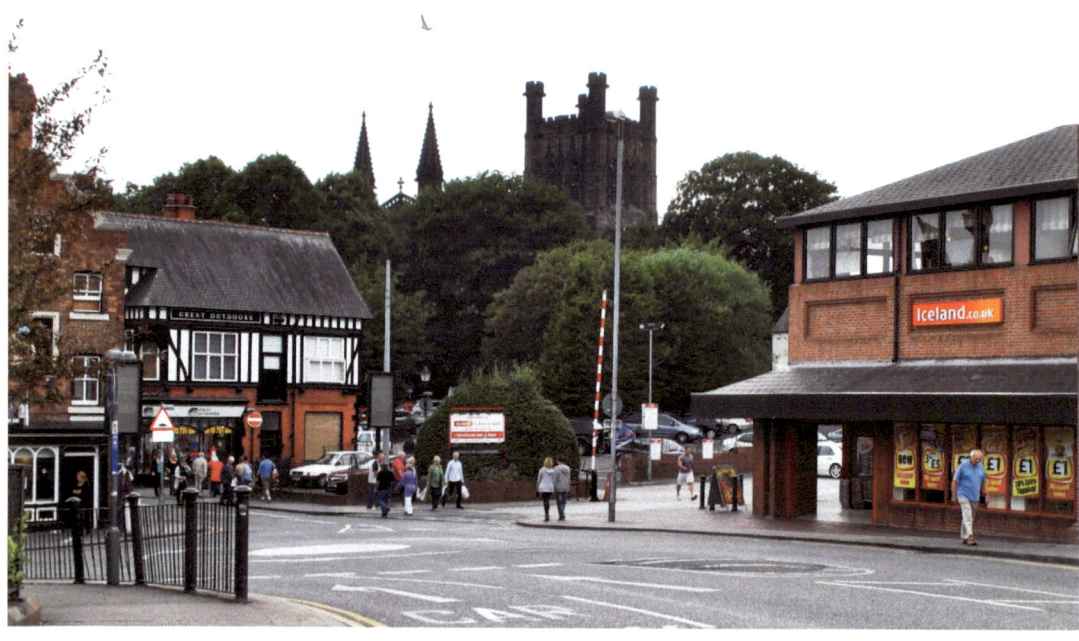

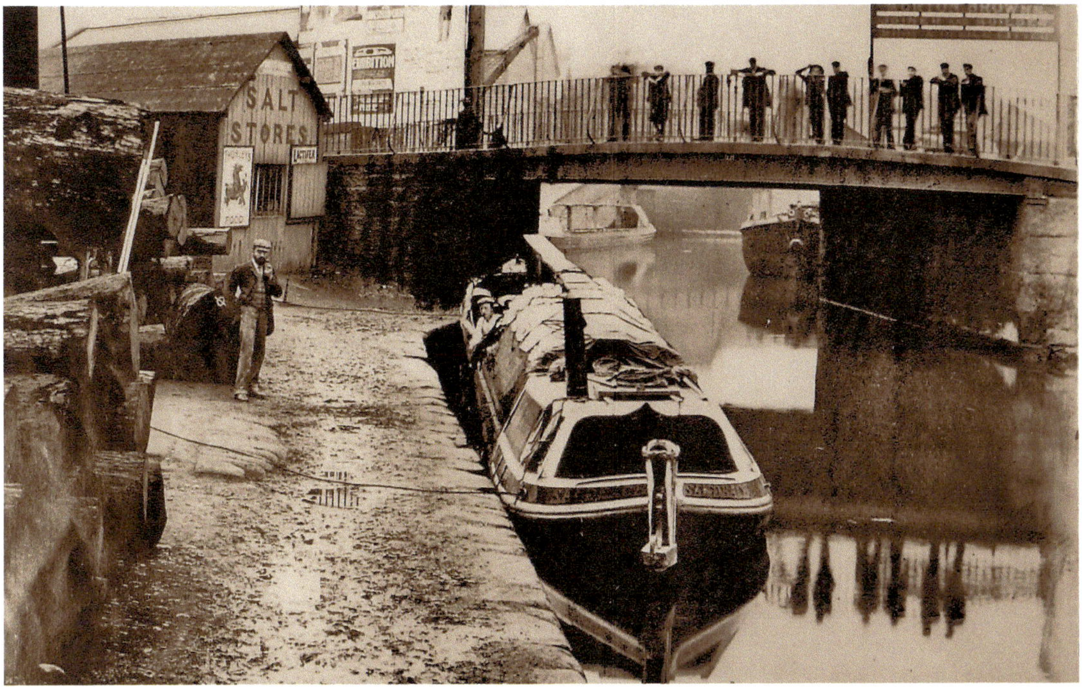

Cow Lane Bridge 1910 and 2010

During the intervening years canal travel has given way to road and rail but in this old photograph we can see canal barges at the wharves that were either side of Cow Lane Bridge. On the right, partly hidden by the bridge, is a wide-bodied canal barge that could only trade between Chester and Ellesmere Port. The main Shropshire Union canal in the opposite direction was of the narrow variety.

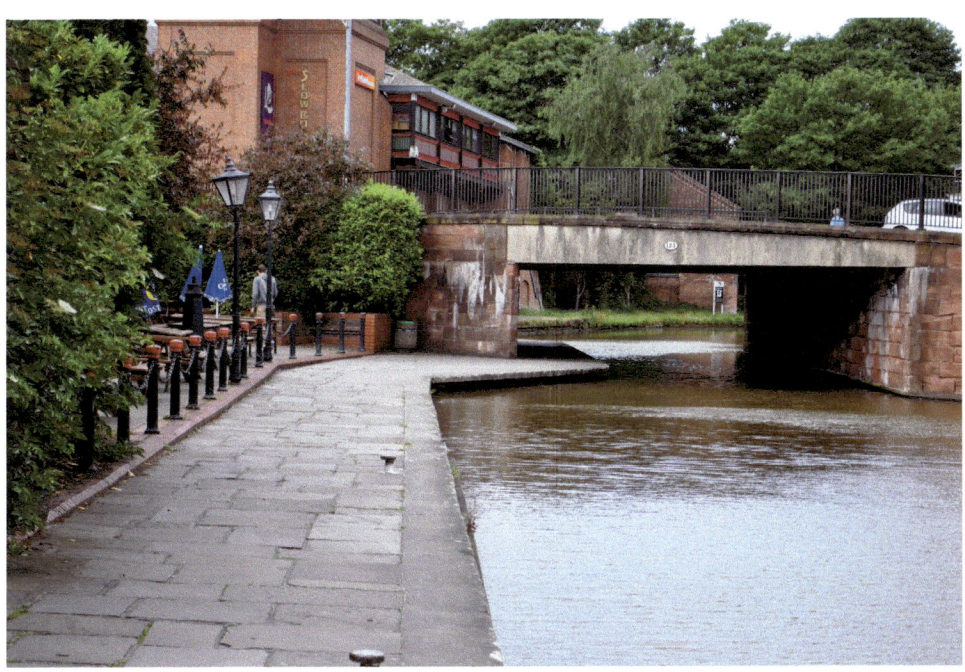

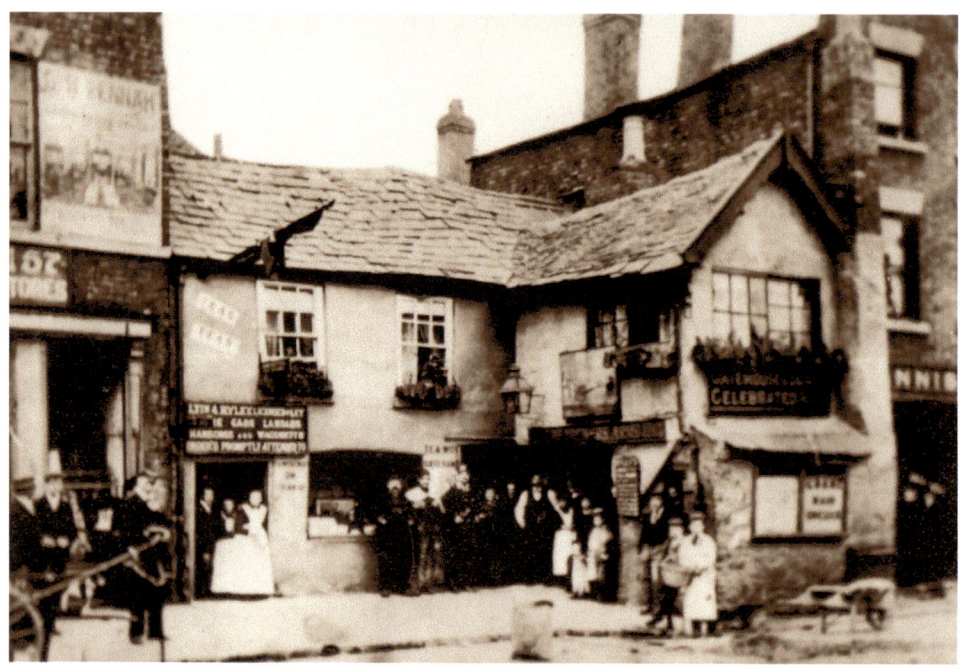

Site of Brewers Arms Foregate Street 1895 and 2010

The Brewers Arms shown in the old photograph was demolished in 1920 and The Green Dragon was erected on the site. When that closed the building became a Curry's store and now houses the Santander Bank. The building to the right of it still exists having had some cosmetic work done to the front.

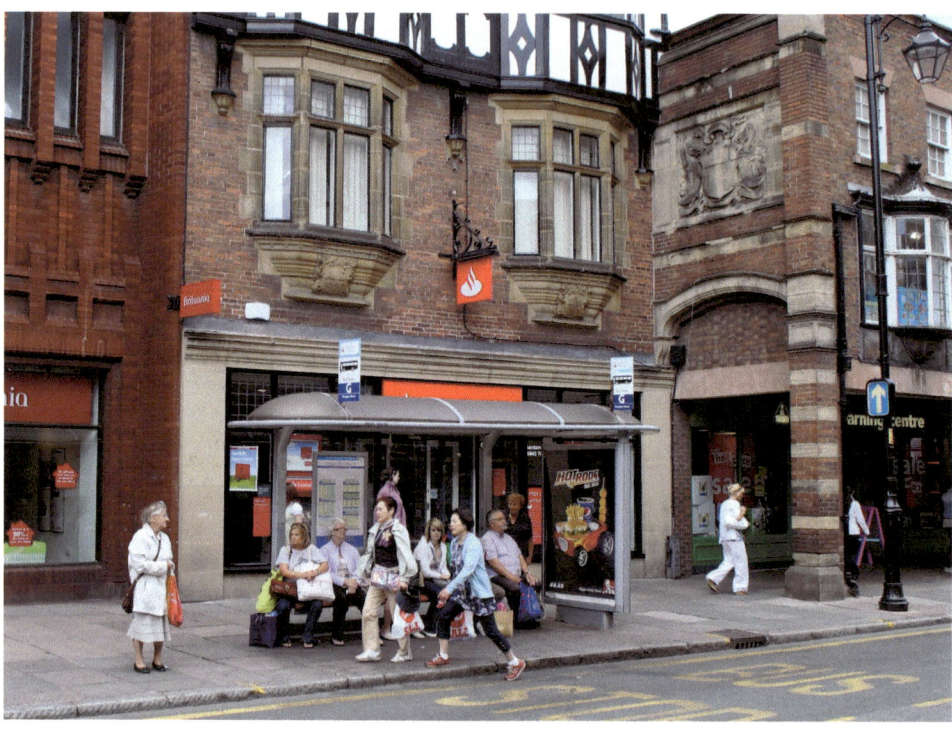

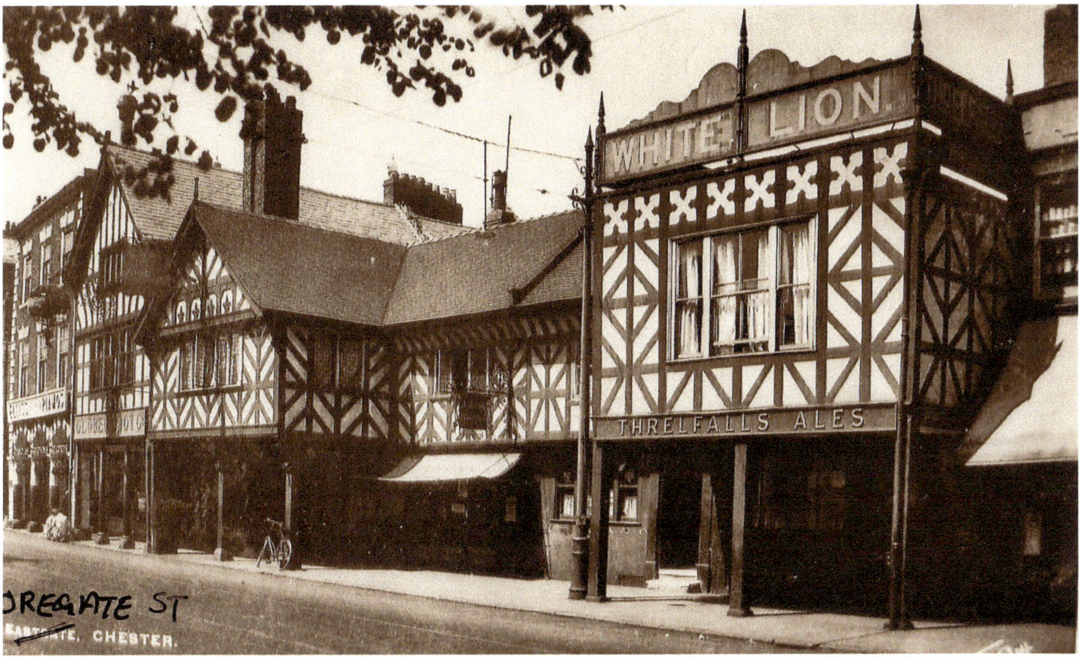

Foregate Street 1920s and 2010

This shot of the lower end of Foregate Street shows in the old photograph the White Lion public house. This pub was bombed during the Second World War and the modern extension built in place of the black and white building that stood there before. Other than the rebuilding of the bombed wing and the change of use, little has altered in the old and new photograph.

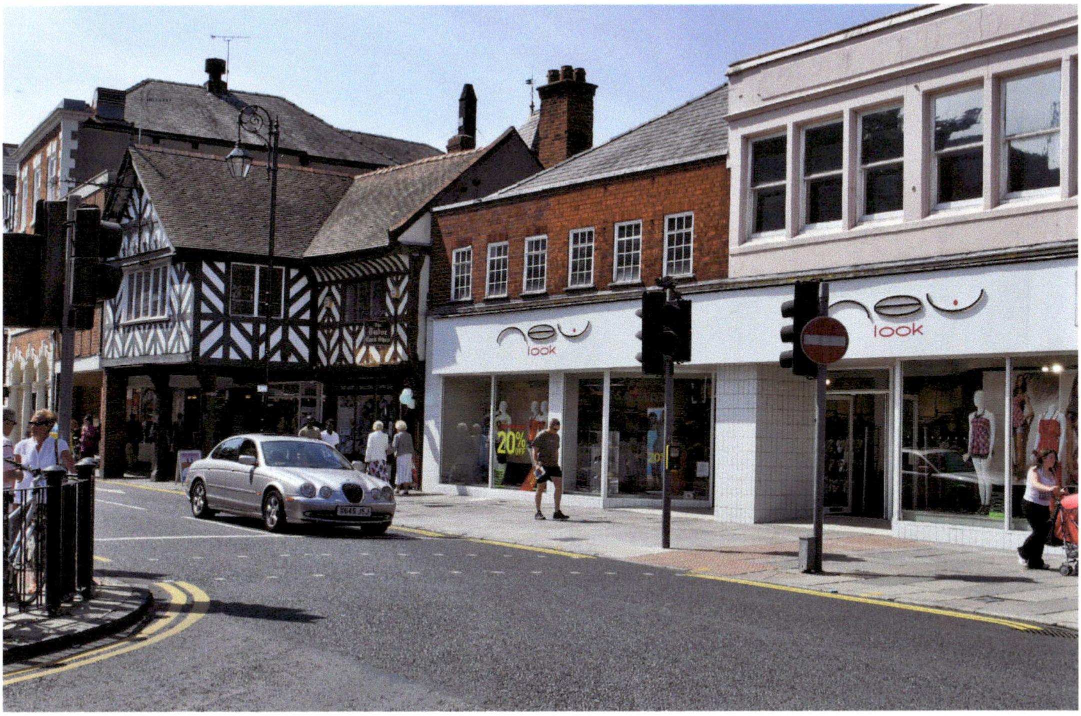

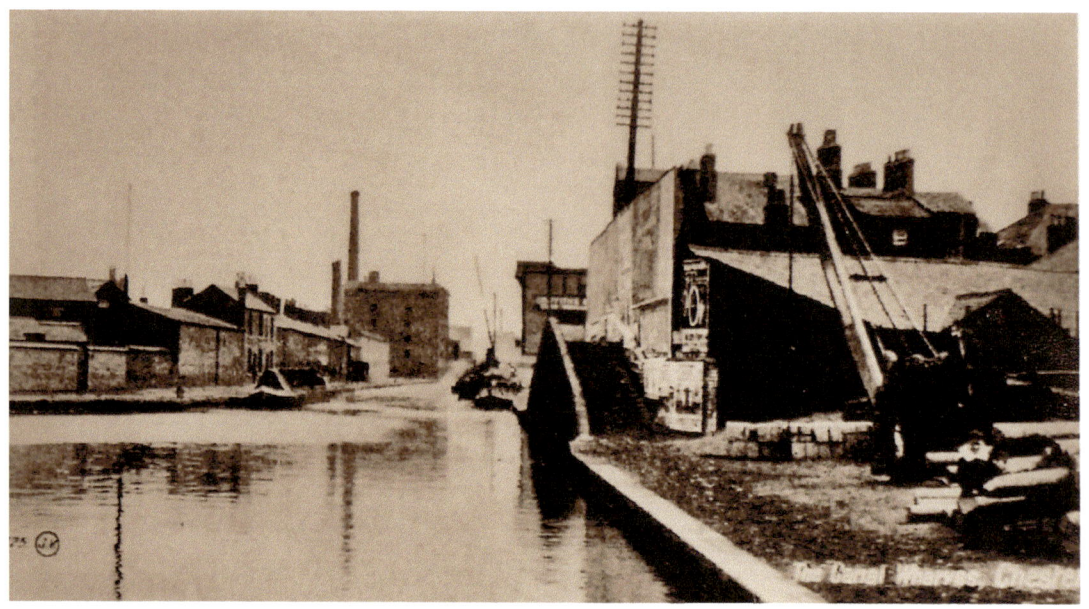

Canal Wharves 1915 and 2009
A look down the Shropshire Union Canal towards the Mill Hotel, the canal runs from Wolverhampton to Ellesmere Port giving access to the River Mersey and later the Manchester ship canal. It passes through Chester and here were many canal warehouses, used when the canal was the main route for goods transportation. The stretch from Chester to Ellesmere Port is a wide canal built originally as the Chester Canal in 1772, it linked up with the Shropshire Union Canal when it was constructed in 1835, the last main line canal to be built.

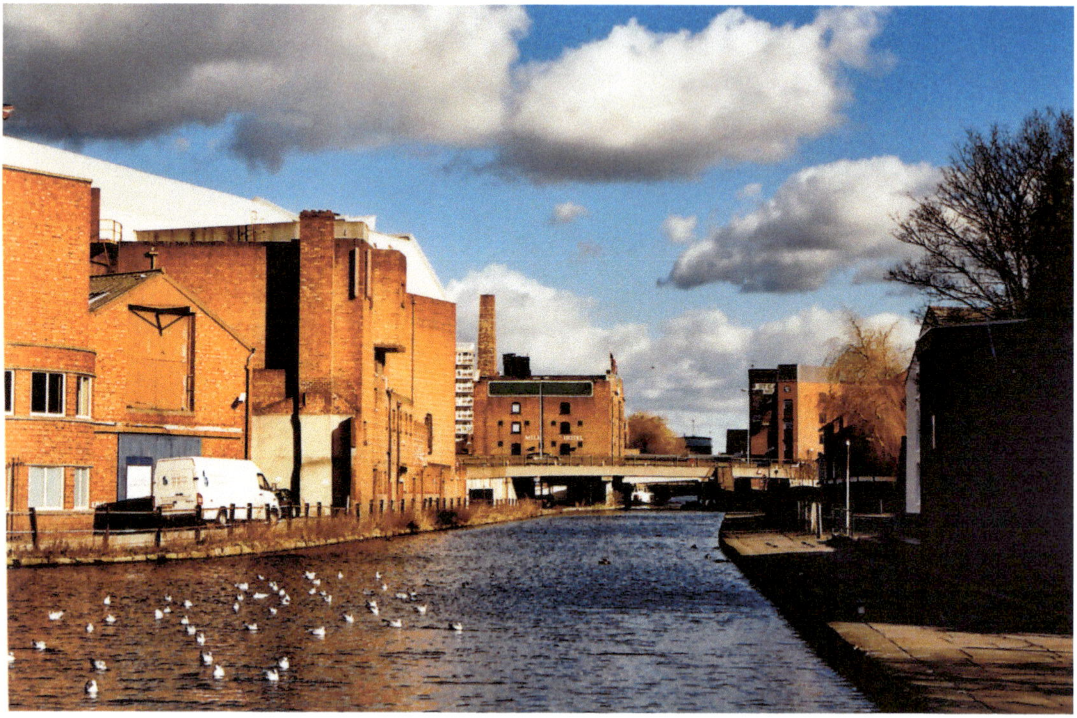

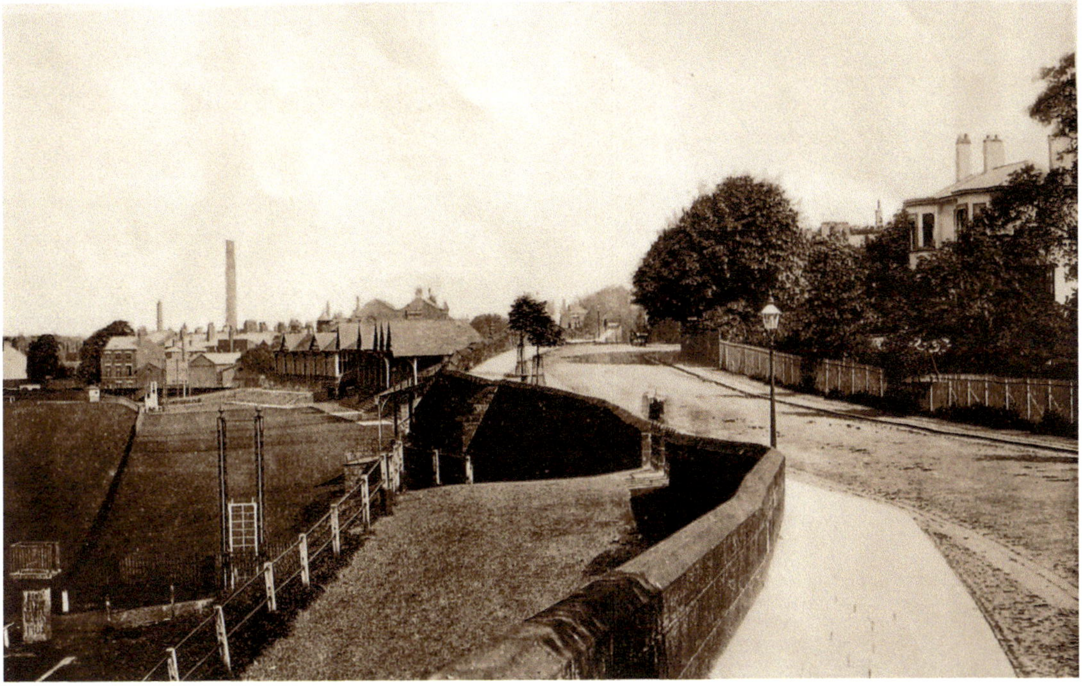

The Roodee and Walls 1950s and 2010
This photograph is a view down Nun's Road towards Watergate and looks across in to the Chester Racecourse known as The Roodee. The old picture shows the grandstand that burnt down on the 28 September 1985. The gasworks chimneys can be seen in the distance.

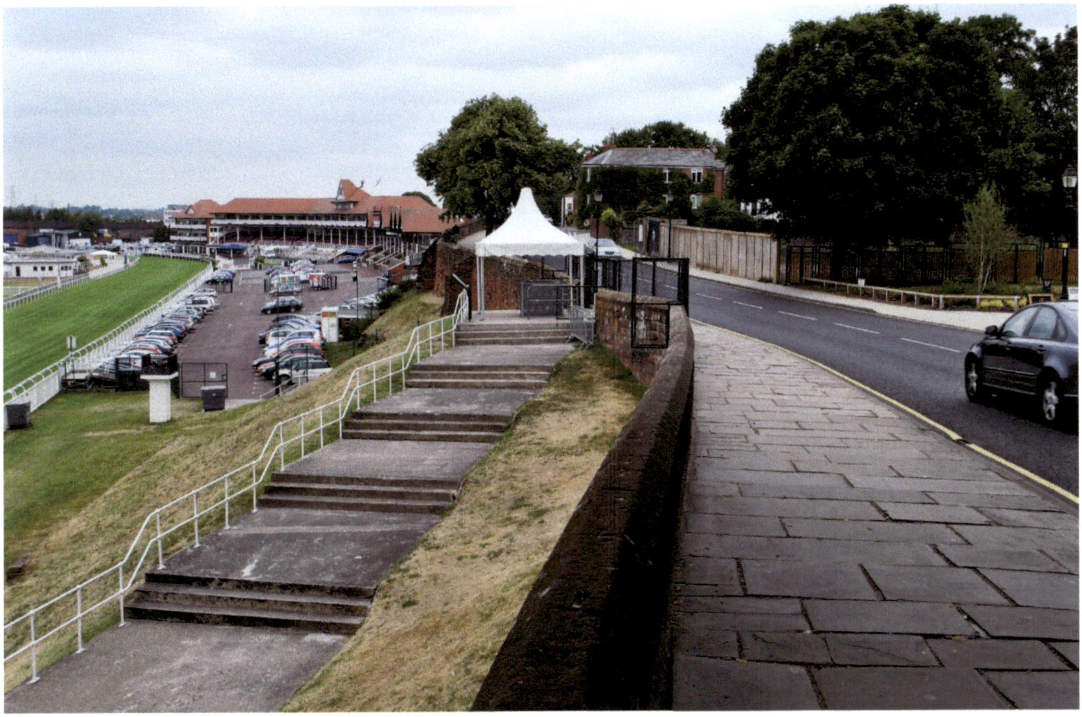

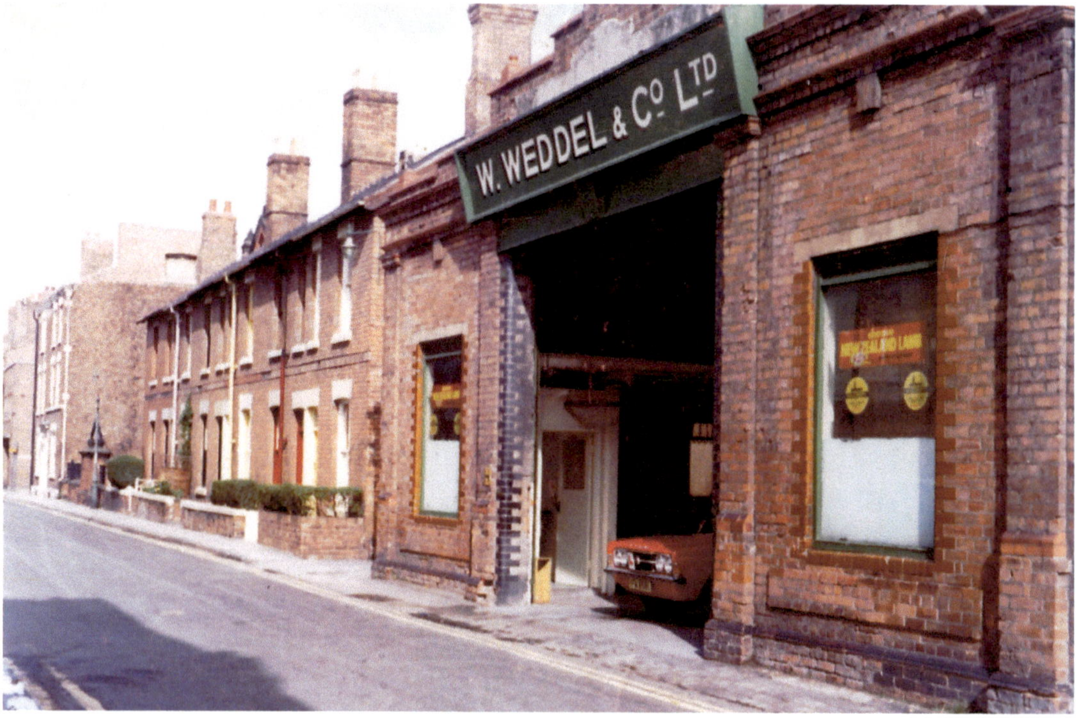

Queen Street 1970 and 2009
Queen Street is in the centre of the city at the rear of Foregate Street. In the old photograph Weddel & Co was situated there and was the cold storage depot for the meat from the abattoir across the road. This abattoir has now gone to make way for the Boots store that is on the site.

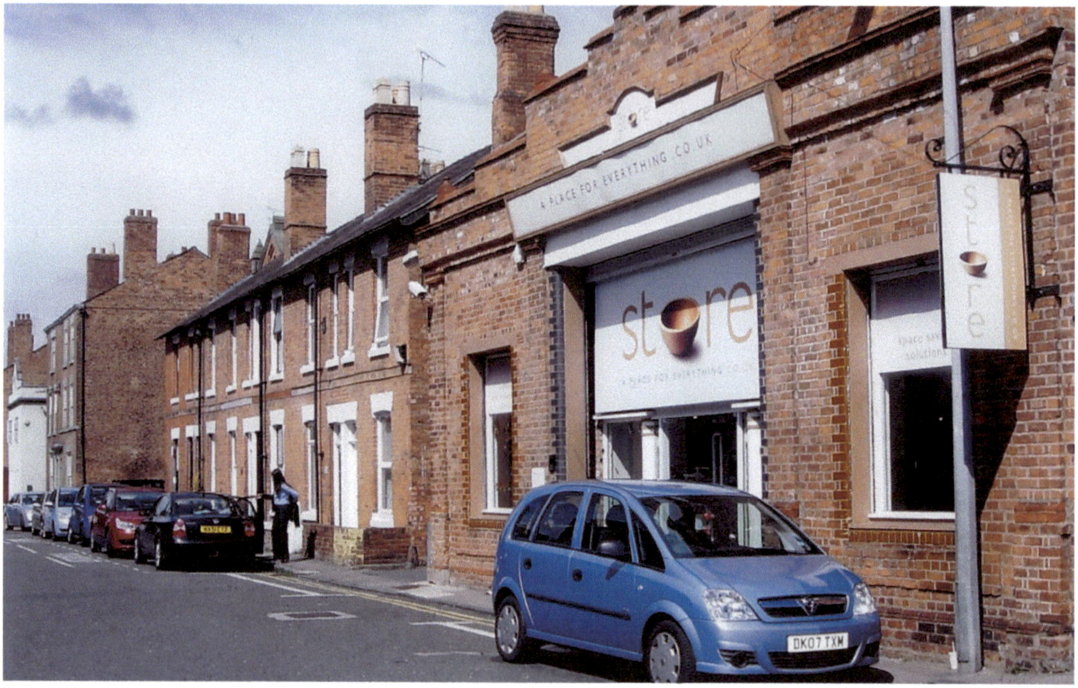

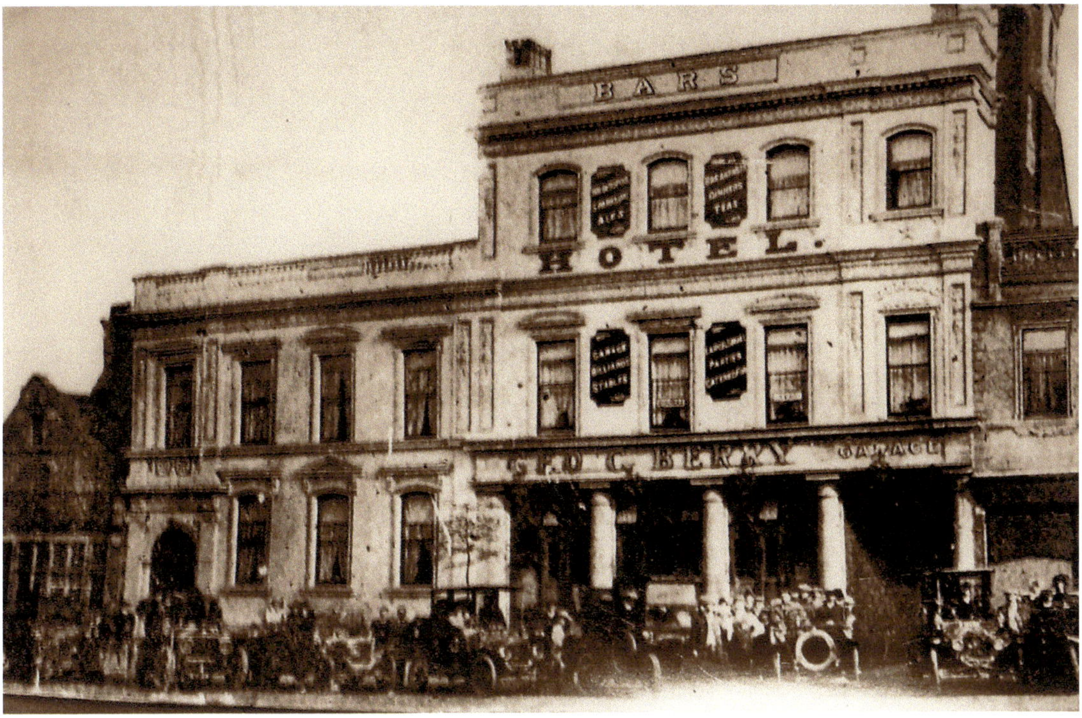

The Bars Hotel 1910 and 2010

The old photograph here is poor but one not to be missed; the Bars Hotel sat astride an area that is still called The Bars to this day. In the Middle Ages this area close to Boughton was known as The Bars because an outer gate to the city was here as part of the city's defences. Note the period line up of cars outside the hotel; it could very well be the start of a rally or they could be at George Berry's garage which was situated there.

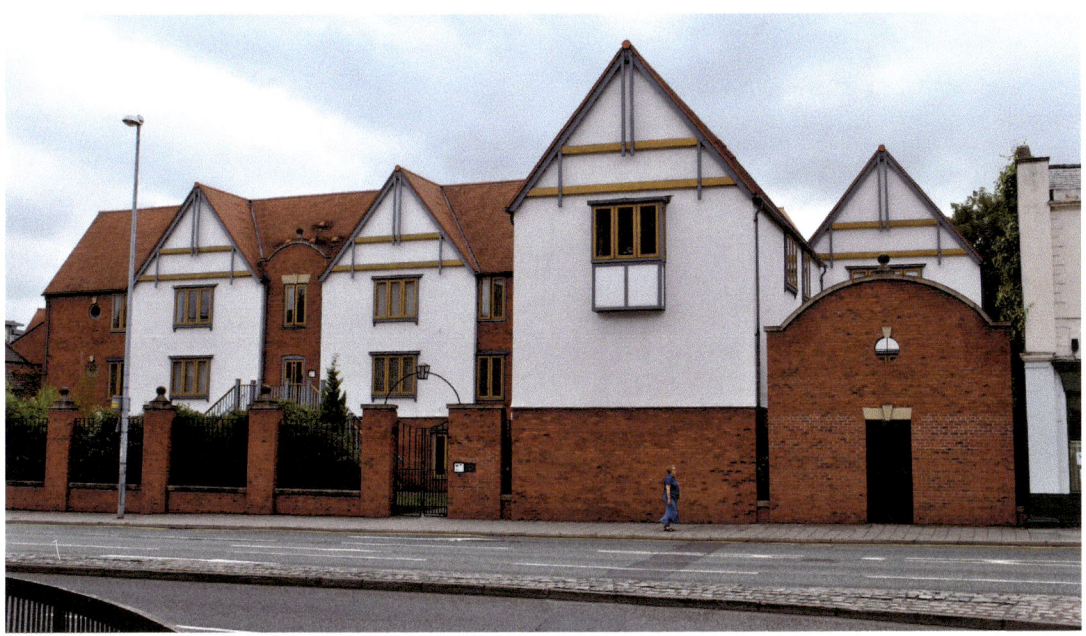

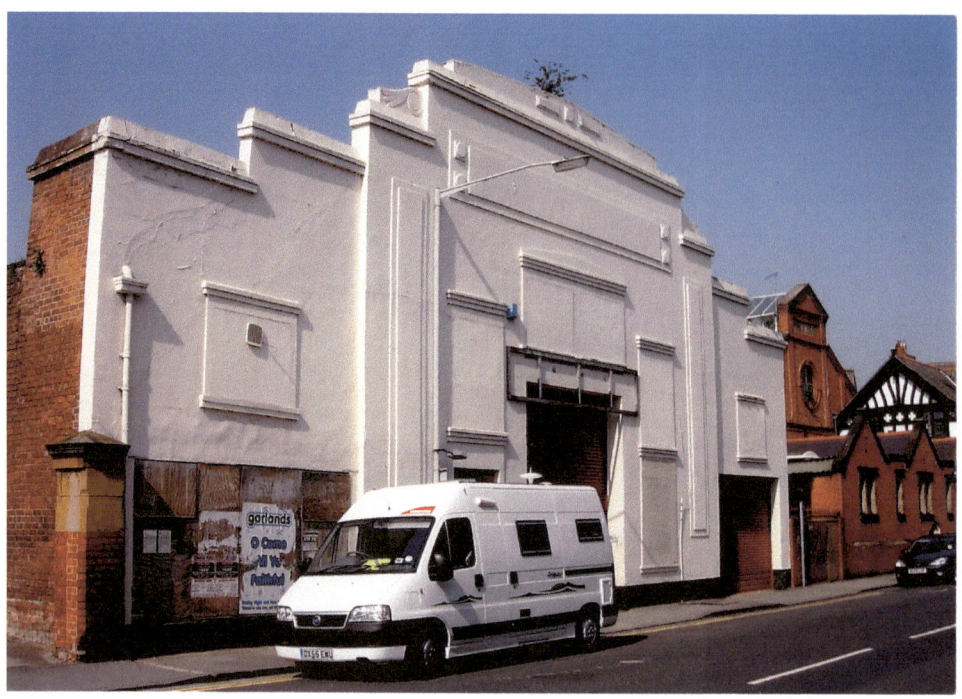

Site of Milton Brothers garage Union Street 2006 and 2010
Milton Brothers garage for car repairs, sales etc and they also provided public address systems for fêtes and gymkhanas. The style of the building would suggest that it has been a cinema but we cannot find any firm evidence of this, no doubt a reader can enlighten us? Either way, the building has gone now and been replaced with what we see in the modern photograph taken at the time of building.

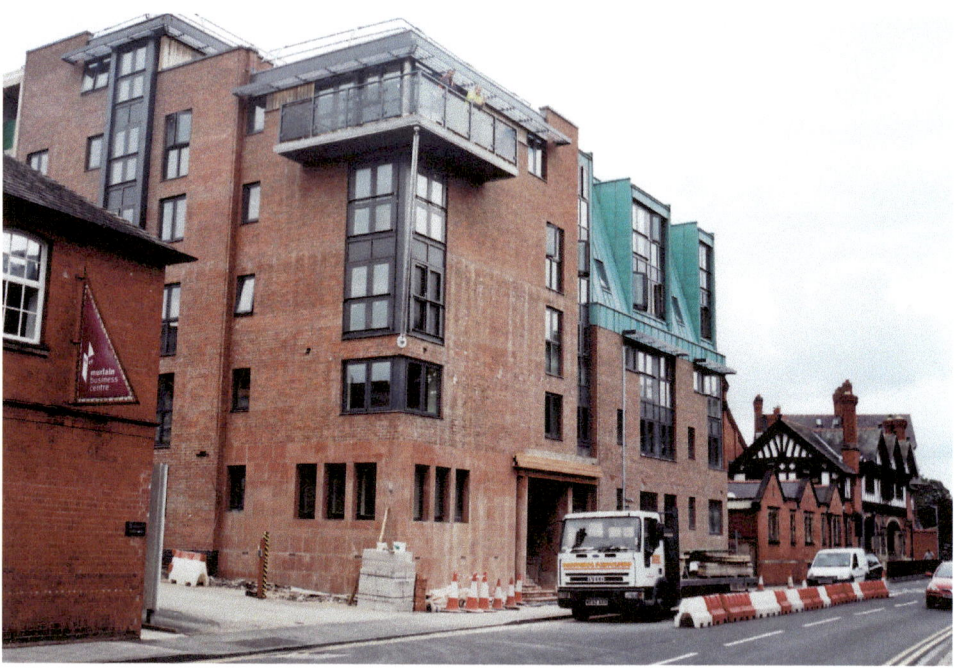

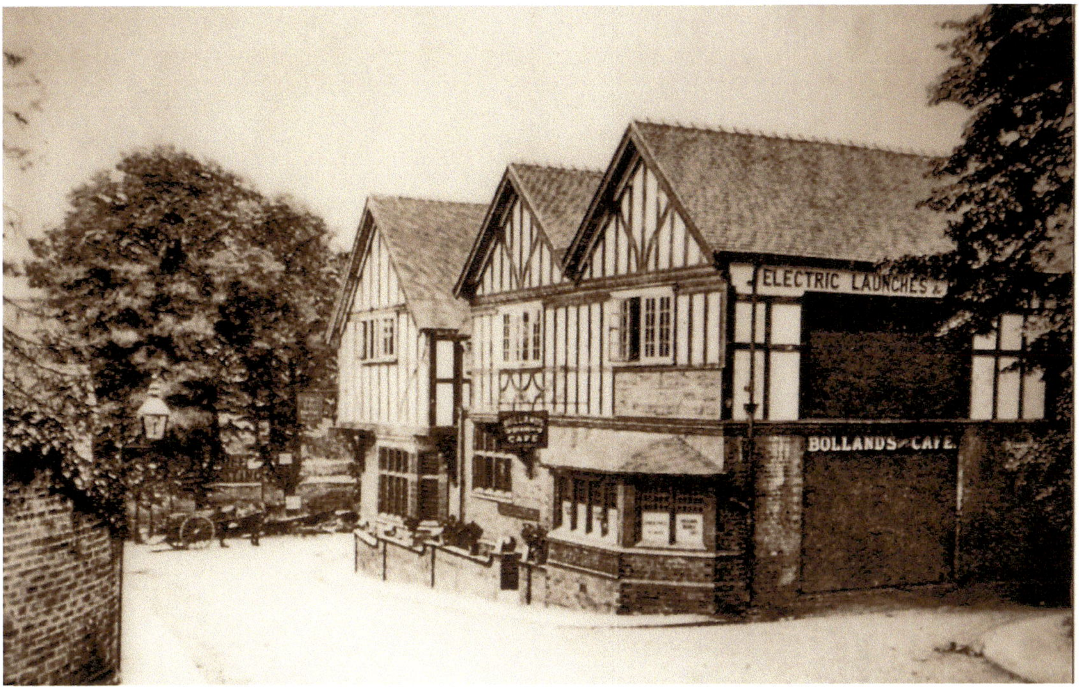

The Groves 1930 and 2010
This view is of the Groves when approaching from Grosvenor Park towards the river with Bolland's café on the right and the Boathouse pub on the left. In the 2010 photograph the Bolland's café building has gone but the Boathouse pub is still there. At the turn of the last century this was a very popular tourist destination and one where the locals would take boat rides or relax and watch the world go by.

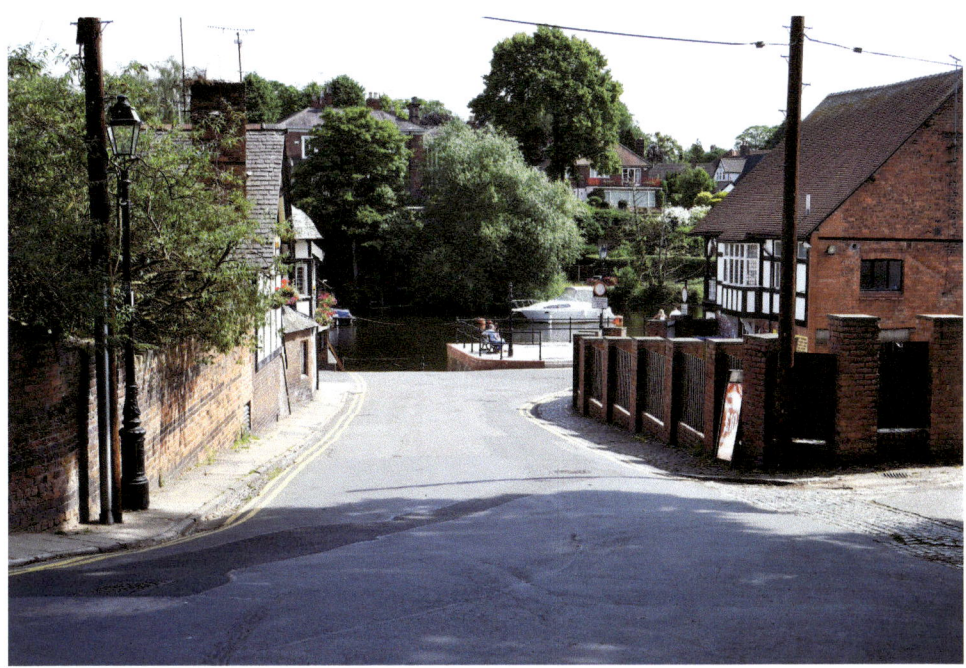

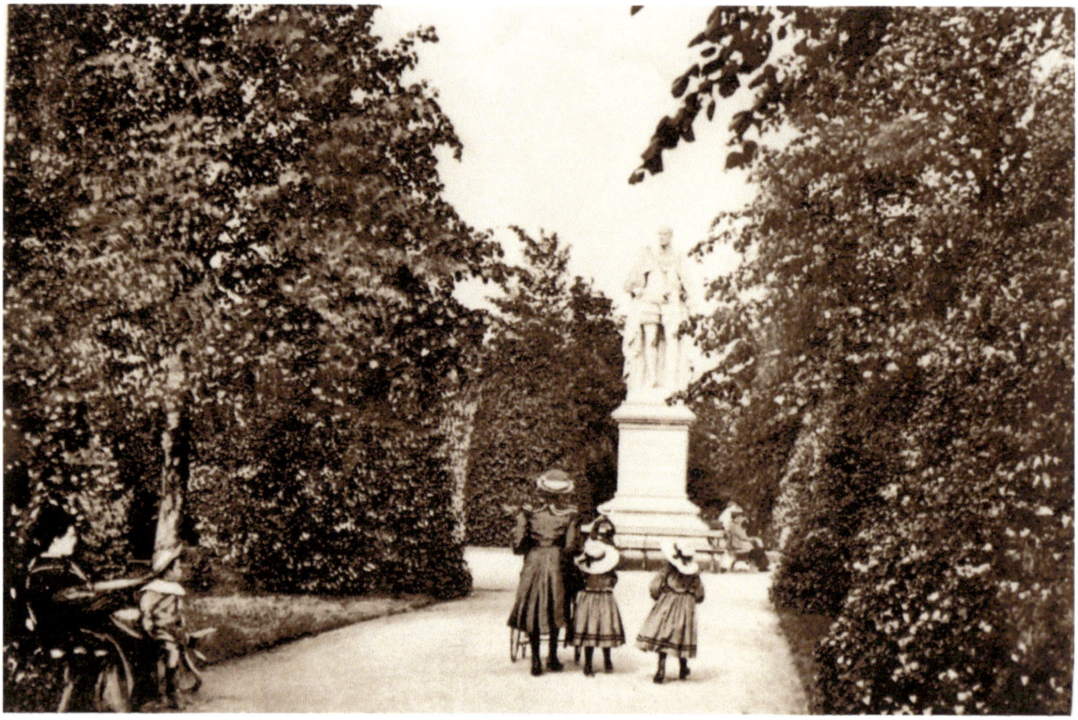

Grosvenor Park 1902 and 2009
Grosvenor Park was a gift to the city from Richard 2nd Marquis of Westminster in 1867. The park covers an area of around 20 acres and was designed by Edward Kemp. The statue in the photograph is of the benefactor and was erected in 1869. The period Edwardian dress of the women and children is an evocative snapshot in time.

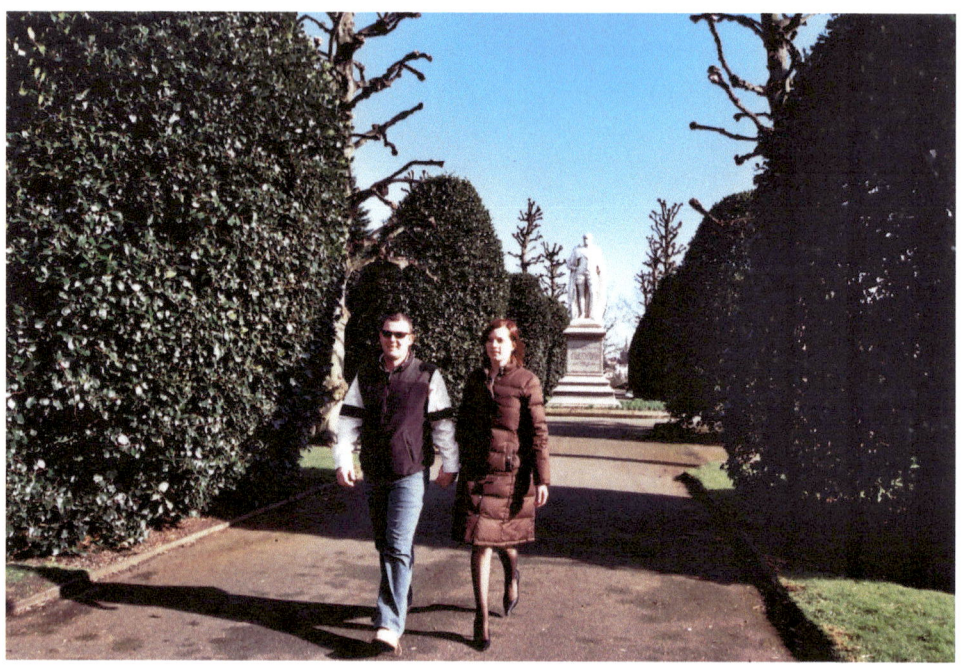

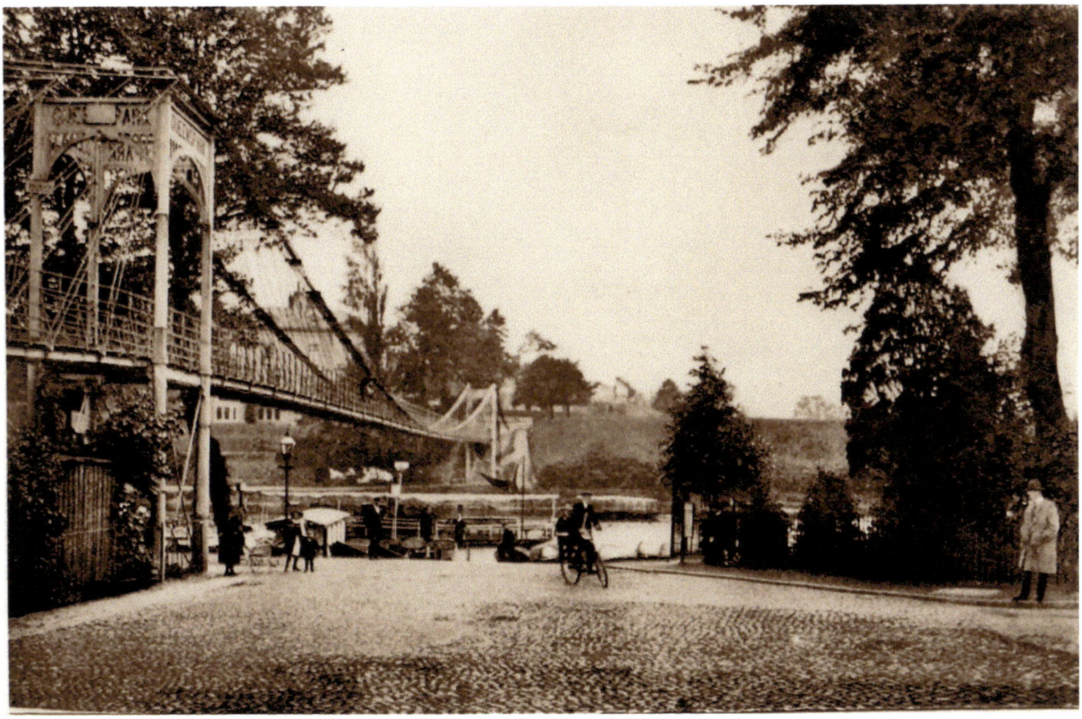

The Chester Suspension Bridge, 1920 and 2010
A first look at this famous Chester landmark that is the route for pedestrians from the Groves to the affluent Queens Park area on the other side of the river two years after the old photograph was taken it would be demolished and the new one erected. This in turn was restored in 1998.

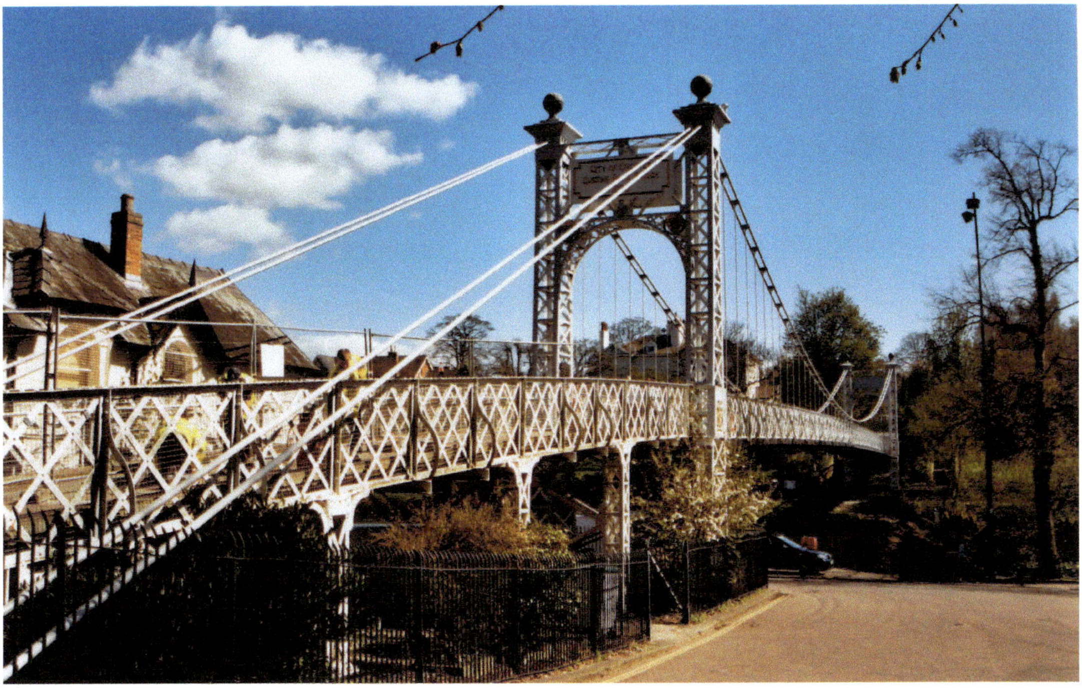

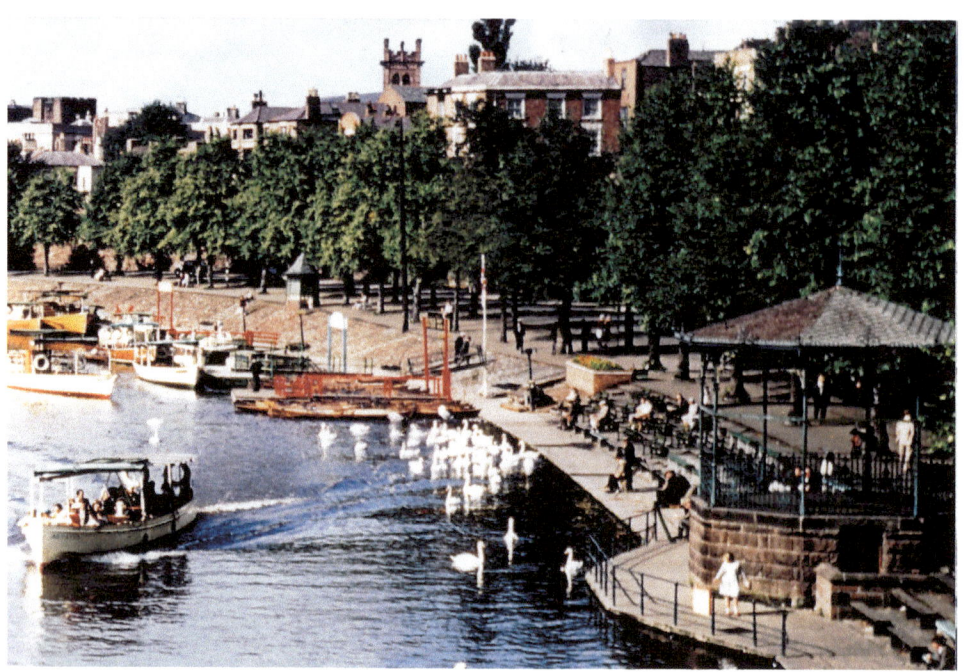

River Dee and the Groves 1960 and 2009
This area was once extremely popular with many boat trips on the river starting from this location. It's still popular with tourists but as the later photograph shows, traffic on the river has decreased albeit that the pleasure boats have become larger! The swan population also seems to have decreased but the bandstand still waits for the musicians to climb aboard and entertain the visitors.

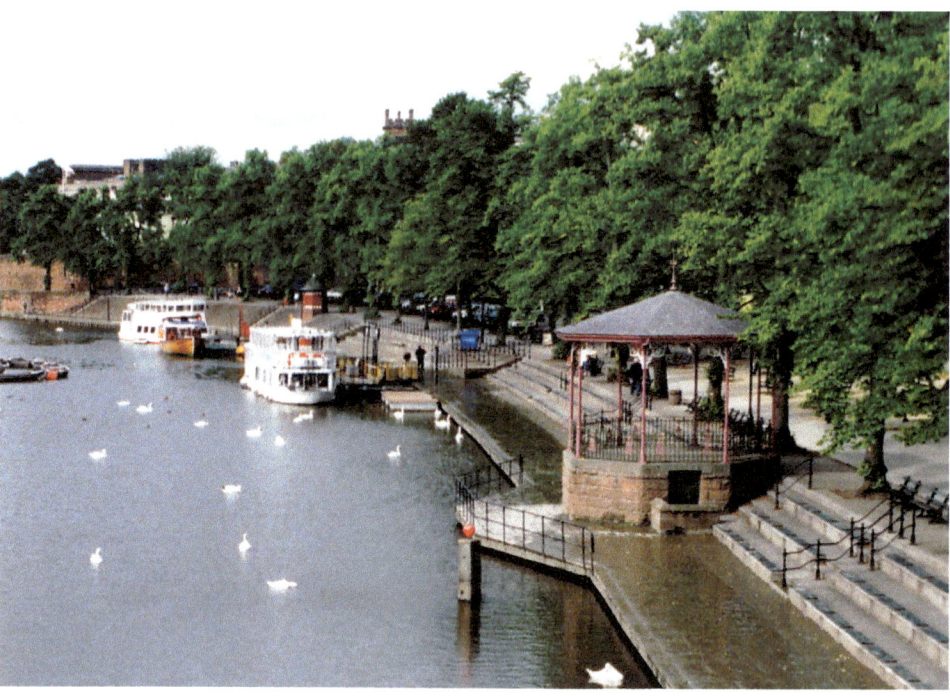

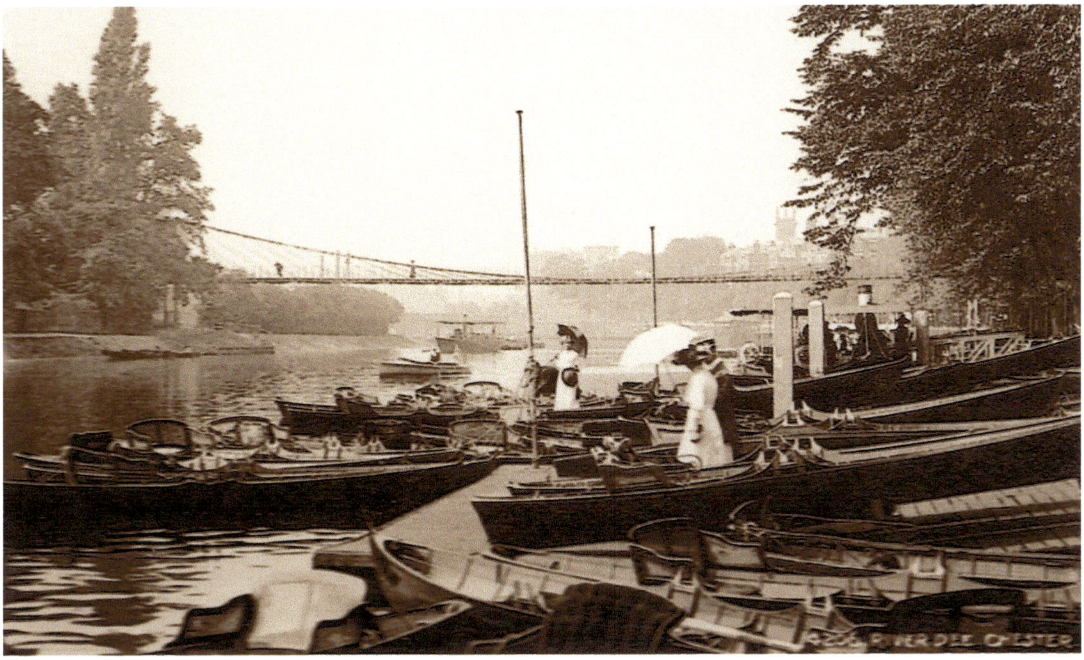

The Groves in 1910 and 2010

100 years separate these two photographs and the change is plain to see. Most of the pontoons holding the many small craft have gone but it is somewhat deceptive as there is still quite a lot of pleasure activity at this spot. In the distance is the tower of St Mary's on the hill Church.

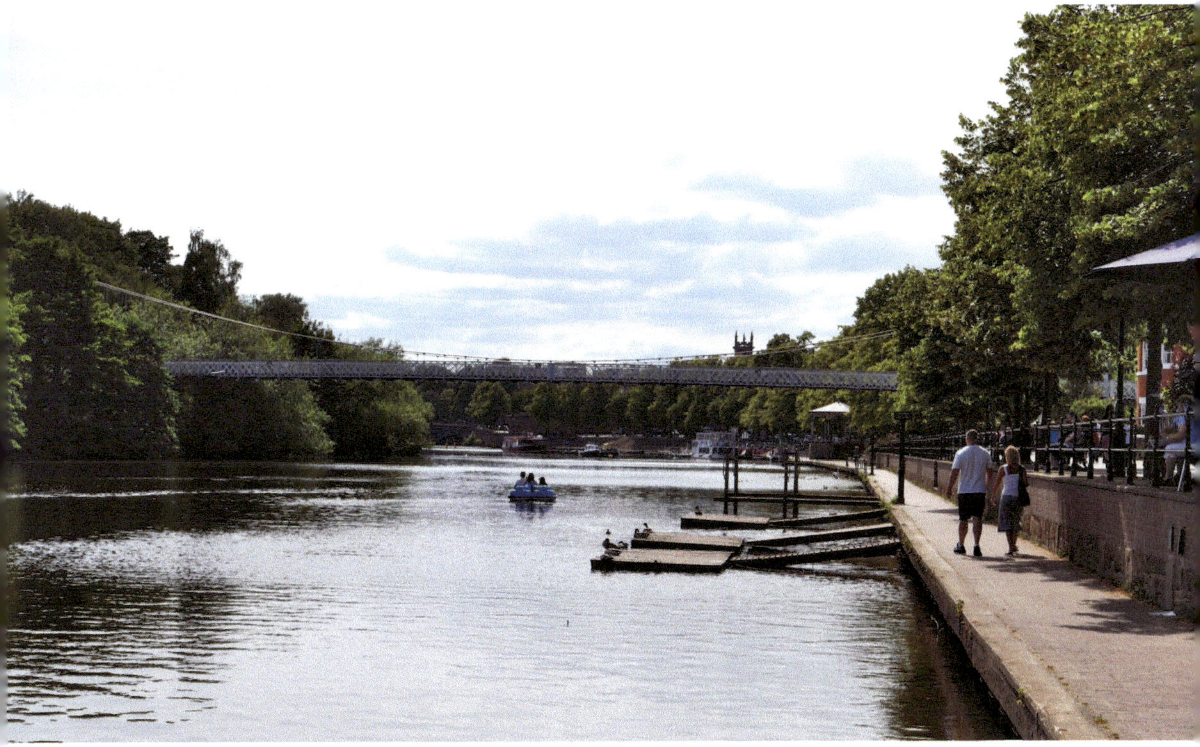

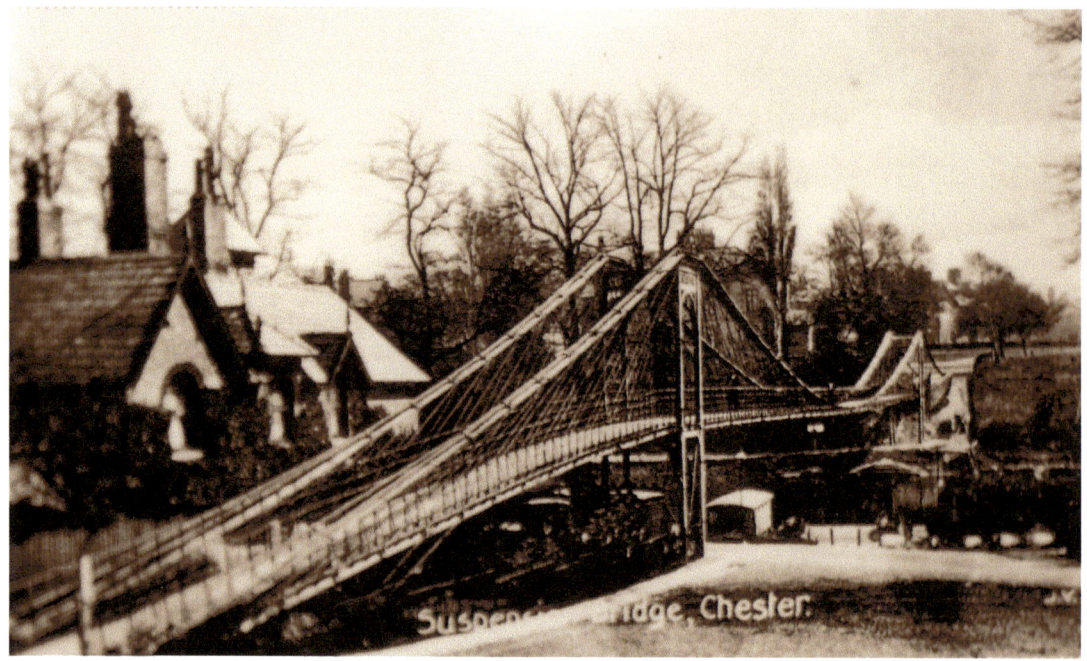

Suspension Bridge 1900 and 2010
Another look at the very attractive Queen's Park suspension bridge that spans the river for pedestrian use. The bridge in the old photograph was erected in 1852 and demolished in August 1922, the new one in the 2010 photograph was designed by Charles Greenwood the city engineer and erected in 1923 and bears a plaque showing the building date.

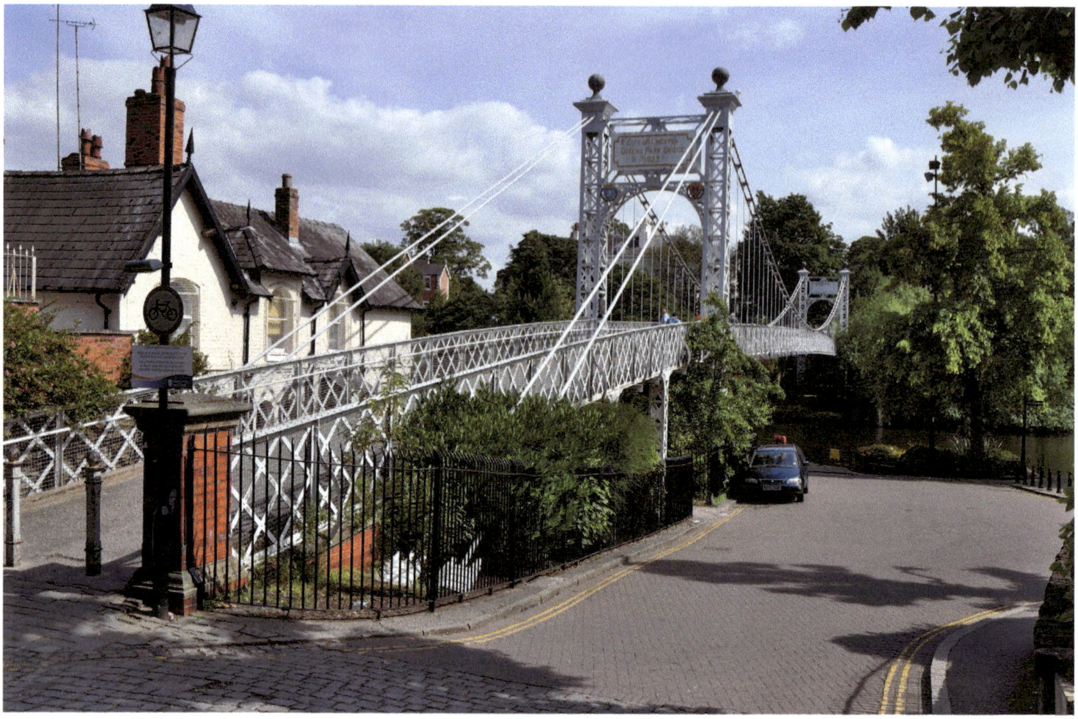

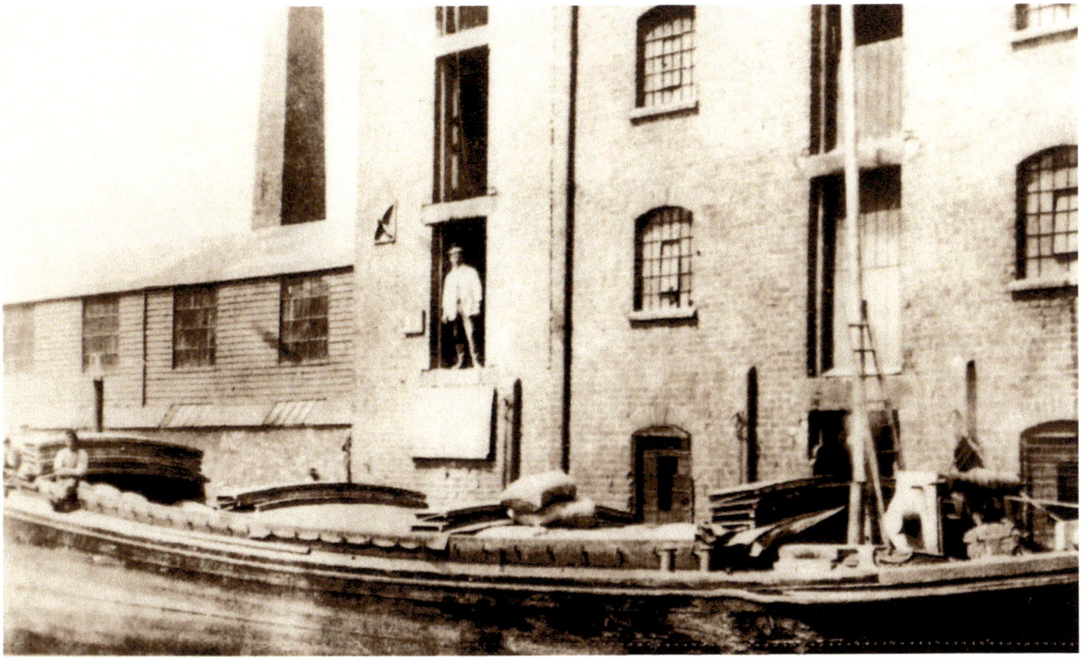

Griffiths Mill near Sellar Street 1890 and 2009
This ancient mill stood empty for many years until re-developed, firstly as a furniture store called Chester Chair and now as The Mill Hotel. The building has been extended with a covered bridge over the canal and additional rooms.

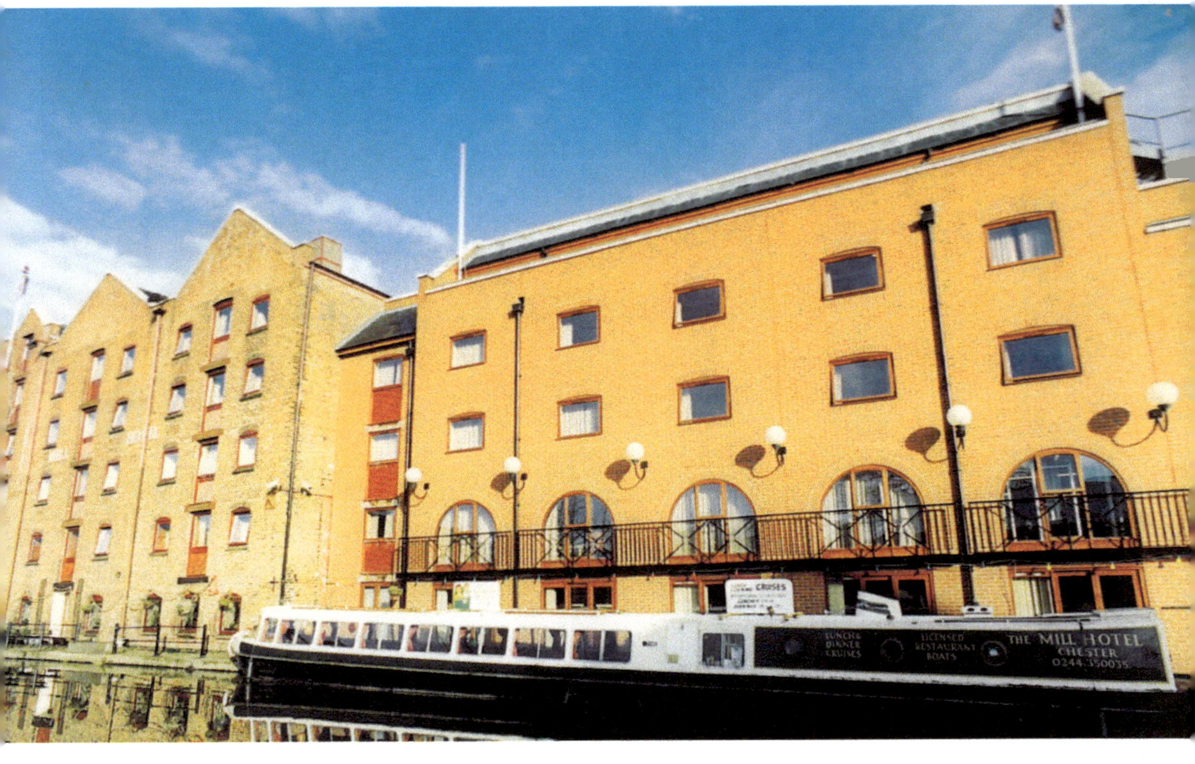

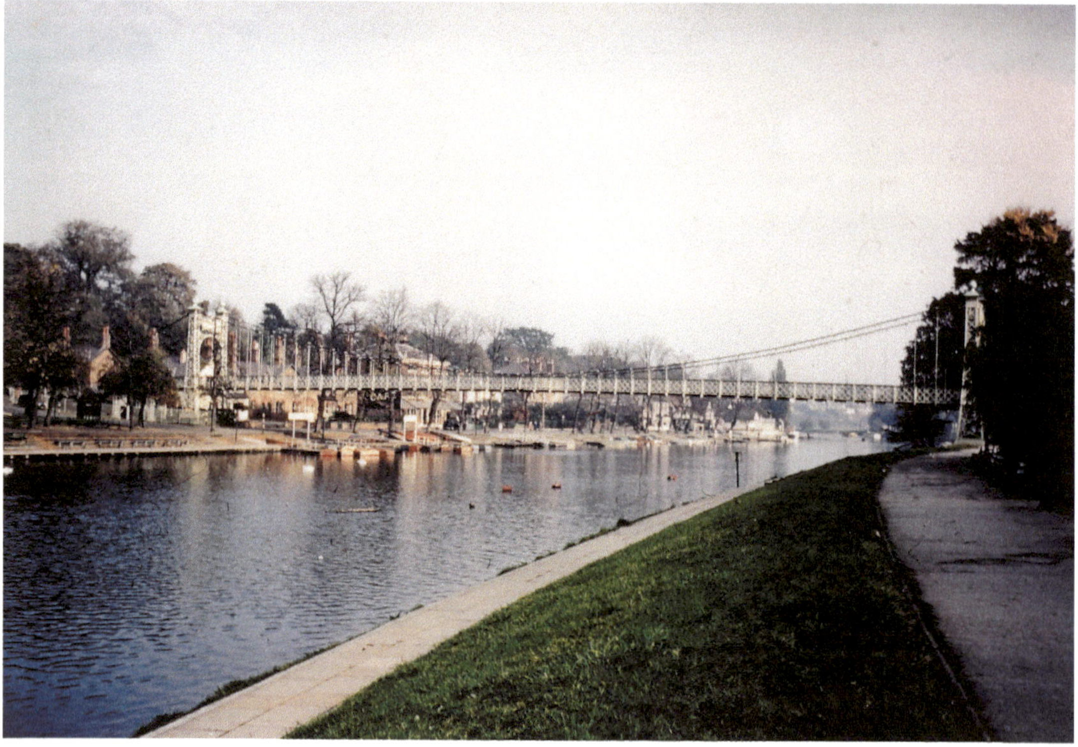

Opposite the Groves 1958 and 2009
This footpath along the south bank of the River Dee is shown in 1958 at which time there was a clear view to the other bank. Now it is completely overgrown with trees and shrubs.

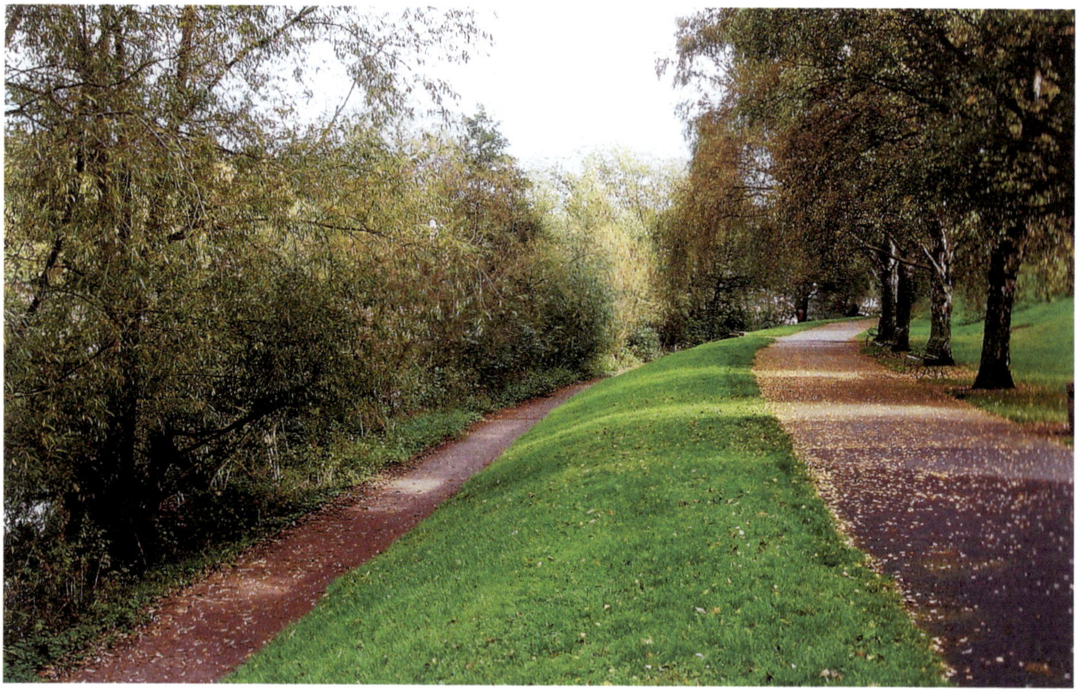

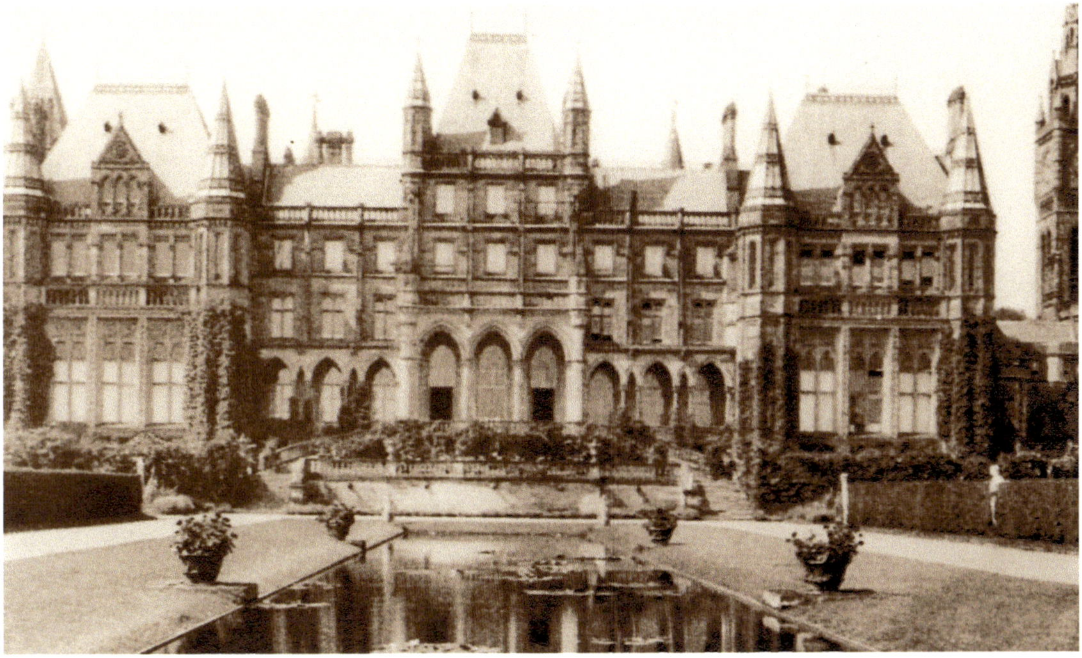

Old and New Eaton Hall 1900 and 2009

Eaton Hall is the principal seat of His Grace the Duke of Westminster. The present hall is the fifth to be built on this site. Used by the Royal Navy in the second war the hall in the old photograph was quite badly damaged and was demolished soon after. The replacement was itself later replaced with the one in the new photograph which was built during 1988/1991 in the French Châteaux style. The church spire has remained *in situ* throughout.

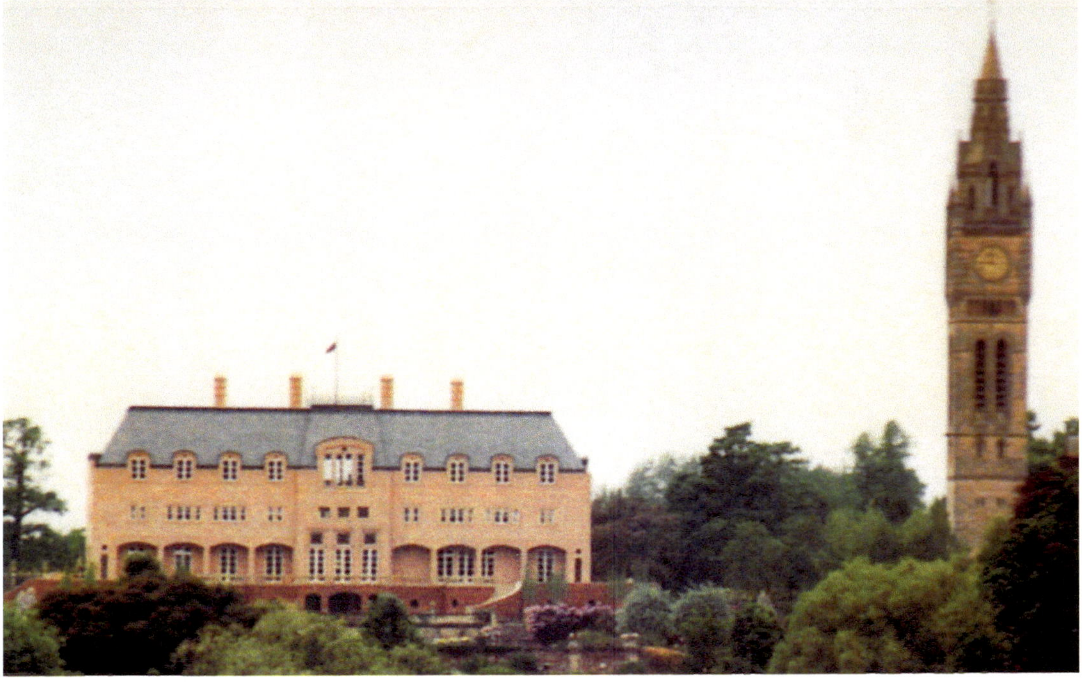

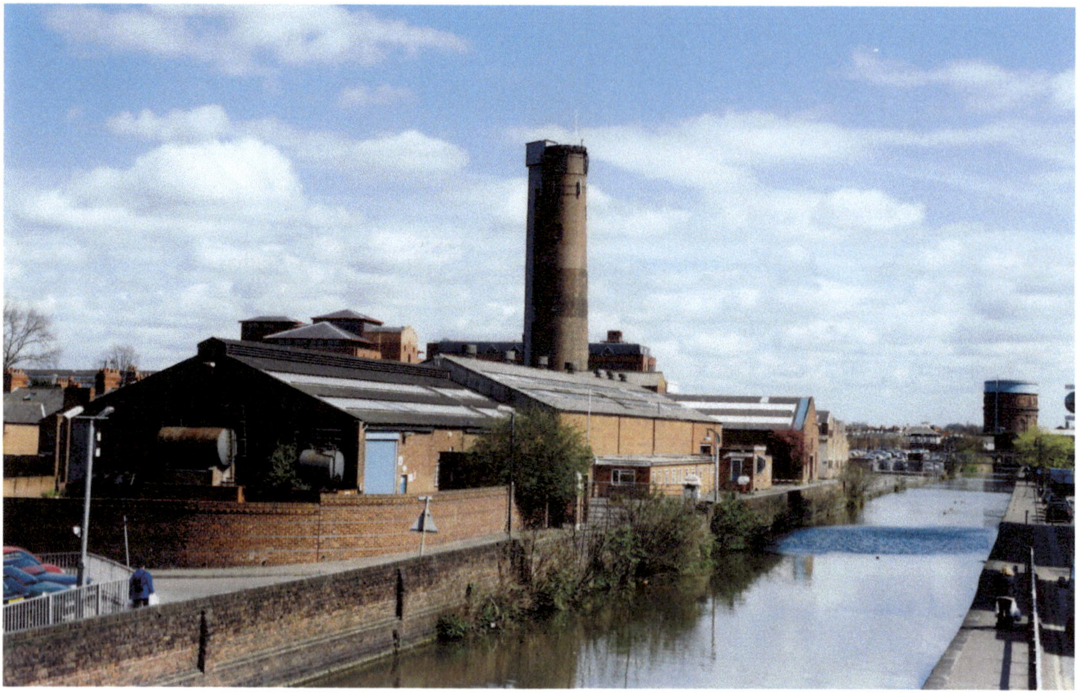

Leadworks and Canal 2002 and 2009
The tall tower in the centre is the Chester Shot Tower which is also known as the Boughton Shot Tower. It stood in the Chester Lead works which was built by Walkers, Parker & Co. in 1799. The tower is the oldest of three remaining shot towers in the UK and probably the oldest such structure still standing in the world. Molten lead was poured through a pierced copper plate or sieve at the top of the tower, with the droplets forming perfect spheres during the fall; the spherical drops were then cooled in a vat of water at the base. The area has now been re-developed around it.

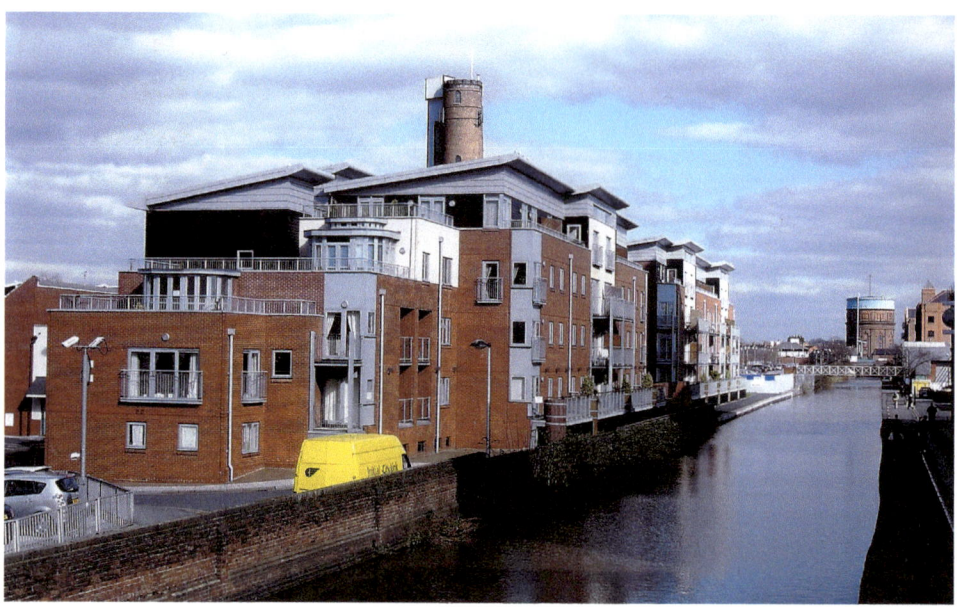

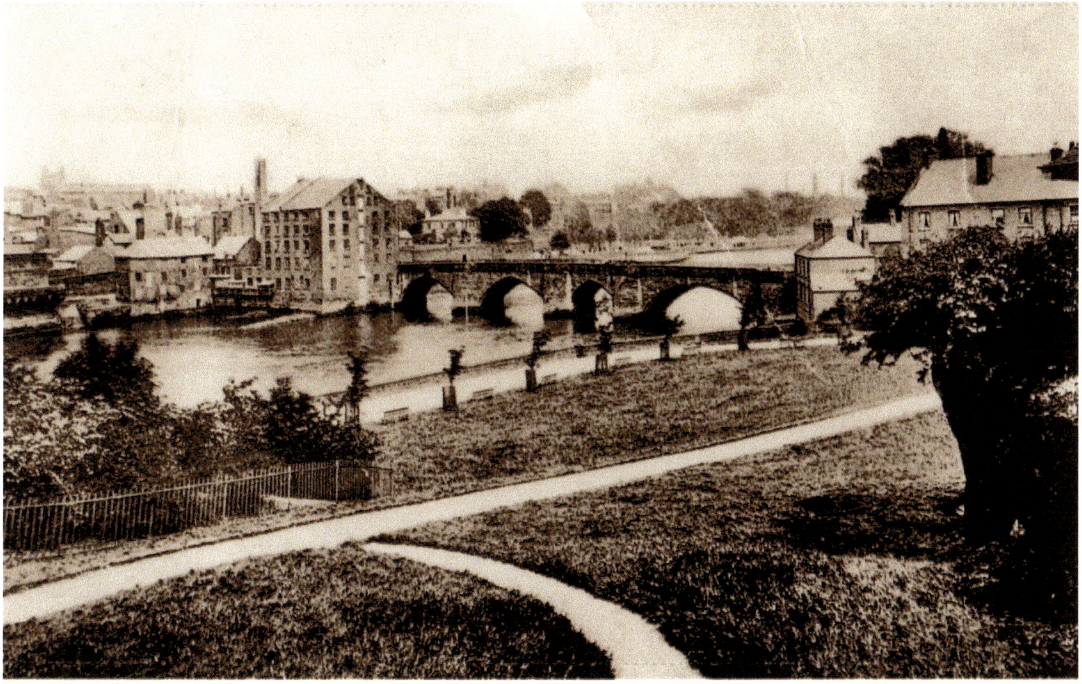

Dee Flour Mills 1903 and 2009
Edgar's field Handbridge named after a tenth-century king was given to the city by the 1st Duke of Westminster in 1892 and the bridge is The Dee Bridge with Watergate in view through the trees and in the old photograph Dee Mills can be seen. There had been corn mills at this location for several centuries and in 1893 the one in the photograph closed down. It was opened again in 1902 by Messrs. Rigby of Frodsham Mill but the attempt failed and the mill closed for good.

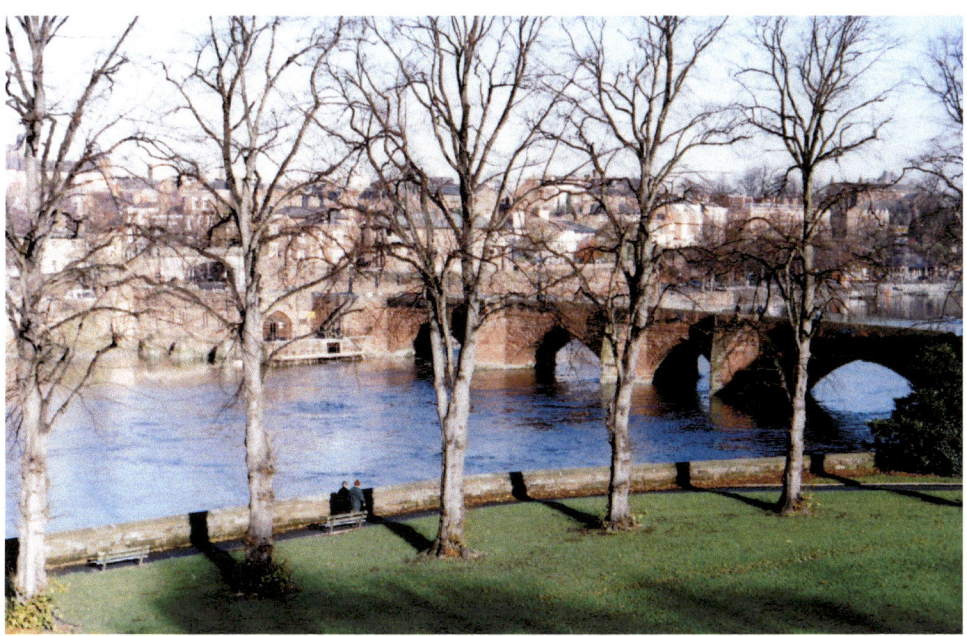

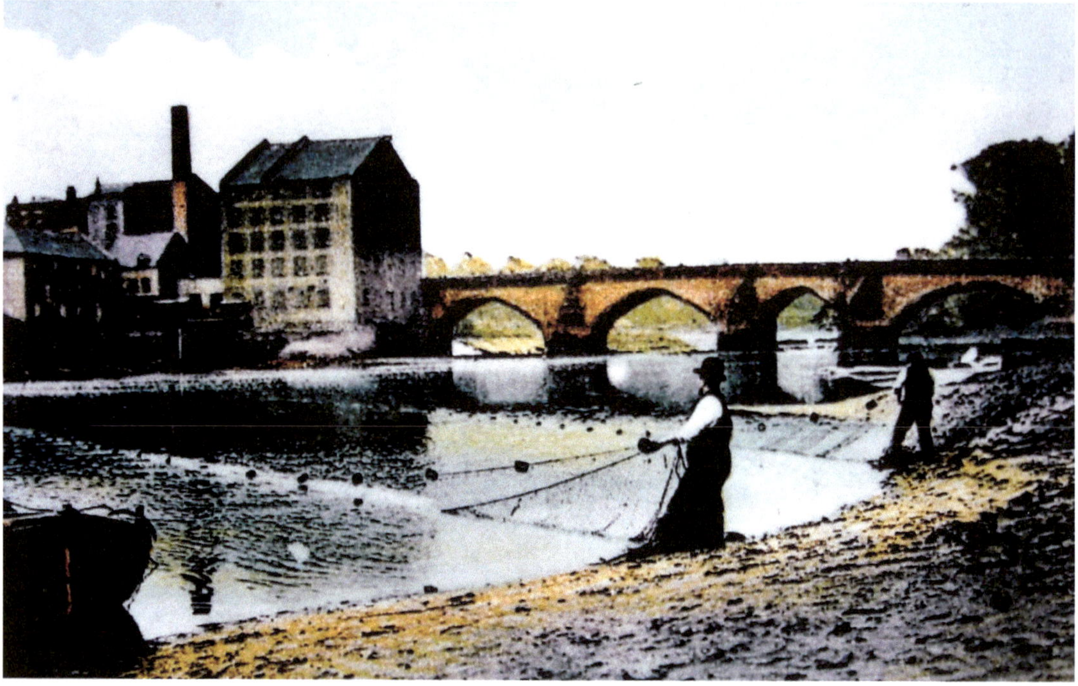

Fishing on the Dee 1900 and 2010
The River Dee as well as once housing Chester Port was well stocked with fish and fishermen made a living catching them for sale. Here in a hand-tinted old photograph we see this underway. In the distance is the Dee Flour Mills and the famous bridge, a good point at which to end this look at Chester through time.

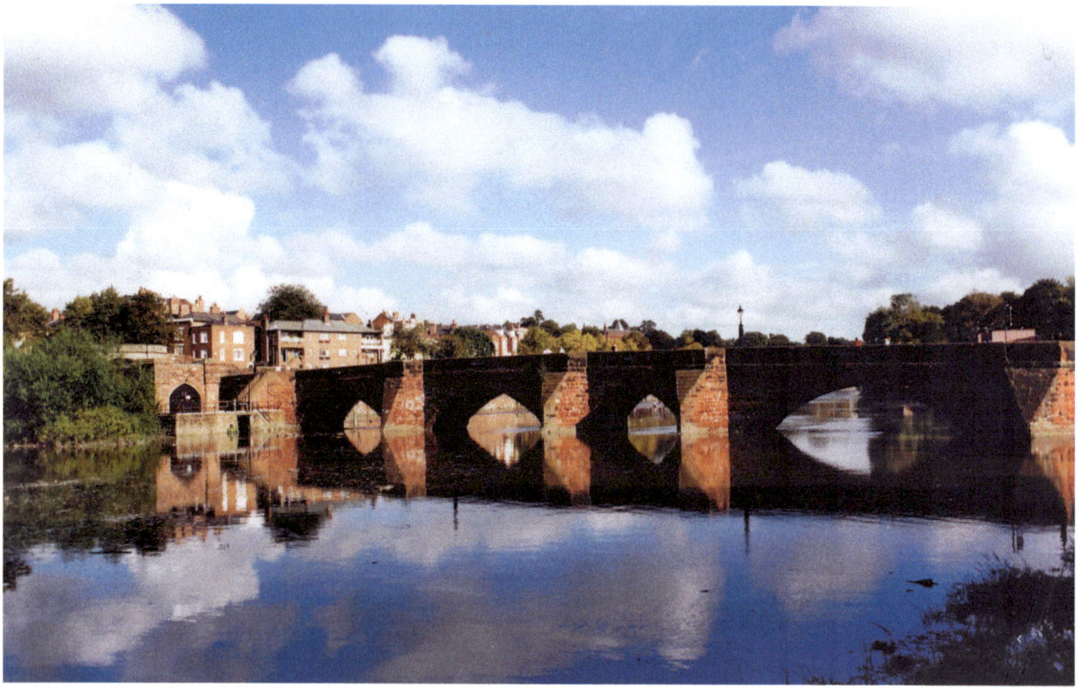